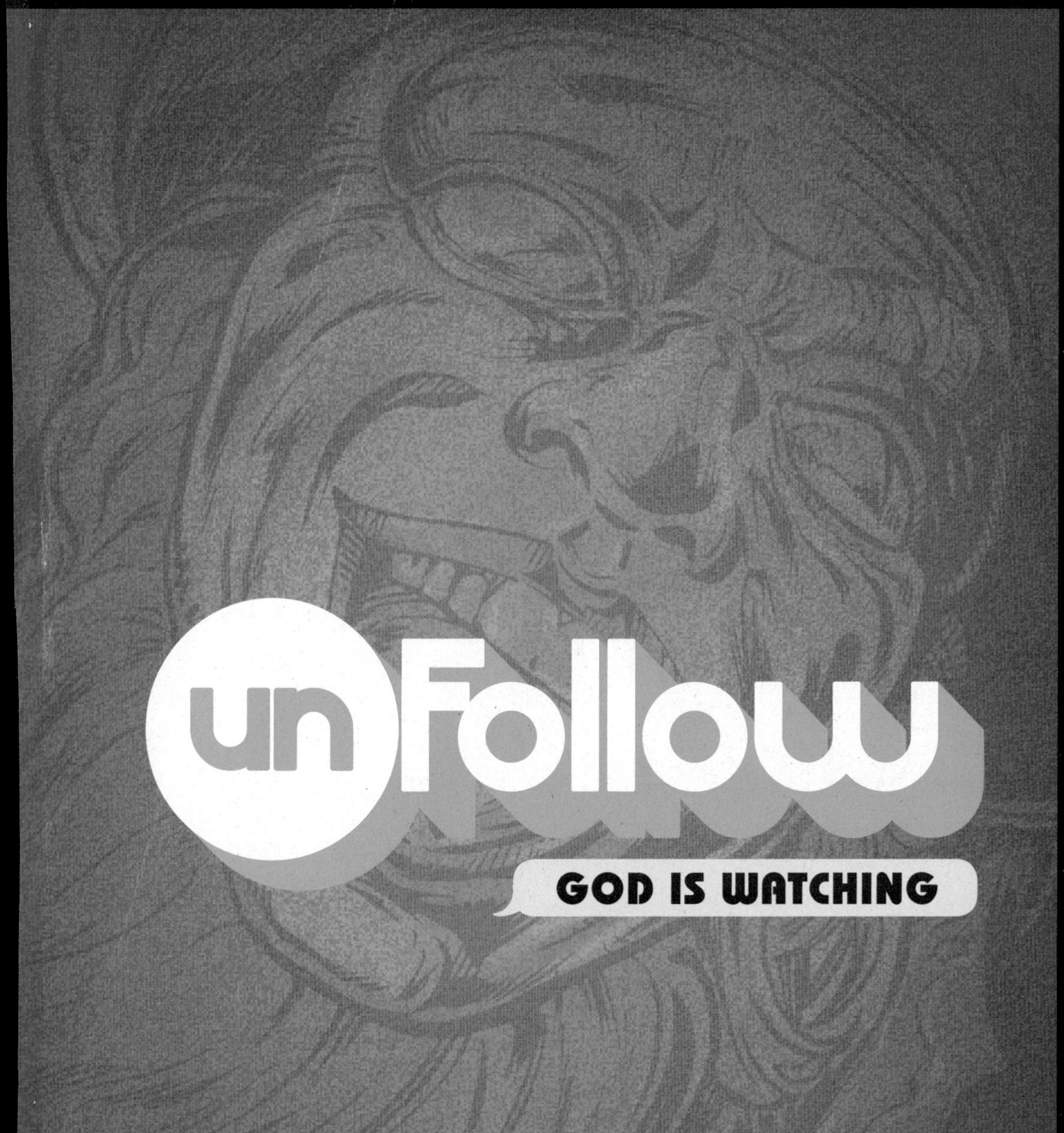
unFollow
GOD IS WATCHING

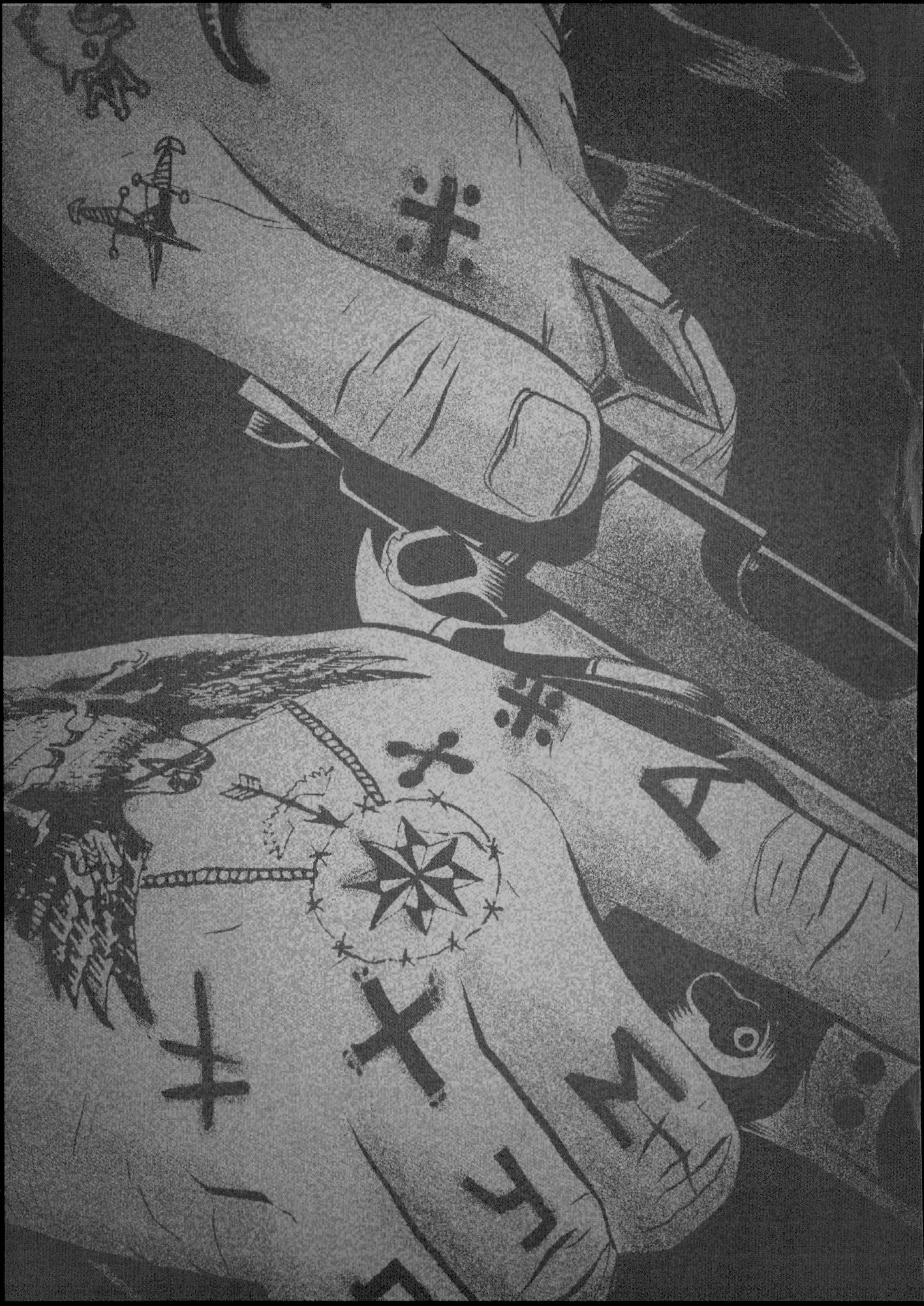

unFollow

GOD IS WATCHING

ROB WILLIAMS Writer

MIKE DOWLING
MARGUERITE SAUVAGE
RYAN KELLY
Artists

QUINTON WINTER
MARGUERITE SAUVAGE
Colorists

CLEM ROBINS
Letterer

MATT TAYLOR
Cover Art and Original Series Covers

UNFOLLOW created by **ROB WILLIAMS** and **MIKE DOWLING**

Ellie Pyle Editor – Original Series
Maggie Howell Assistant Editor – Original Series
Jamie S. Rich Group Editor – Vertigo Comics
Jeb Woodard Group Editor – Collected Editions
Scott Nybakken Editor – Collected Edition
Steve Cook Design Director – Books
Damian Ryland Publication Design

Diane Nelson President
Dan DiDio Publisher
Jim Lee Publisher
Geoff Johns President & Chief Creative Officer
Amit Desai Executive VP – Business & Marketing Strategy, Direct to Consumer & Global Franchise Management
Sam Ades Senior VP – Direct to Consumer
Bobbie Chase VP – Talent Development
Mark Chiarello Senior VP – Art, Design & Collected Editions
John Cunningham Senior VP – Sales & Trade Marketing
Anne DePies Senior VP – Business Strategy, Finance & Administration
Don Falletti VP – Manufacturing Operations
Lawrence Ganem VP – Editorial Administration & Talent Relations
Alison Gill Senior VP – Manufacturing & Operations
Hank Kanalz Senior VP – Editorial Strategy & Administration
Jay Kogan VP – Legal Affairs
Thomas Loftus VP – Business Affairs
Jack Mahan VP – Business Affairs
Nick Napolitano VP – Manufacturing Administration
Eddie Scannell VP – Consumer Marketing
Courtney Simmons Senior VP – Publicity & Communications
Jim (Ski) Sokolowski VP – Comic Book Specialty Sales & Trade Marketing
Nancy Spears VP – Mass, Book, Digital Sales & Trade Marketing

Logo design by **Tom Muller**

UNFOLLOW: GOD IS WATCHING

DC Comics 2900 West Alameda Avenue, Burbank, CA 91505
Printed in Canada. First Printing. ISBN: 978-1-4012-6723-0

Library of Congress Cataloging-in-Publication Data is available.

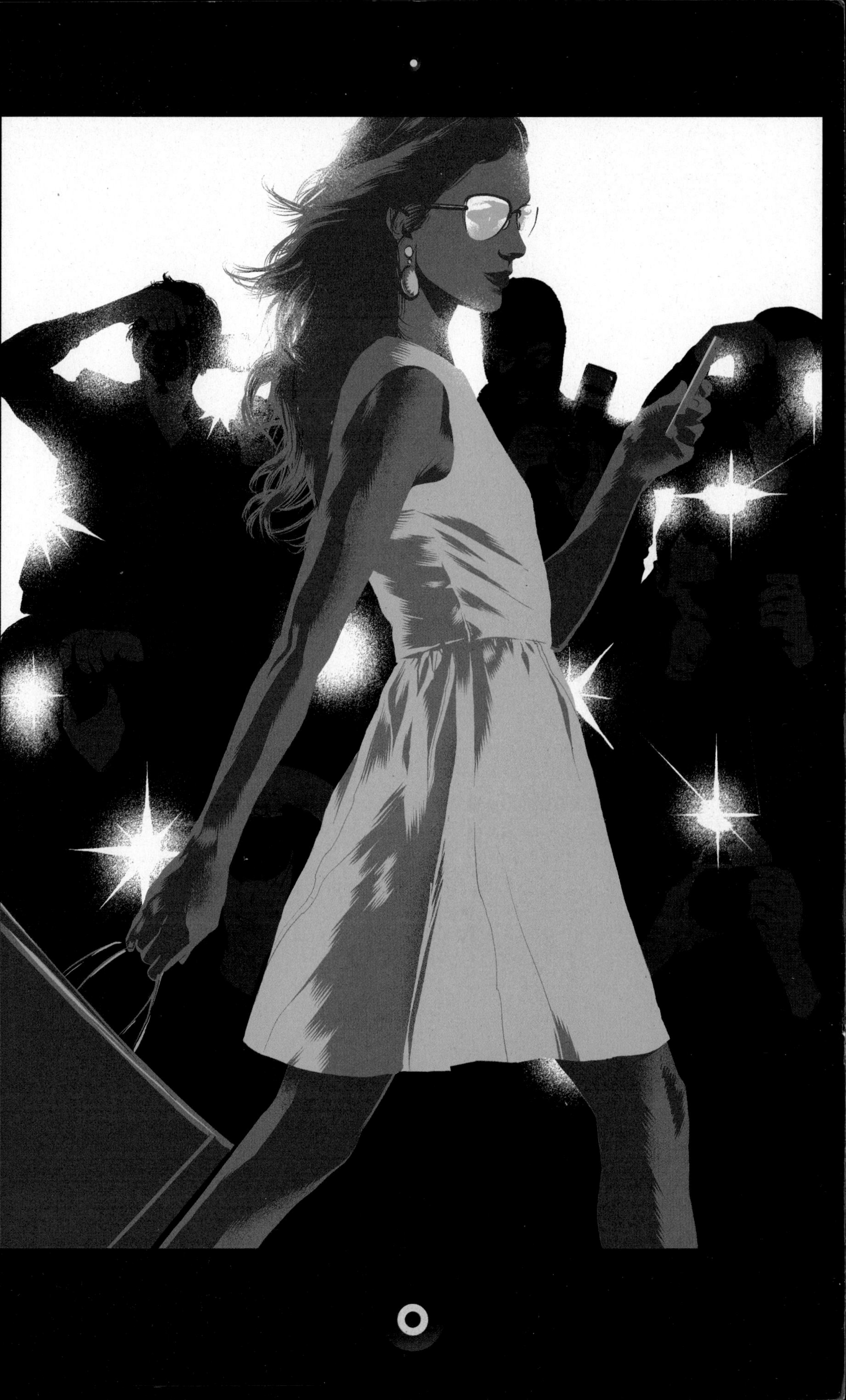

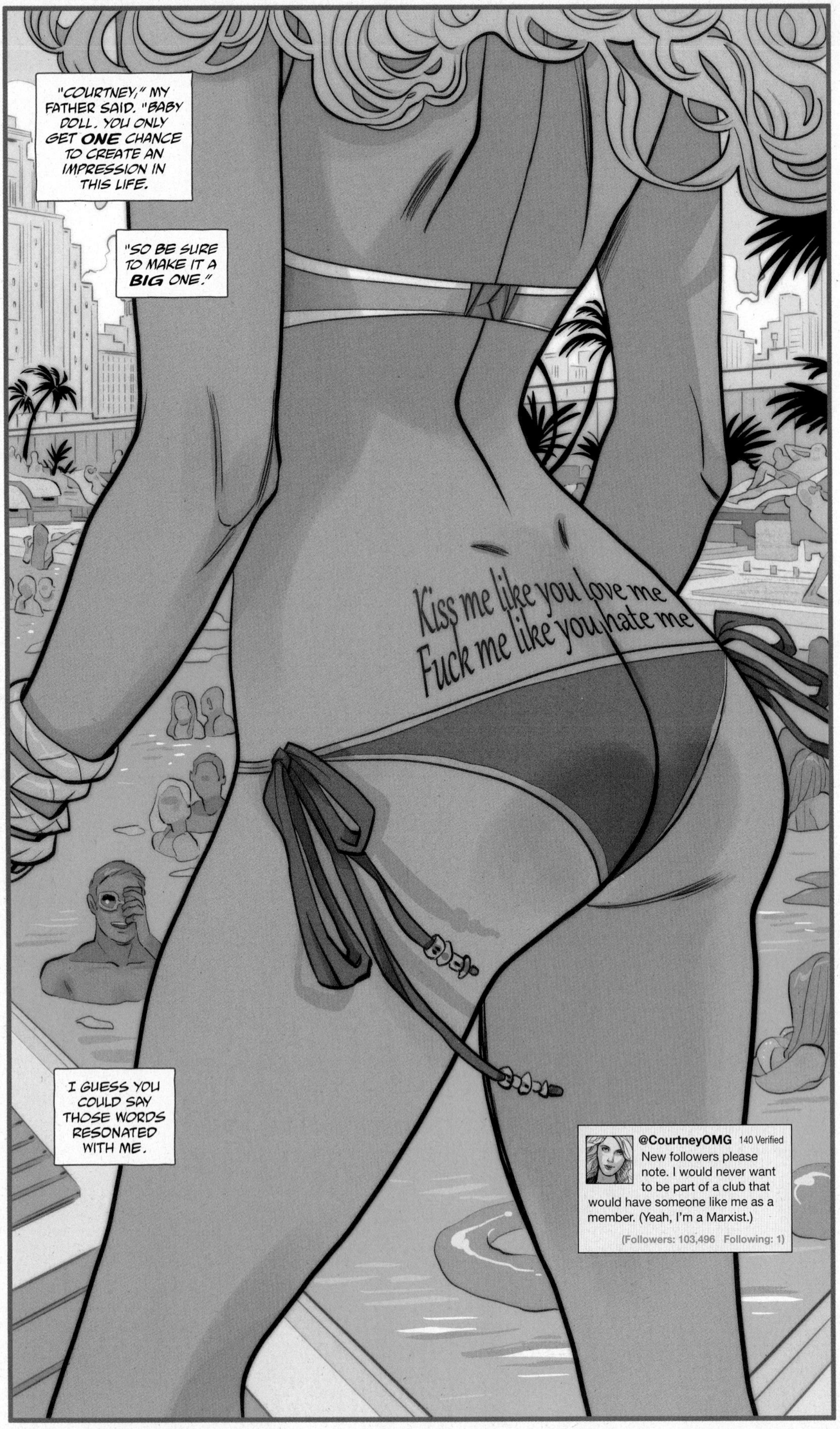

"COURTNEY," MY FATHER SAID. "BABY DOLL. YOU ONLY GET ONE CHANCE TO CREATE AN IMPRESSION IN THIS LIFE.
"SO BE SURE TO MAKE IT A BIG ONE."
Kiss me like you love me
Fuck me like you hate me
I GUESS YOU COULD SAY THOSE WORDS RESONATED WITH ME.
@CourtneyOMG 140 Verified
New followers please note. I would never want to be part of a club that would have someone like me as a member. (Yeah, I'm a Marxist.)
(Followers: 103,496 Following: 1)

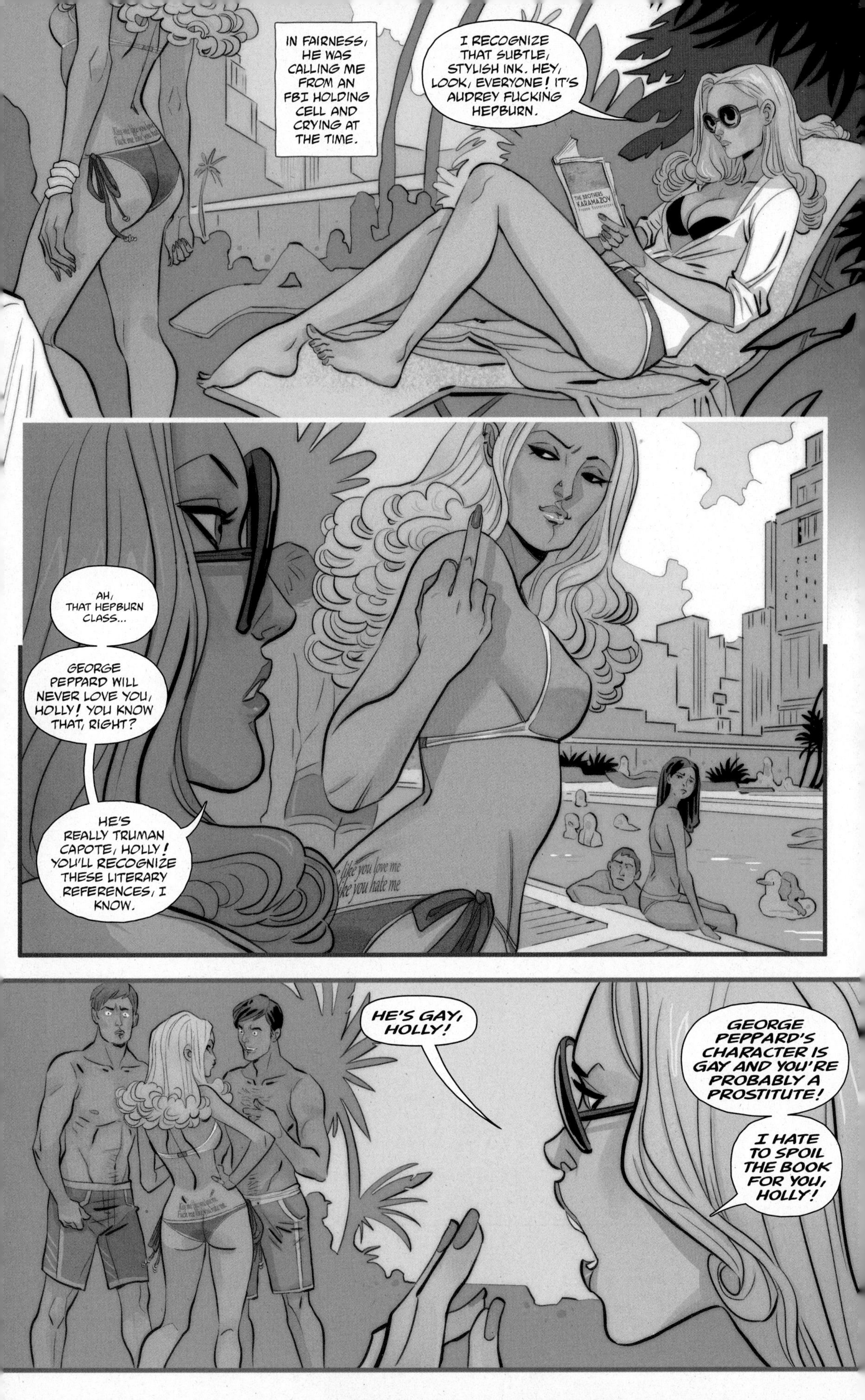
IN FAIRNESS, HE WAS CALLING ME FROM AN FBI HOLDING CELL AND CRYING AT THE TIME.
I RECOGNIZE THAT SUBTLE, STYLISH INK. HEY, LOOK, EVERYONE! IT'S AUDREY FUCKING HEPBURN.
THE BROTHERS KARAMAZOV
AH, THAT HEPBURN CLASS...
GEORGE PEPPARD WILL NEVER LOVE YOU, HOLLY! YOU KNOW THAT, RIGHT?
HE'S REALLY TRUMAN CAPOTE, HOLLY! YOU'LL RECOGNIZE THESE LITERARY REFERENCES, I KNOW.
HE'S GAY, HOLLY!
GEORGE PEPPARD'S CHARACTER IS GAY AND YOU'RE PROBABLY A PROSTITUTE!
I HATE TO SPOIL THE BOOK FOR YOU, HOLLY!

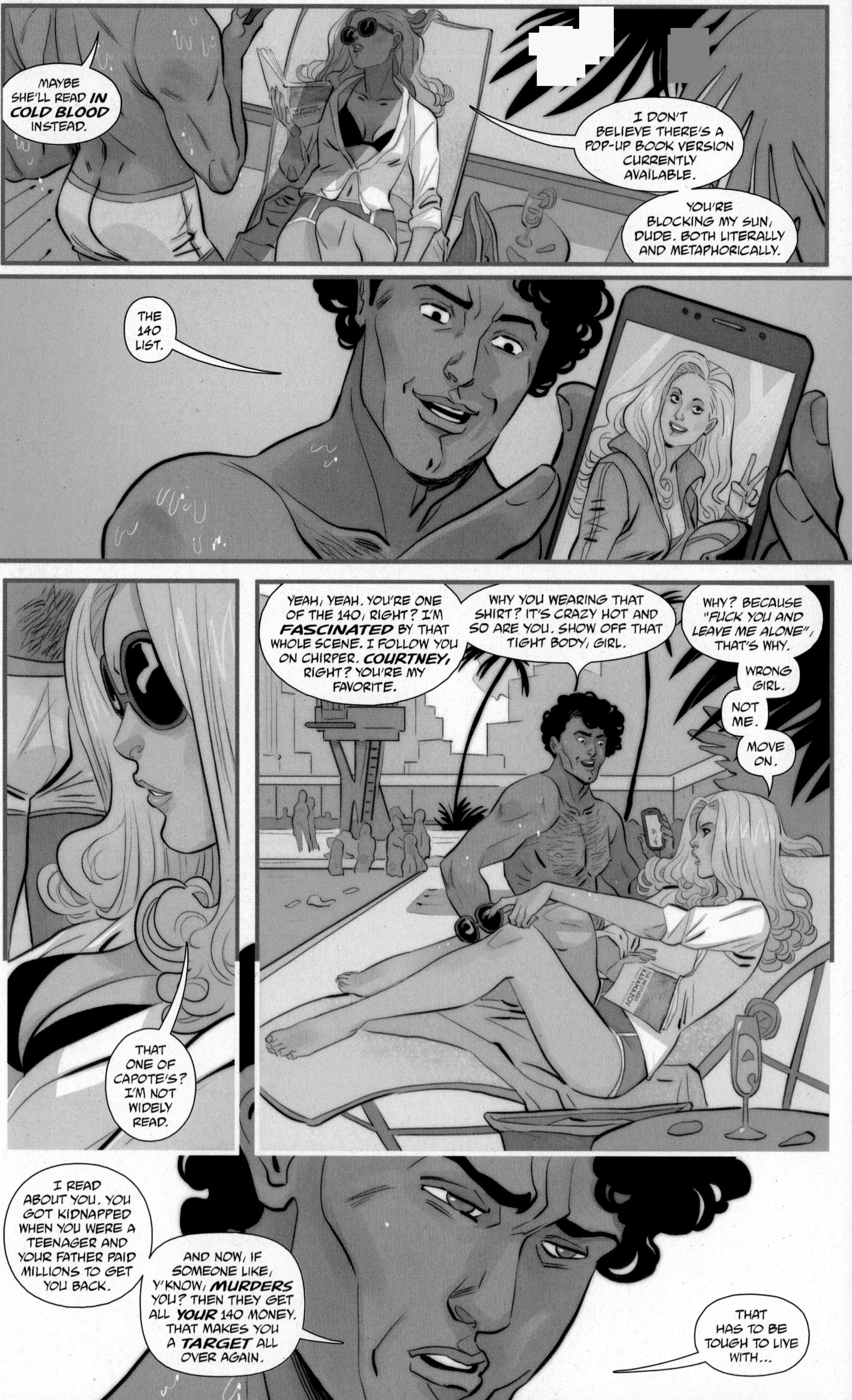
MAYBE SHE'LL READ **IN COLD BLOOD** INSTEAD.
I DON'T BELIEVE THERE'S A POP-UP BOOK VERSION CURRENTLY AVAILABLE.
YOU'RE BLOCKING MY SUN, DUDE. BOTH LITERALLY AND METAPHORICALLY.
THE 140 LIST.
THAT ONE OF CAPOTE'S? I'M NOT WIDELY READ.
YEAH, YEAH. YOU'RE ONE OF THE 140, RIGHT? I'M ***FASCINATED*** BY THAT WHOLE SCENE. I FOLLOW YOU ON CHIRPER. ***COURTNEY,*** RIGHT? YOU'RE MY FAVORITE.
WHY YOU WEARING THAT SHIRT? IT'S CRAZY HOT AND SO ARE YOU. SHOW OFF THAT TIGHT BODY, GIRL.
WHY? BECAUSE "*FUCK YOU AND LEAVE ME ALONE*", THAT'S WHY.
WRONG GIRL.
NOT ME.
MOVE ON.
I READ ABOUT YOU. YOU GOT KIDNAPPED WHEN YOU WERE A TEENAGER AND YOUR FATHER PAID MILLIONS TO GET YOU BACK.
AND NOW, IF SOMEONE LIKE, Y'KNOW, ***MURDERS*** YOU? THEN THEY GET ALL ***YOUR*** 140 MONEY. THAT MAKES YOU A ***TARGET*** ALL OVER AGAIN.
THAT HAS TO BE TOUGH TO LIVE WITH...

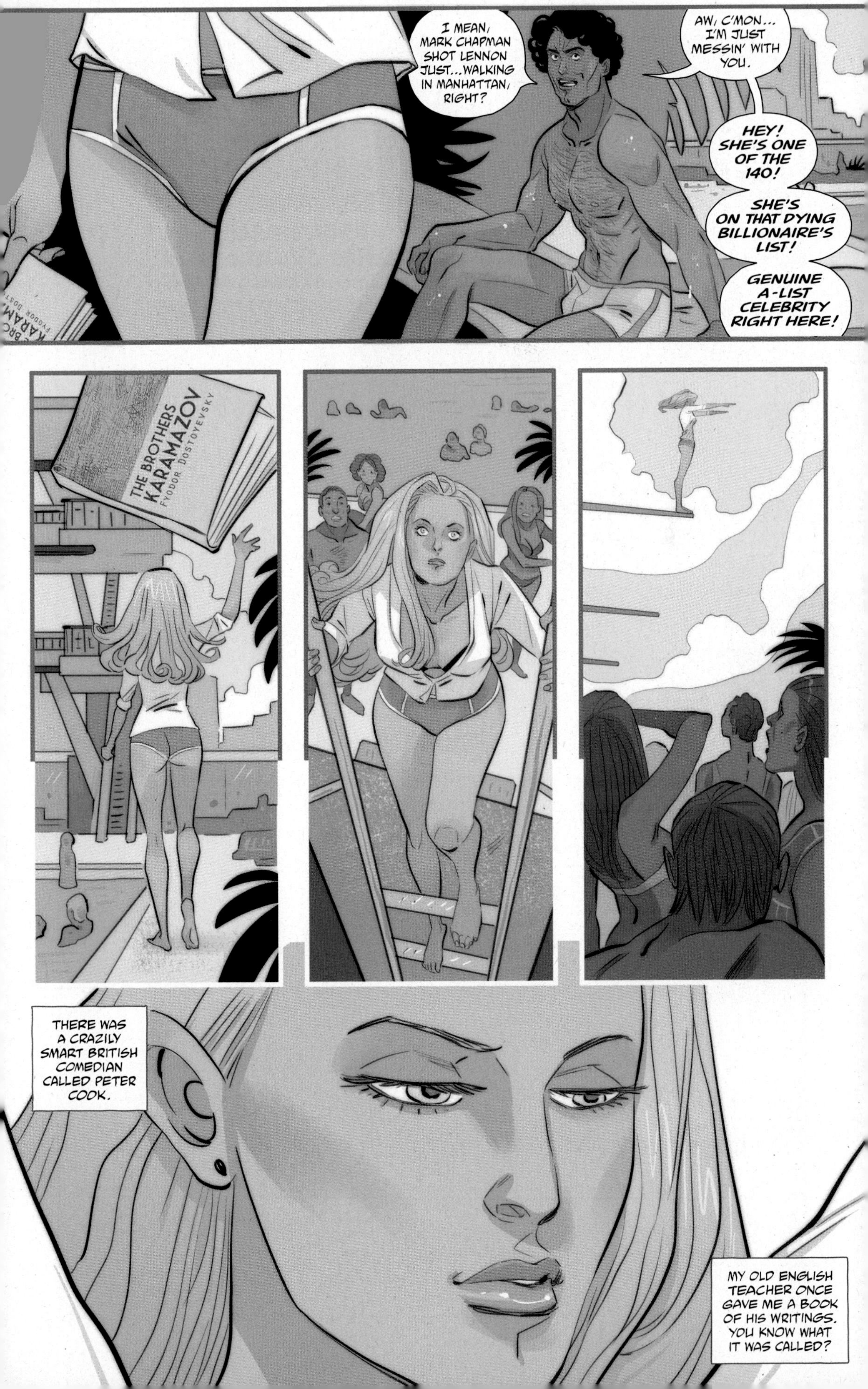
I MEAN, MARK CHAPMAN SHOT LENNON JUST...WALKING IN MANHATTAN, RIGHT?
AW, C'MON... I'M JUST MESSIN' WITH YOU.
HEY! SHE'S ONE OF THE 140!
SHE'S ON THAT DYING BILLIONAIRE'S LIST!
GENUINE A-LIST CELEBRITY RIGHT HERE!
THE BROTHERS KARAMAZOV
FYODOR DOSTOYEVSKY
THERE WAS A CRAZILY SMART BRITISH COMEDIAN CALLED PETER COOK.
MY OLD ENGLISH TEACHER ONCE GAVE ME A BOOK OF HIS WRITINGS. YOU KNOW WHAT IT WAS CALLED?

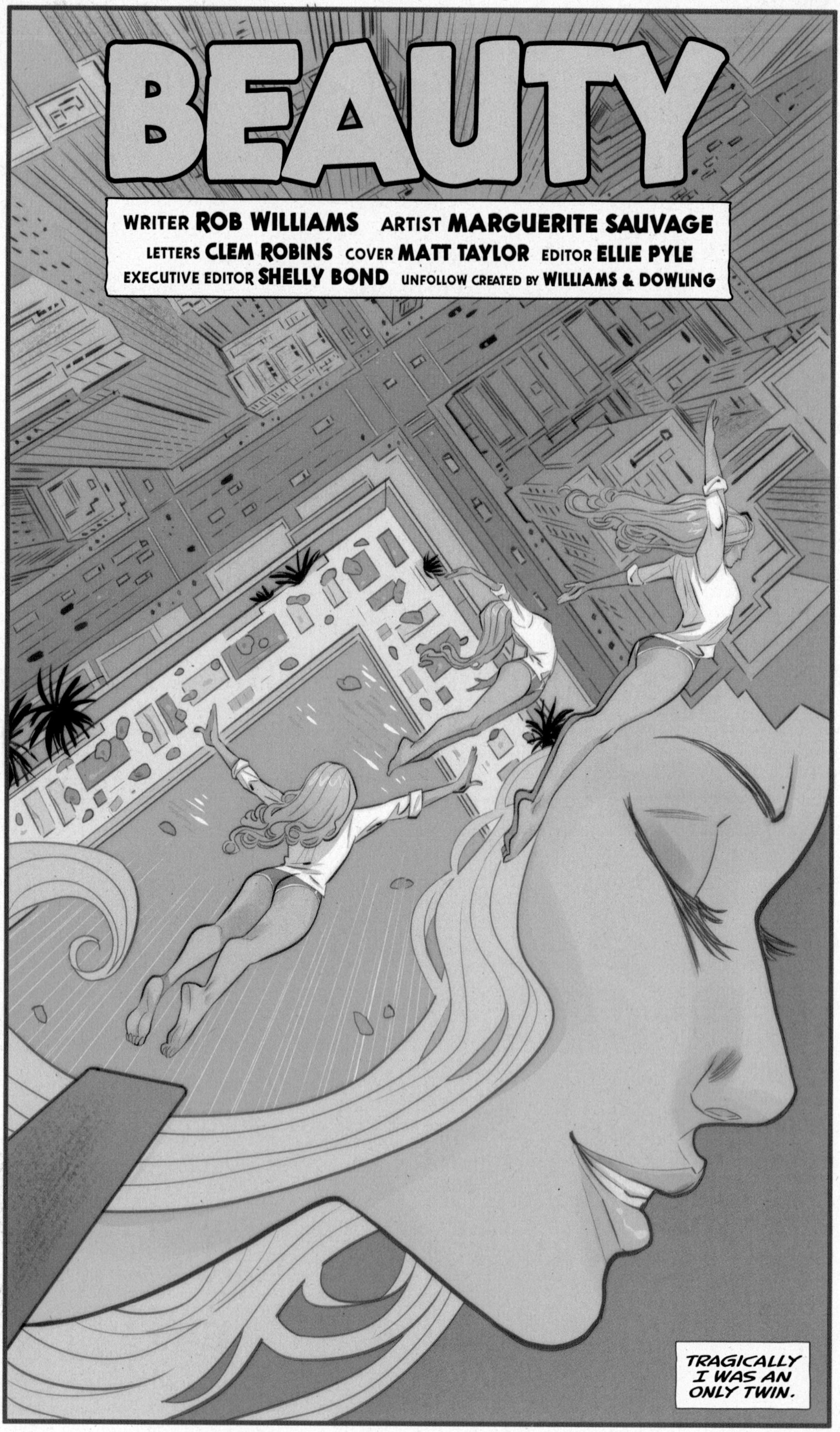
BEAUTY
WRITER ROB WILLIAMS ARTIST MARGUERITE SAUVAGE
LETTERS CLEM ROBINS COVER MATT TAYLOR EDITOR ELLIE PYLE
EXECUTIVE EDITOR SHELLY BOND UNFOLLOW CREATED BY WILLIAMS & DOWLING
TRAGICALLY I WAS AN ONLY TWIN.

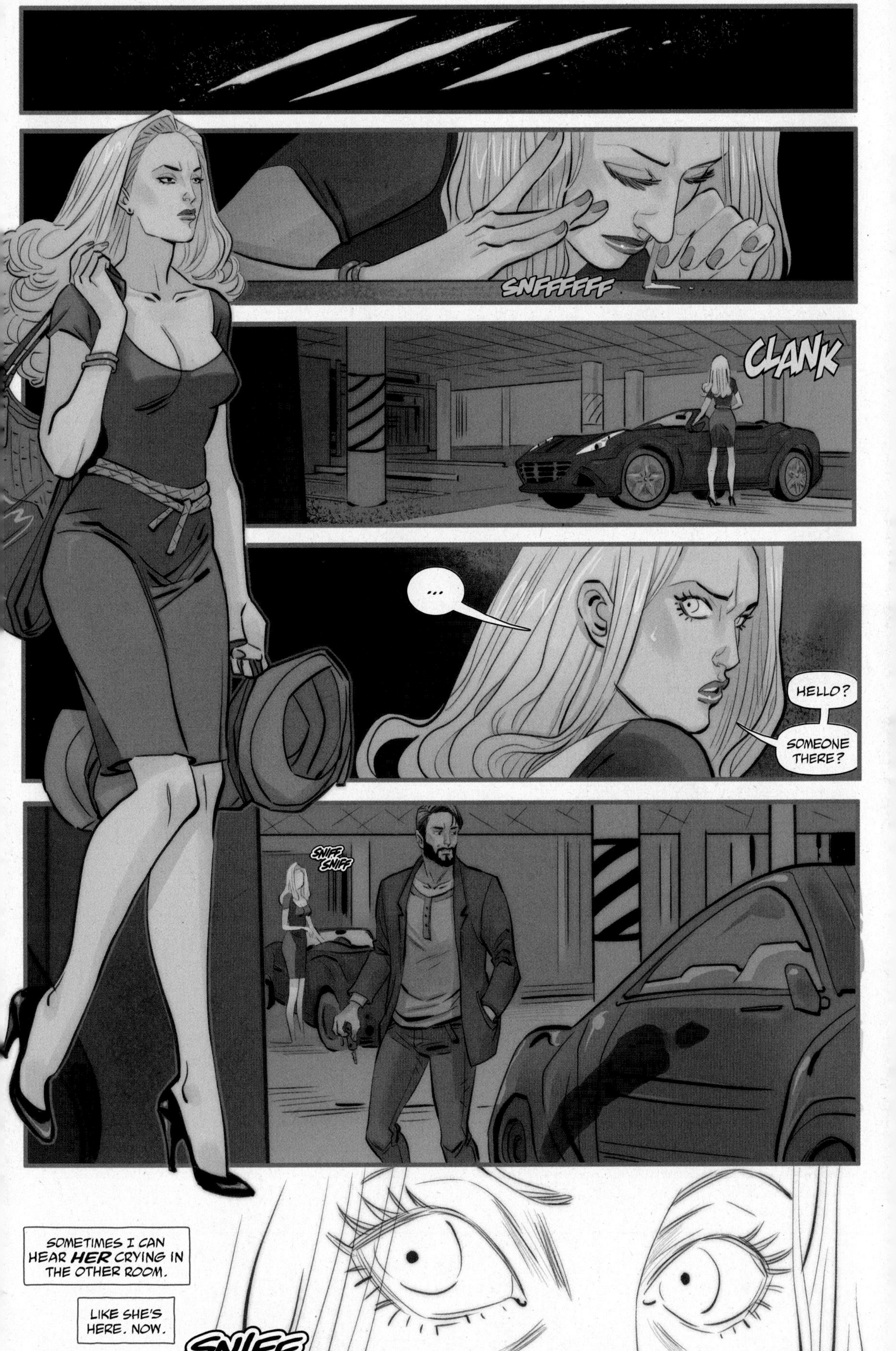
SNFFFFFF
CLANK
...
HELLO?
SOMEONE THERE?
SNIFF SNIFF
SOMETIMES I CAN HEAR HER CRYING IN THE OTHER ROOM.
LIKE SHE'S HERE. NOW.
SNIFF SNIFF

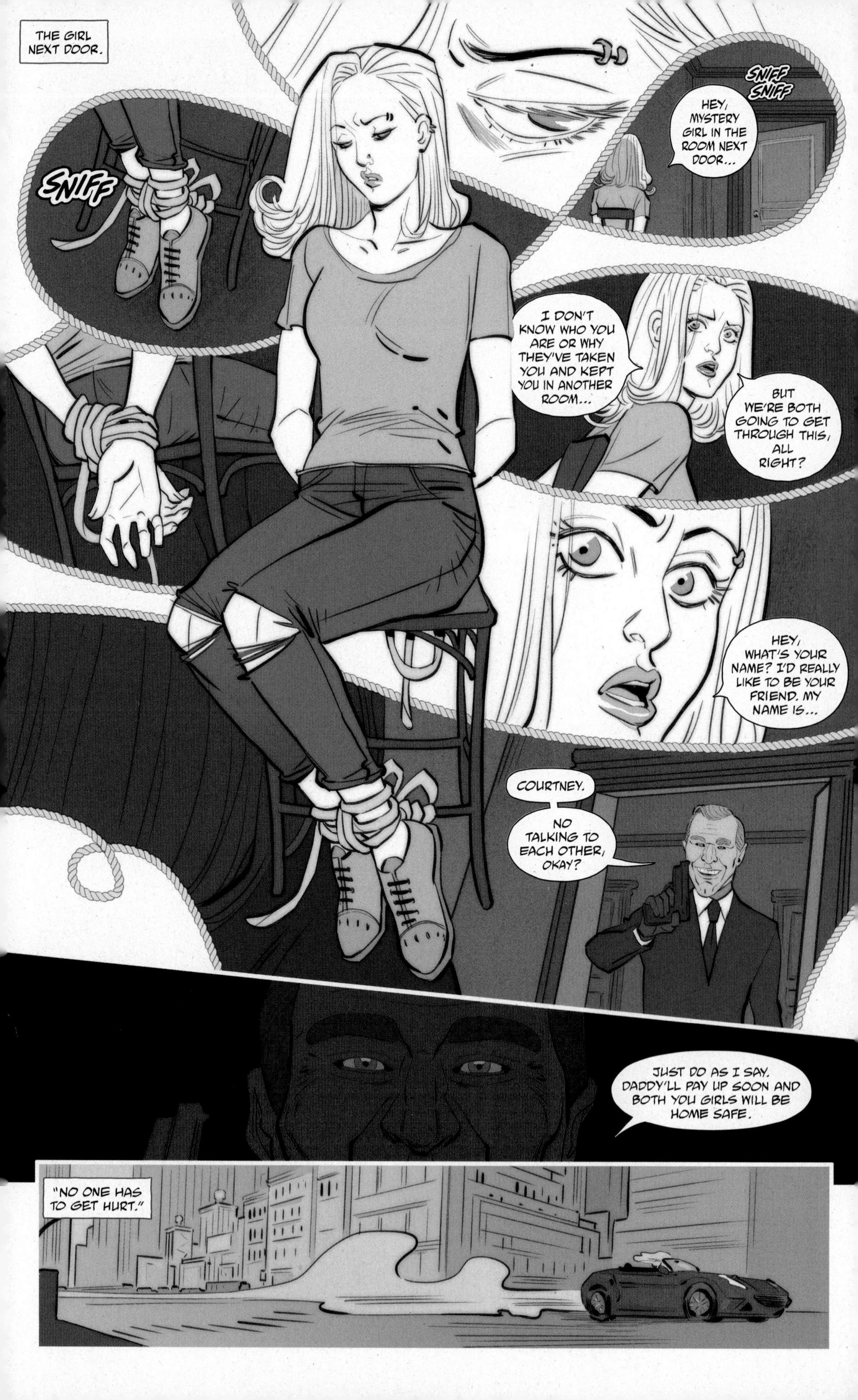
THE GIRL NEXT DOOR.
SNIFF SNIFF
HEY, MYSTERY GIRL IN THE ROOM NEXT DOOR...
SNIFF
I DON'T KNOW WHO YOU ARE OR WHY THEY'VE TAKEN YOU AND KEPT YOU IN ANOTHER ROOM...
BUT WE'RE BOTH GOING TO GET THROUGH THIS, ALL RIGHT?
HEY, WHAT'S YOUR NAME? I'D REALLY LIKE TO BE YOUR FRIEND. MY NAME IS...
COURTNEY.
NO TALKING TO EACH OTHER, OKAY?
JUST DO AS I SAY. DADDY'LL PAY UP SOON AND BOTH YOU GIRLS WILL BE HOME SAFE.
"NO ONE HAS TO GET HURT."

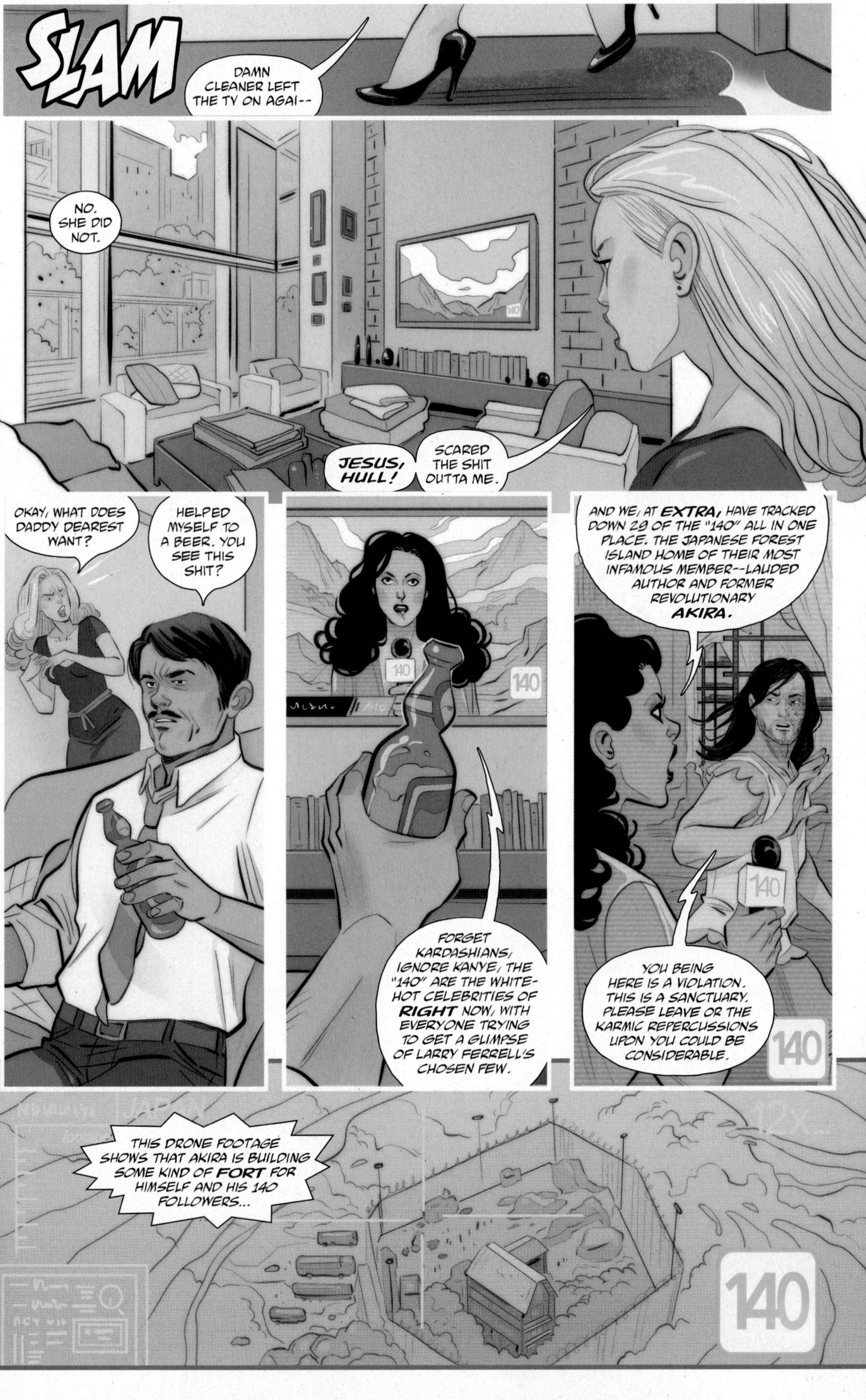
SLAM
DAMN CLEANER LEFT THE TV ON AGAI--
NO. SHE DID NOT.
JESUS, HULL!
SCARED THE SHIT OUTTA ME.
OKAY, WHAT DOES DADDY DEAREST WANT?
HELPED MYSELF TO A BEER. YOU SEE THIS SHIT?
140
FORGET KARDASHIANS, IGNORE KANYE, THE "140" ARE THE WHITE-HOT CELEBRITIES OF RIGHT NOW, WITH EVERYONE TRYING TO GET A GLIMPSE OF LARRY FERRELL'S CHOSEN FEW.
AND WE, AT EXTRA, HAVE TRACKED DOWN 29 OF THE "140" ALL IN ONE PLACE. THE JAPANESE FOREST ISLAND HOME OF THEIR MOST INFAMOUS MEMBER--LAUDED AUTHOR AND FORMER REVOLUTIONARY AKIRA.
YOU BEING HERE IS A VIOLATION. THIS IS A SANCTUARY. PLEASE LEAVE OR THE KARMIC REPERCUSSIONS UPON YOU COULD BE CONSIDERABLE.
140
JAPAN
12X
THIS DRONE FOOTAGE SHOWS THAT AKIRA IS BUILDING SOME KIND OF FORT FOR HIMSELF AND HIS 140 FOLLOWERS...
140

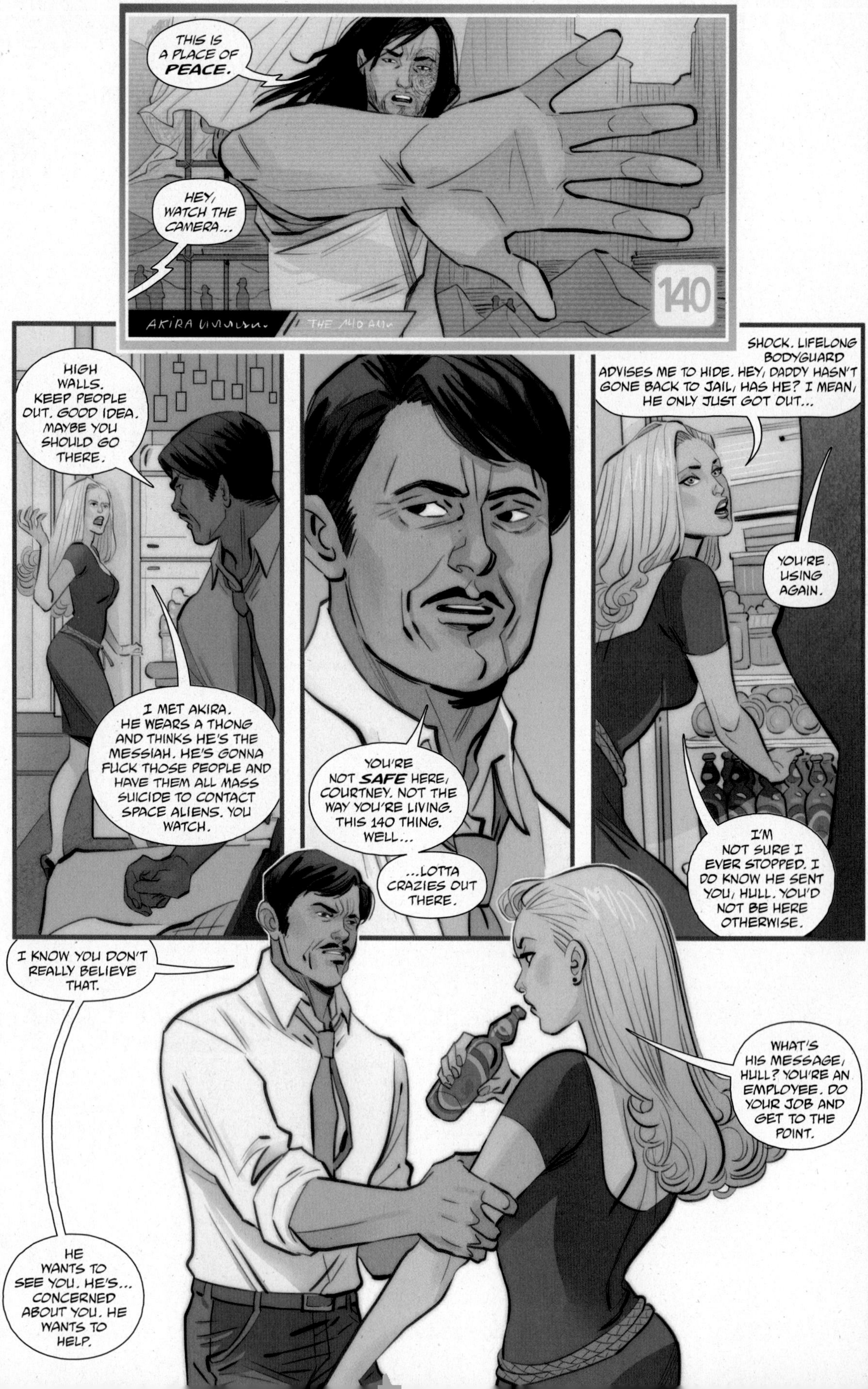
THIS IS A PLACE OF **PEACE.**
HEY, WATCH THE CAMERA...
140
HIGH WALLS. KEEP PEOPLE OUT. GOOD IDEA. MAYBE YOU SHOULD GO THERE.
I MET AKIRA. HE WEARS A THONG AND THINKS HE'S THE MESSIAH. HE'S GONNA FUCK THOSE PEOPLE AND HAVE THEM ALL MASS SUICIDE TO CONTACT SPACE ALIENS. YOU WATCH.
YOU'RE NOT ***SAFE*** HERE, COURTNEY. NOT THE WAY YOU'RE LIVING. THIS 140 THING. WELL...
...LOTTA CRAZIES OUT THERE.
SHOCK. LIFELONG BODYGUARD ADVISES ME TO HIDE. HEY, DADDY HASN'T GONE BACK TO JAIL, HAS HE? I MEAN, HE ONLY JUST GOT OUT...
YOU'RE USING AGAIN.
I'M NOT SURE I EVER STOPPED. I DO KNOW HE SENT YOU, HULL. YOU'D NOT BE HERE OTHERWISE.
I KNOW YOU DON'T REALLY BELIEVE THAT.
WHAT'S HIS MESSAGE, HULL? YOU'RE AN EMPLOYEE. DO YOUR JOB AND GET TO THE POINT.
HE WANTS TO SEE YOU. HE'S... CONCERNED ABOUT YOU. HE WANTS TO HELP.

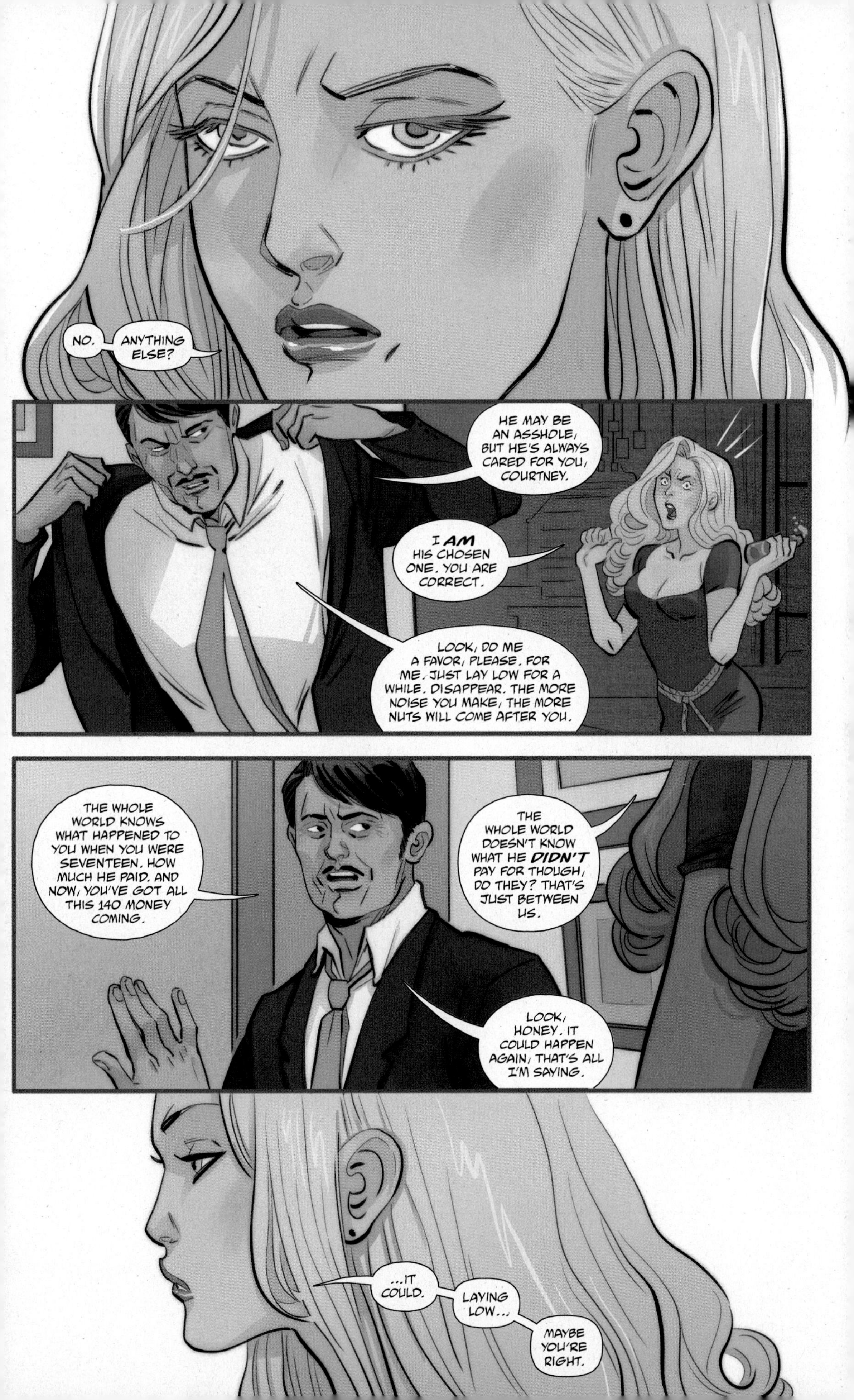
NO.
ANYTHING ELSE?
HE MAY BE AN ASSHOLE, BUT HE'S ALWAYS CARED FOR YOU, COURTNEY.
I **AM** HIS CHOSEN ONE. YOU ARE CORRECT.
LOOK, DO ME A FAVOR, PLEASE. FOR ME. JUST LAY LOW FOR A WHILE. DISAPPEAR. THE MORE NOISE YOU MAKE, THE MORE NUTS WILL COME AFTER YOU.
THE WHOLE WORLD KNOWS WHAT HAPPENED TO YOU WHEN YOU WERE SEVENTEEN. HOW MUCH HE PAID. AND NOW, YOU'VE GOT ALL THIS 140 MONEY COMING.
THE WHOLE WORLD DOESN'T KNOW WHAT HE ***DIDN'T*** PAY FOR THOUGH, DO THEY? THAT'S JUST BETWEEN US.
LOOK, HONEY. IT COULD HAPPEN AGAIN, THAT'S ALL I'M SAYING.
...IT COULD.
LAYING LOW...
MAYBE YOU'RE RIGHT.

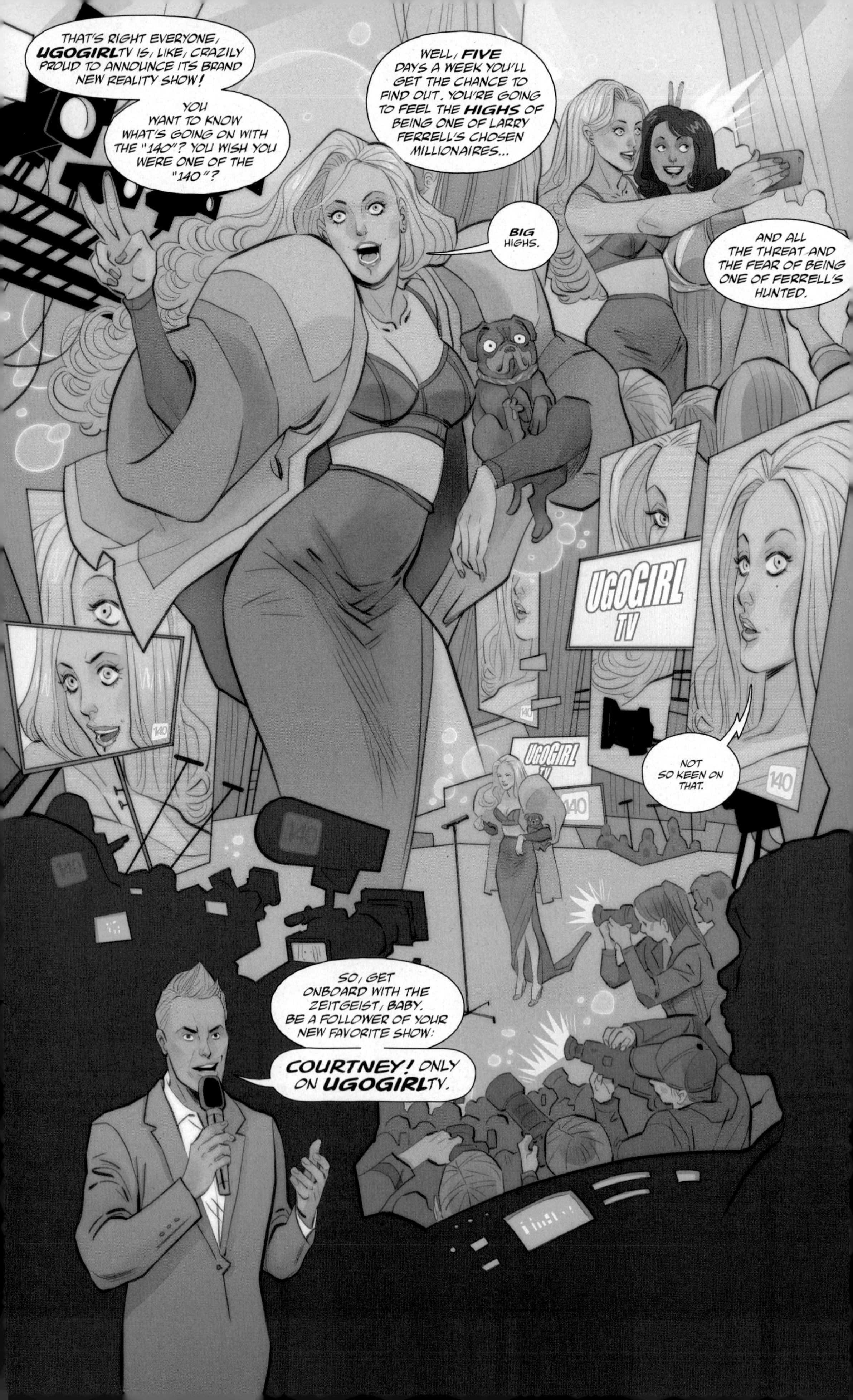
THAT'S RIGHT EVERYONE, UGOGIRLTV IS, LIKE, CRAZILY PROUD TO ANNOUNCE ITS BRAND NEW REALITY SHOW!
YOU WANT TO KNOW WHAT'S GOING ON WITH THE "140"? YOU WISH YOU WERE ONE OF THE "140"?
WELL, FIVE DAYS A WEEK YOU'LL GET THE CHANCE TO FIND OUT. YOU'RE GOING TO FEEL THE HIGHS OF BEING ONE OF LARRY FERRELL'S CHOSEN MILLIONAIRES...
BIG HIGHS.
AND ALL THE THREAT AND THE FEAR OF BEING ONE OF FERRELL'S HUNTED.
UGOGIRL TV
140
NOT SO KEEN ON THAT.
UGOGIRL TV
SO, GET ONBOARD WITH THE ZEITGEIST, BABY. BE A FOLLOWER OF YOUR NEW FAVORITE SHOW:
COURTNEY! ONLY ON UGOGIRLTV.

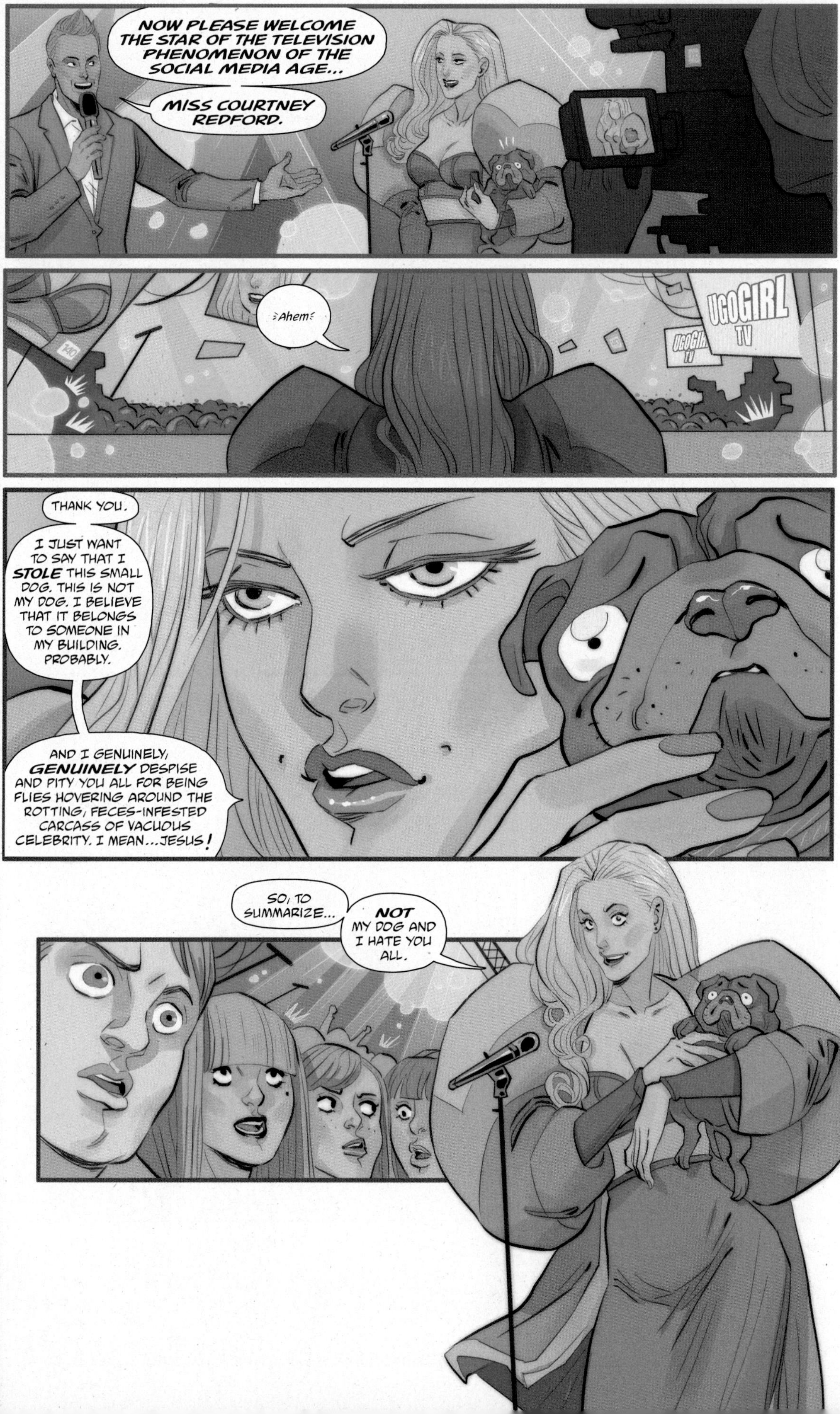
NOW PLEASE WELCOME THE STAR OF THE TELEVISION PHENOMENON OF THE SOCIAL MEDIA AGE...
MISS COURTNEY REDFORD.
Ahem
UGOGIRL TV
UGOGIRL TV
THANK YOU.
I JUST WANT TO SAY THAT I STOLE THIS SMALL DOG. THIS IS NOT MY DOG. I BELIEVE THAT IT BELONGS TO SOMEONE IN MY BUILDING. PROBABLY.
AND I GENUINELY, GENUINELY DESPISE AND PITY YOU ALL FOR BEING FLIES HOVERING AROUND THE ROTTING, FECES-INFESTED CARCASS OF VACUOUS CELEBRITY. I MEAN...JESUS!
SO, TO SUMMARIZE...
NOT MY DOG AND I HATE YOU ALL.

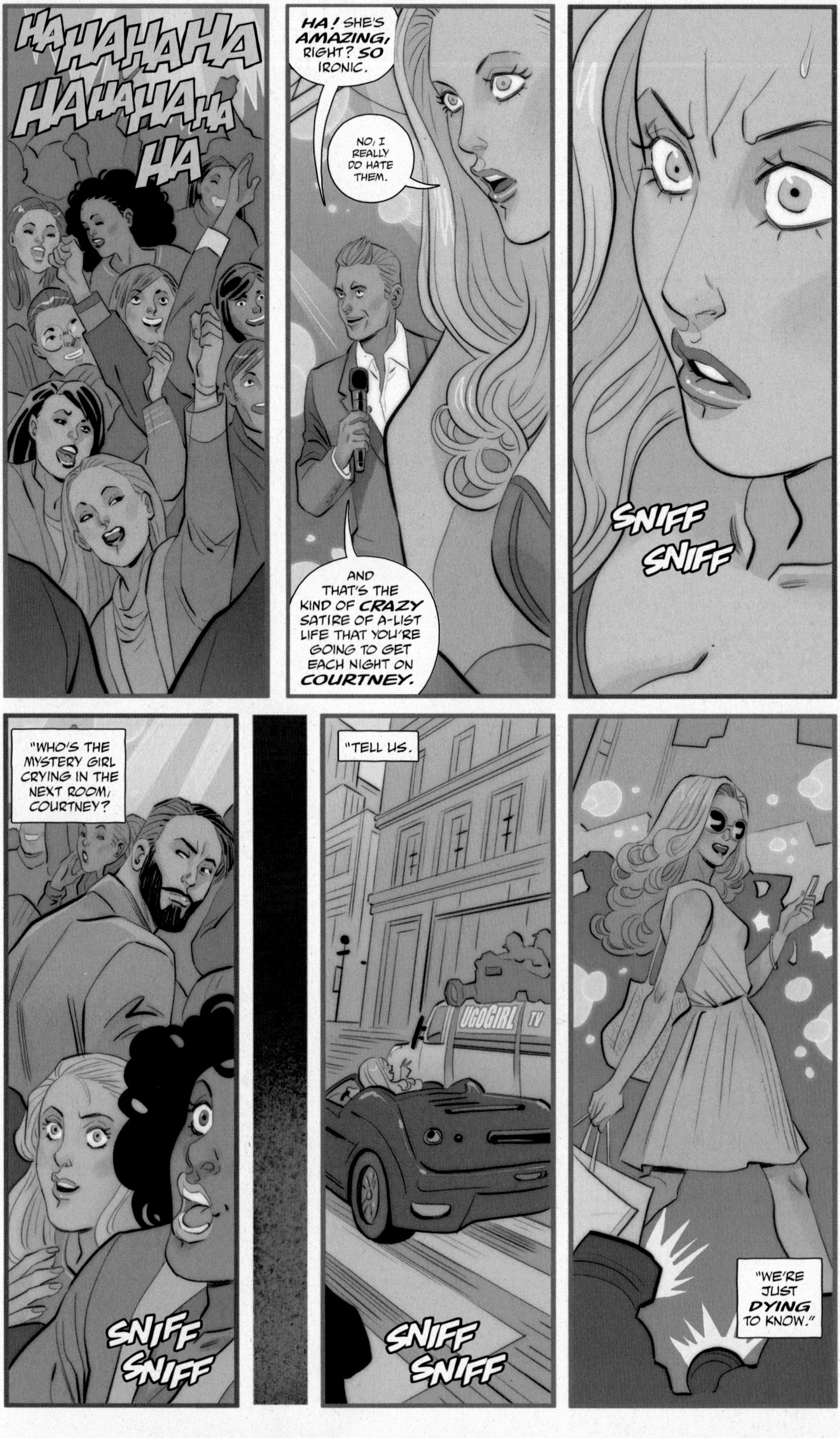
HA HAHAHAHA HAHAHAHAHA HA
HA! SHE'S AMAZING, RIGHT? SO IRONIC.
NO, I REALLY DO HATE THEM.
AND THAT'S THE KIND OF CRAZY SATIRE OF A-LIST LIFE THAT YOU'RE GOING TO GET EACH NIGHT ON COURTNEY.
SNIFF SNIFF
"WHO'S THE MYSTERY GIRL CRYING IN THE NEXT ROOM, COURTNEY?
SNIFF SNIFF
"TELL US.
UGOGIRL TV
SNIFF SNIFF
"WE'RE JUST DYING TO KNOW."

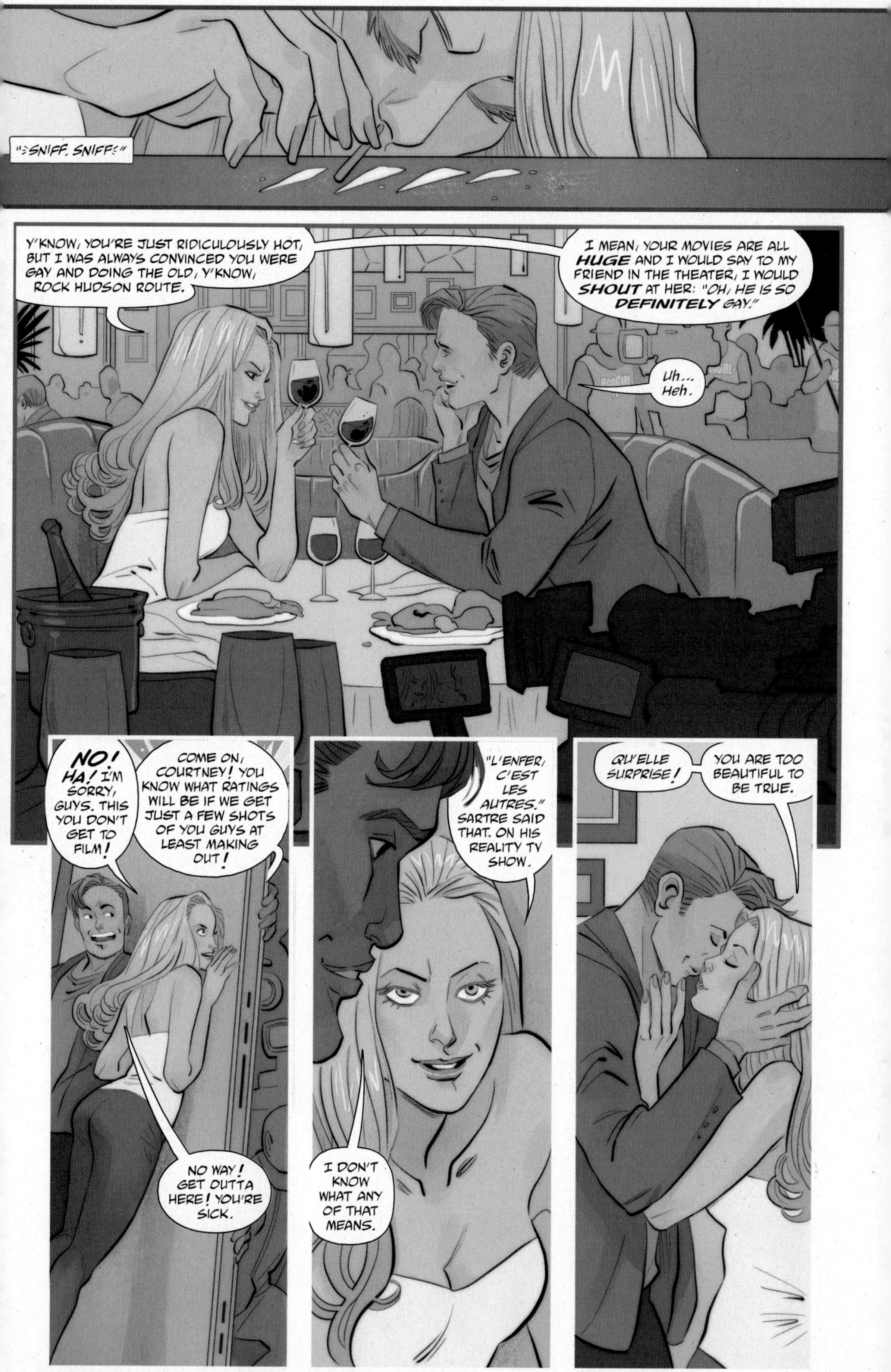
"SNIFF. SNIFF"
Y'KNOW, YOU'RE JUST RIDICULOUSLY HOT, BUT I WAS ALWAYS CONVINCED YOU WERE GAY AND DOING THE OLD, Y'KNOW, ROCK HUDSON ROUTE.
I MEAN, YOUR MOVIES ARE ALL HUGE AND I WOULD SAY TO MY FRIEND IN THE THEATER, I WOULD SHOUT AT HER: "OH, HE IS SO DEFINITELY GAY."
Uh... Heh.
NO! HA! I'M SORRY, GUYS. THIS YOU DON'T GET TO FILM!
COME ON, COURTNEY! YOU KNOW WHAT RATINGS WILL BE IF WE GET JUST A FEW SHOTS OF YOU GUYS AT LEAST MAKING OUT!
NO WAY! GET OUTTA HERE! YOU'RE SICK.
"L'ENFER, C'EST LES AUTRES." SARTRE SAID THAT. ON HIS REALITY TV SHOW.
I DON'T KNOW WHAT ANY OF THAT MEANS.
QU'ELLE SURPRISE!
YOU ARE TOO BEAUTIFUL TO BE TRUE.

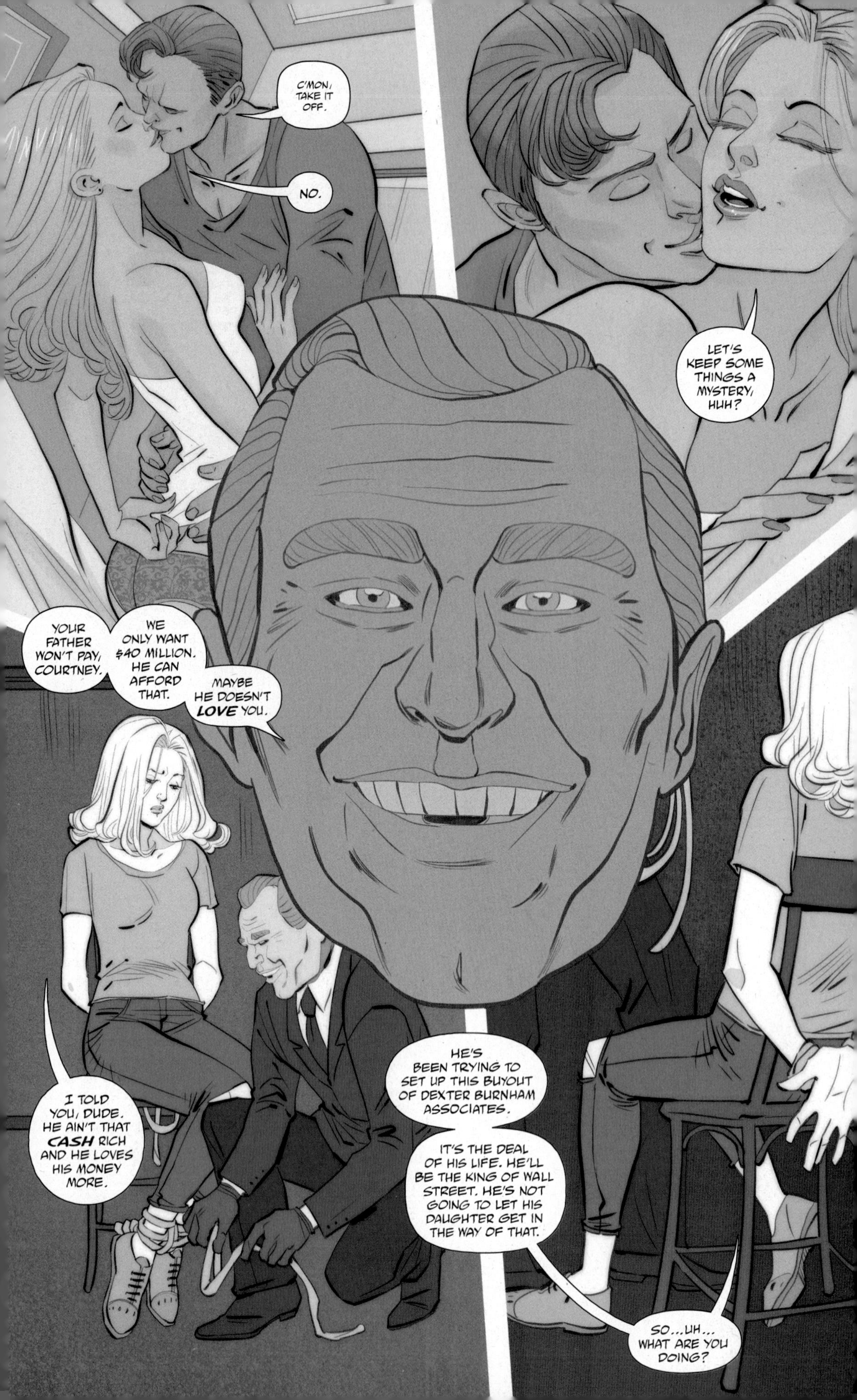
C'MON, TAKE IT OFF.
NO.
LET'S KEEP SOME THINGS A MYSTERY, HUH?
YOUR FATHER WON'T PAY, COURTNEY.
WE ONLY WANT $40 MILLION. HE CAN AFFORD THAT.
MAYBE HE DOESN'T LOVE YOU.
I TOLD YOU, DUDE. HE AIN'T THAT CASH RICH AND HE LOVES HIS MONEY MORE.
HE'S BEEN TRYING TO SET UP THIS BUYOUT OF DEXTER BURNHAM ASSOCIATES.
IT'S THE DEAL OF HIS LIFE. HE'LL BE THE KING OF WALL STREET. HE'S NOT GOING TO LET HIS DAUGHTER GET IN THE WAY OF THAT.
SO...UH... WHAT ARE YOU DOING?

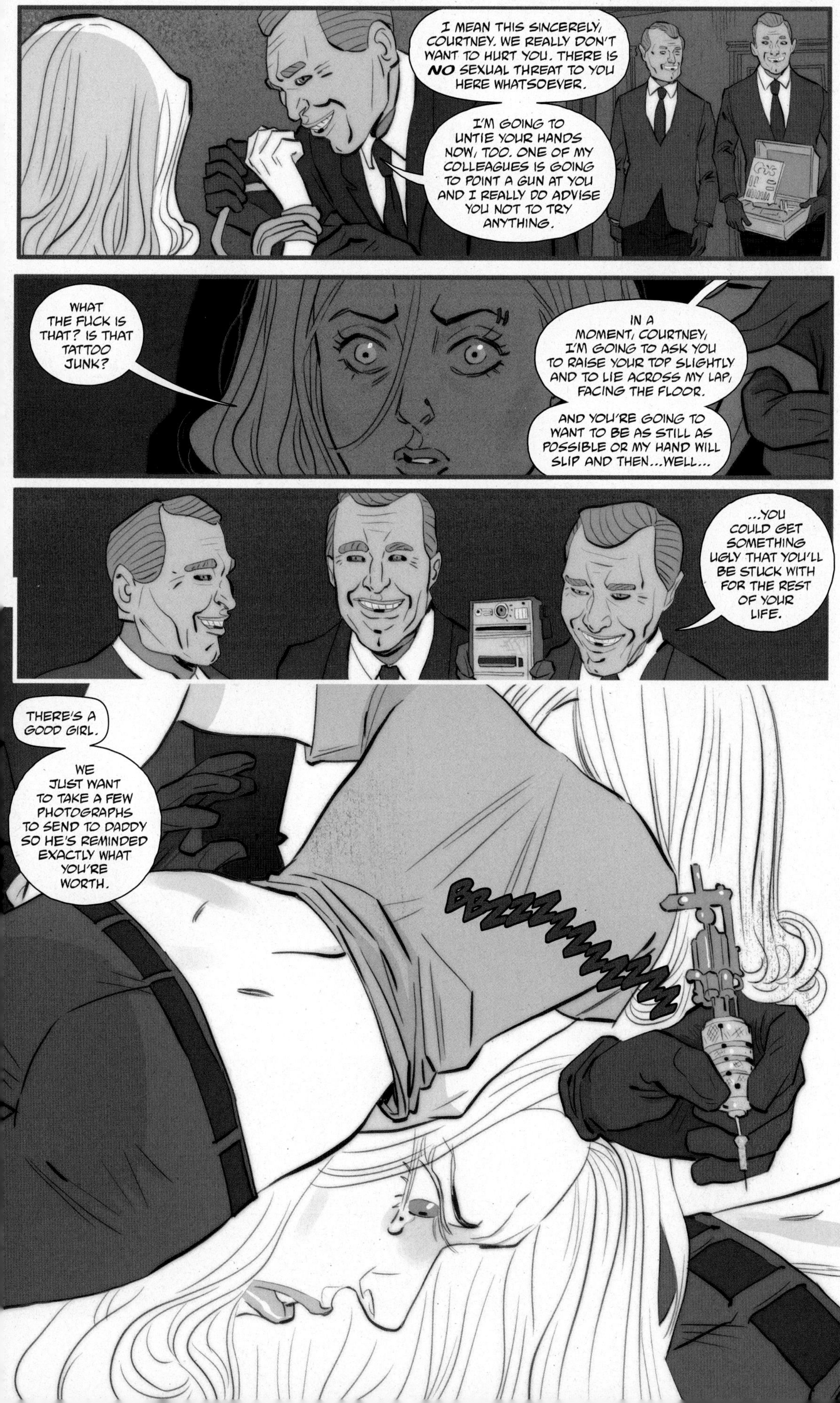
I MEAN THIS SINCERELY, COURTNEY. WE REALLY DON'T WANT TO HURT YOU. THERE IS **NO** SEXUAL THREAT TO YOU HERE WHATSOEVER.
I'M GOING TO UNTIE YOUR HANDS NOW, TOO. ONE OF MY COLLEAGUES IS GOING TO POINT A GUN AT YOU AND I REALLY DO ADVISE YOU NOT TO TRY ANYTHING.
WHAT THE FUCK IS THAT? IS THAT TATTOO JUNK?
IN A MOMENT, COURTNEY, I'M GOING TO ASK YOU TO RAISE YOUR TOP SLIGHTLY AND TO LIE ACROSS MY LAP, FACING THE FLOOR.
AND YOU'RE GOING TO WANT TO BE AS STILL AS POSSIBLE OR MY HAND WILL SLIP AND THEN...WELL...
...YOU COULD GET SOMETHING UGLY THAT YOU'LL BE STUCK WITH FOR THE REST OF YOUR LIFE.
THERE'S A GOOD GIRL.
WE JUST WANT TO TAKE A FEW PHOTOGRAPHS TO SEND TO DADDY SO HE'S REMINDED EXACTLY WHAT YOU'RE WORTH.
BBZZZZMMMMMM

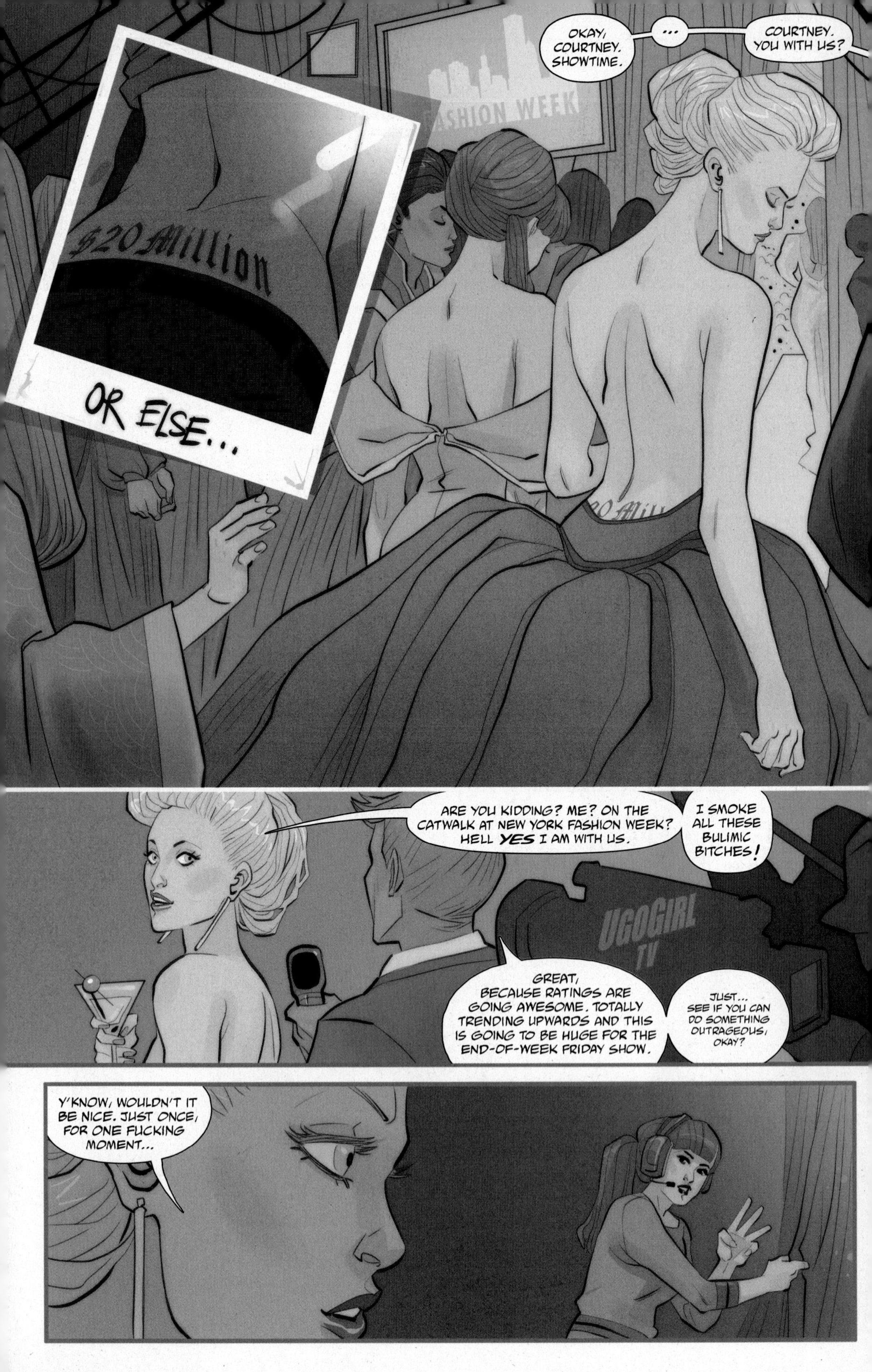
$20 Million
OR ELSE...
FASHION WEEK
OKAY, COURTNEY. SHOWTIME.
...
COURTNEY. YOU WITH US?
ARE YOU KIDDING? ME? ON THE CATWALK AT NEW YORK FASHION WEEK? HELL YES I AM WITH US.
I SMOKE ALL THESE BULIMIC BITCHES!
UGOGIRL TV
GREAT, BECAUSE RATINGS ARE GOING AWESOME. TOTALLY TRENDING UPWARDS AND THIS IS GOING TO BE HUGE FOR THE END-OF-WEEK FRIDAY SHOW.
JUST... SEE IF YOU CAN DO SOMETHING OUTRAGEOUS, OKAY?
Y'KNOW, WOULDN'T IT BE NICE. JUST ONCE, FOR ONE FUCKING MOMENT...

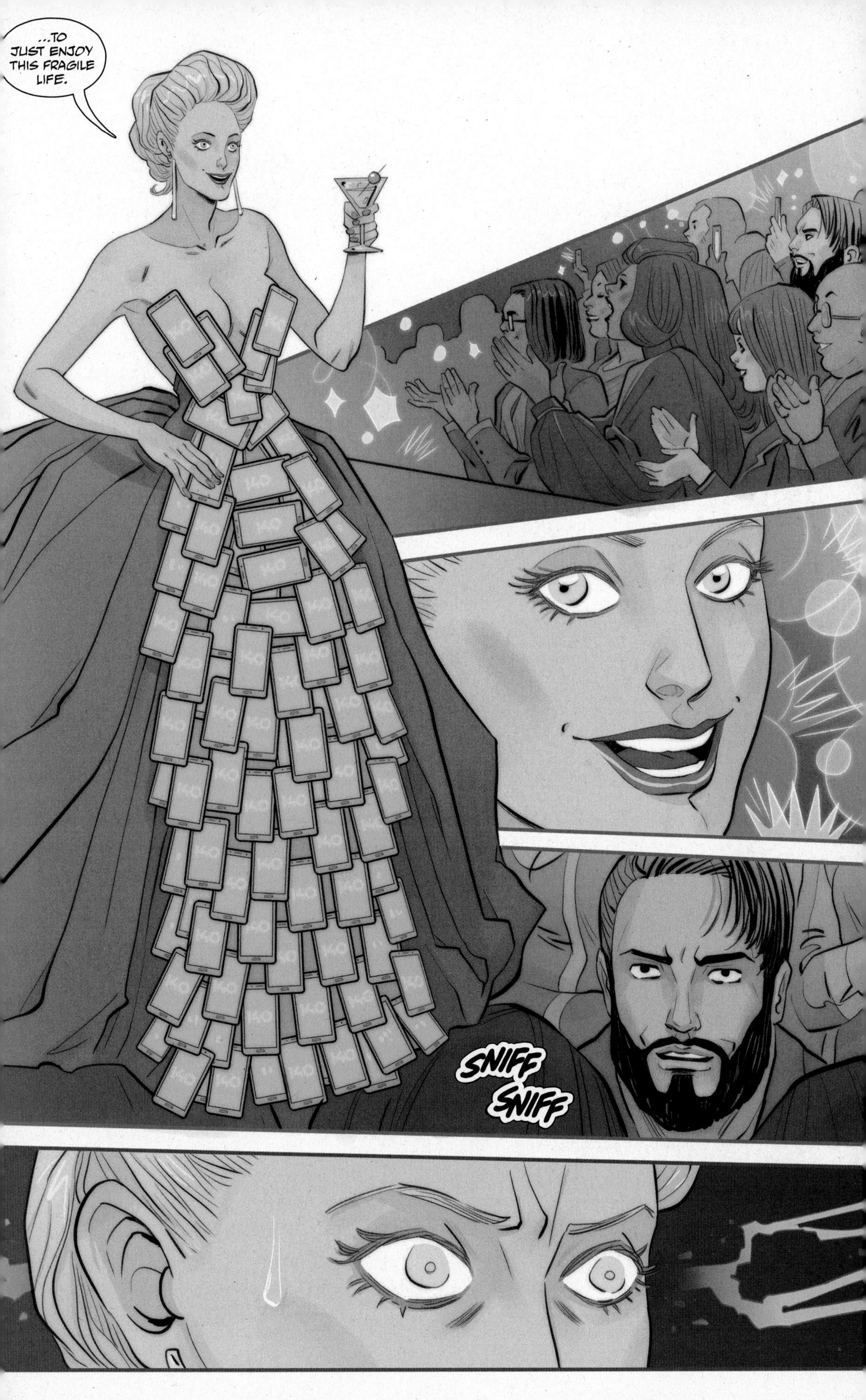
...TO JUST ENJOY THIS FRAGILE LIFE.
SNIFF SNIFF

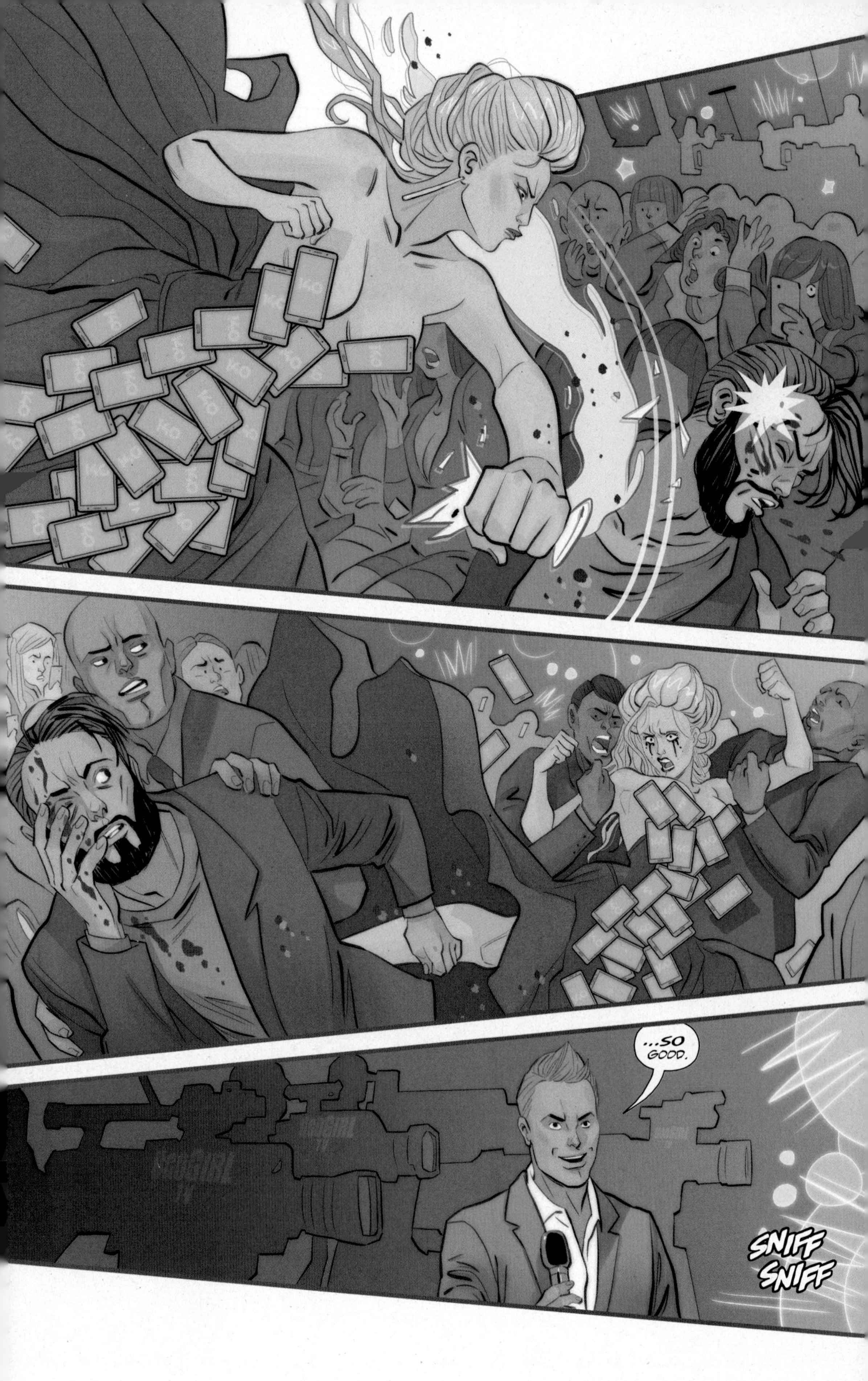
...SO GOOD.
SNIFF SNIFF

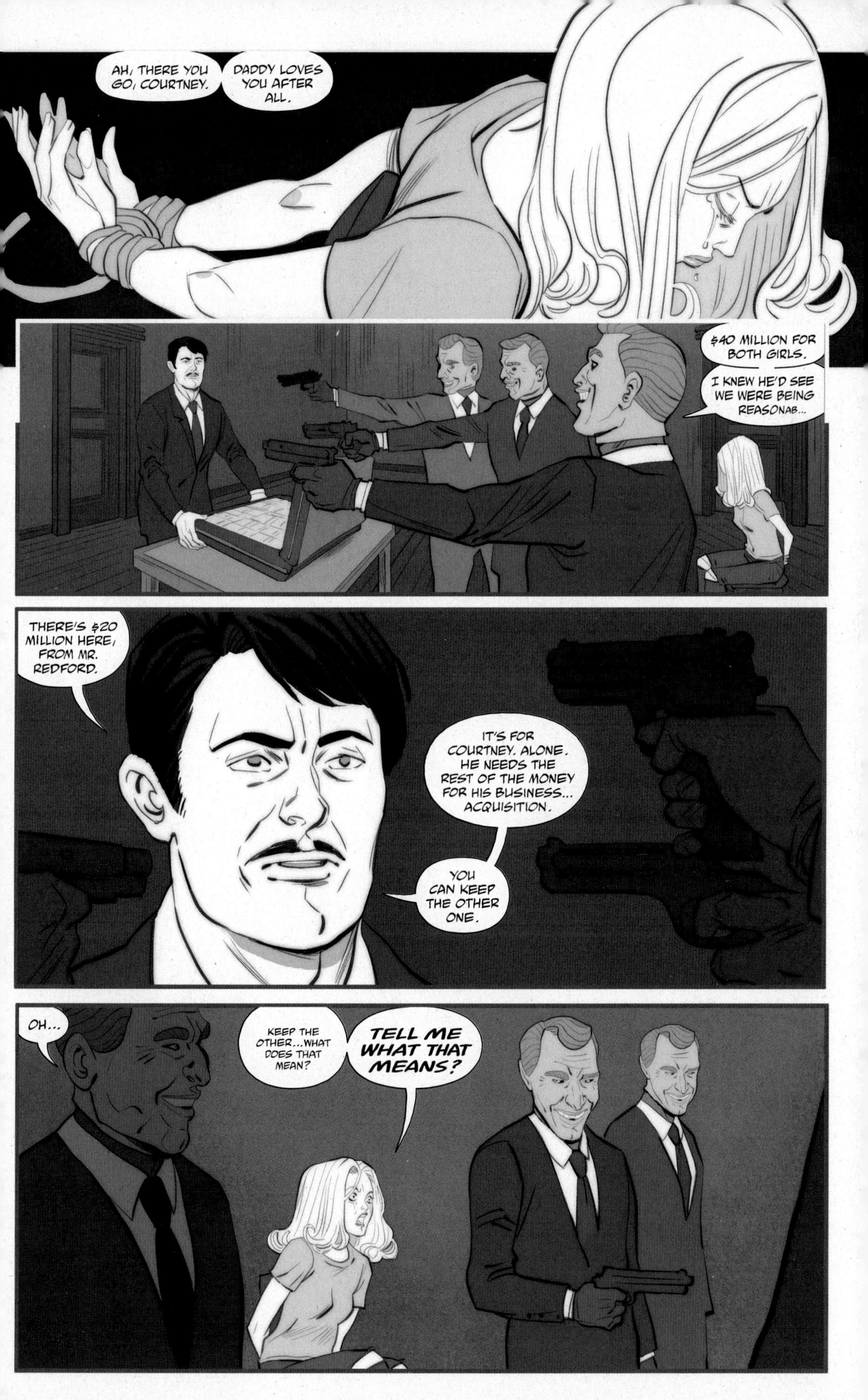
AH, THERE YOU GO, COURTNEY.
DADDY LOVES YOU AFTER ALL.
$40 MILLION FOR BOTH GIRLS.
I KNEW HE'D SEE WE WERE BEING REASONAB...
THERE'S $20 MILLION HERE, FROM MR. REDFORD.
IT'S FOR COURTNEY. ALONE. HE NEEDS THE REST OF THE MONEY FOR HIS BUSINESS... ACQUISITION.
YOU CAN KEEP THE OTHER ONE.
OH...
KEEP THE OTHER...WHAT DOES THAT MEAN?
TELL ME WHAT THAT MEANS?

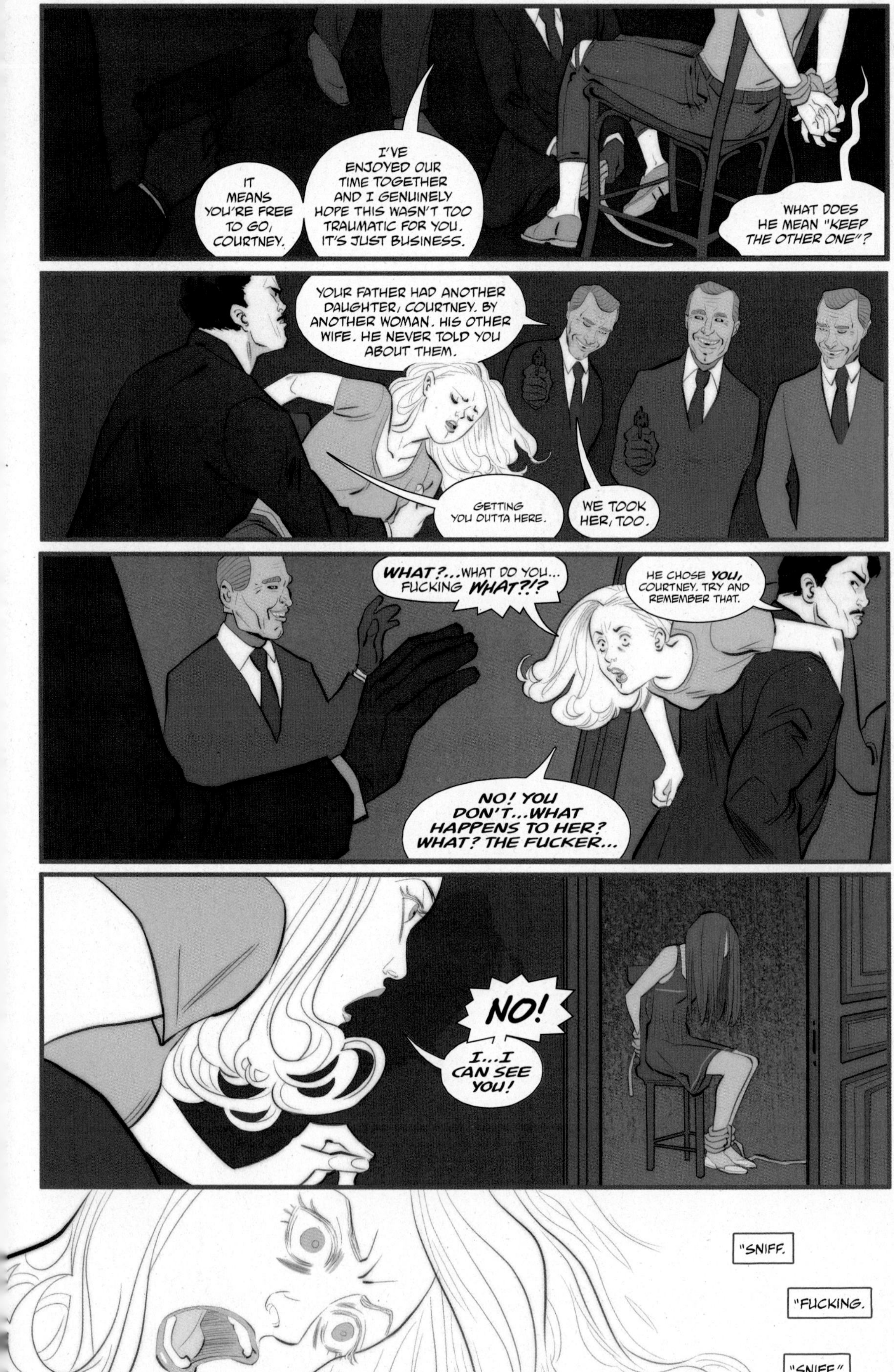
WHAT DOES HE MEAN "KEEP THE OTHER ONE"?
I'VE ENJOYED OUR TIME TOGETHER AND I GENUINELY HOPE THIS WASN'T TOO TRAUMATIC FOR YOU. IT'S JUST BUSINESS.
IT MEANS YOU'RE FREE TO GO, COURTNEY.
YOUR FATHER HAD ANOTHER DAUGHTER, COURTNEY. BY ANOTHER WOMAN. HIS OTHER WIFE. HE NEVER TOLD YOU ABOUT THEM.
WE TOOK HER, TOO.
GETTING YOU OUTTA HERE.
WHAT?...WHAT DO YOU... FUCKING WHAT?!?
HE CHOSE YOU, COURTNEY. TRY AND REMEMBER THAT.
NO! YOU DON'T...WHAT HAPPENS TO HER? WHAT? THE FUCKER...
NO!
I...I CAN SEE YOU!
"SNIFF.
"FUCKING.
"SNIFF."

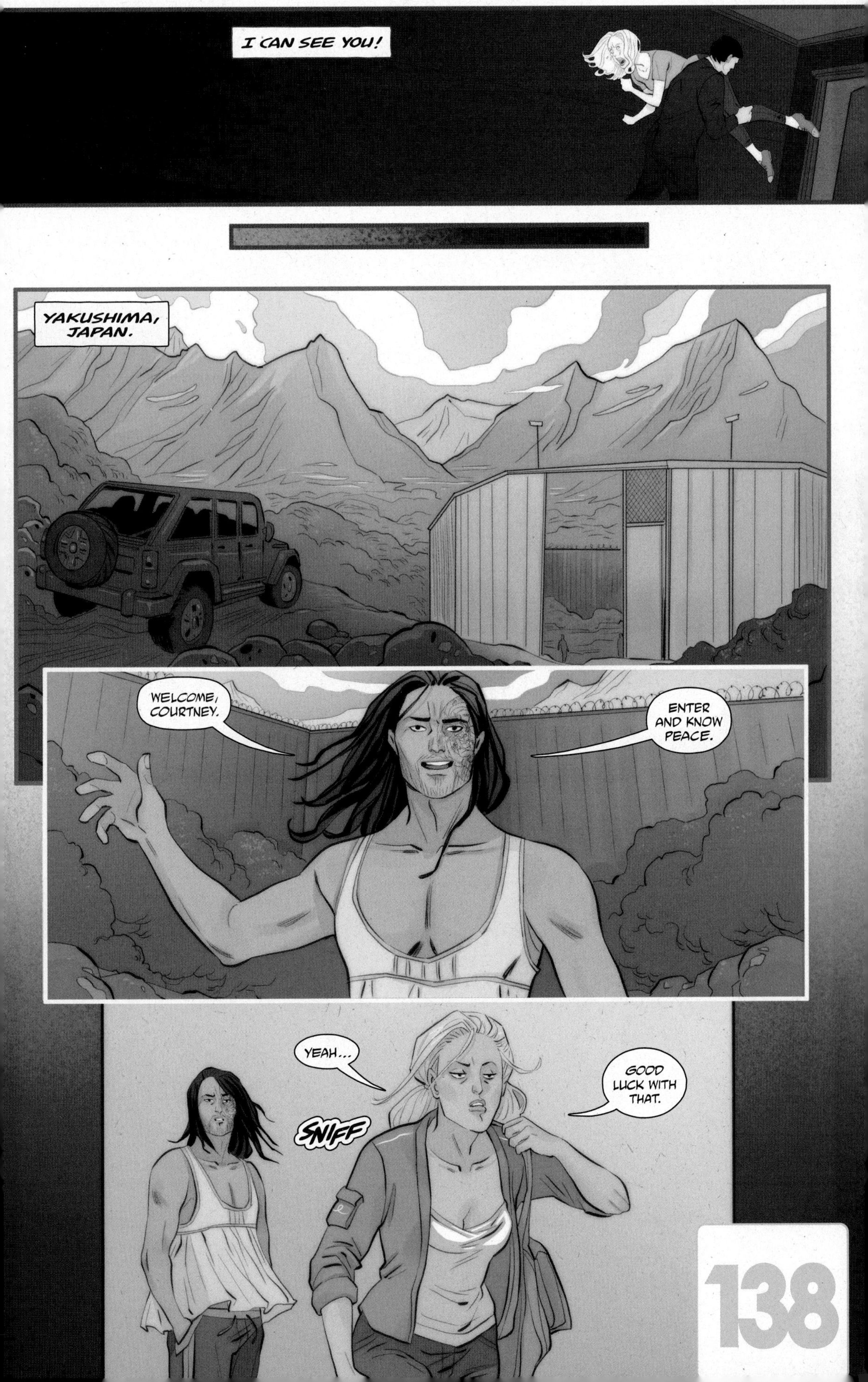
I CAN SEE YOU!
YAKUSHIMA, JAPAN.
WELCOME, COURTNEY.
ENTER AND KNOW PEACE.
YEAH...
GOOD LUCK WITH THAT.
SNIFF
138

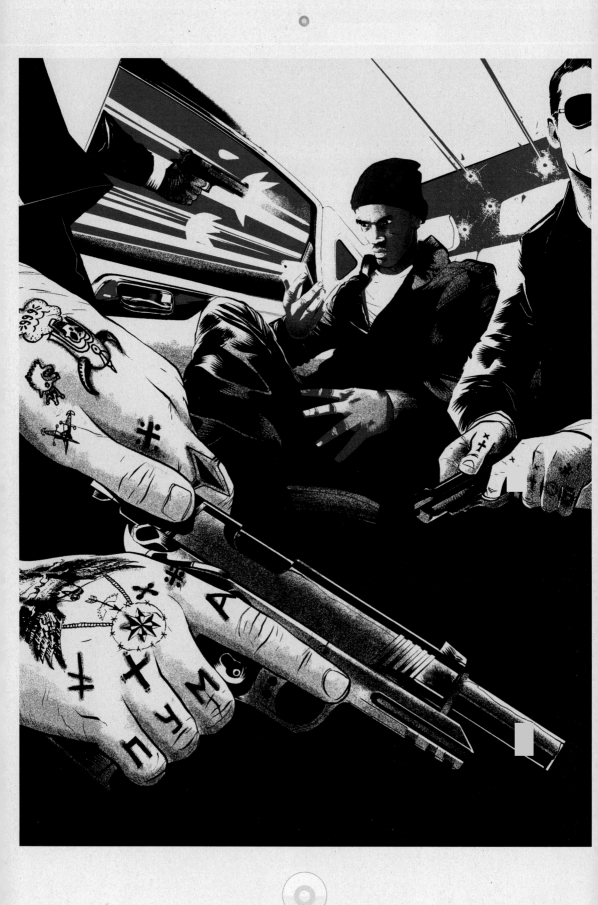

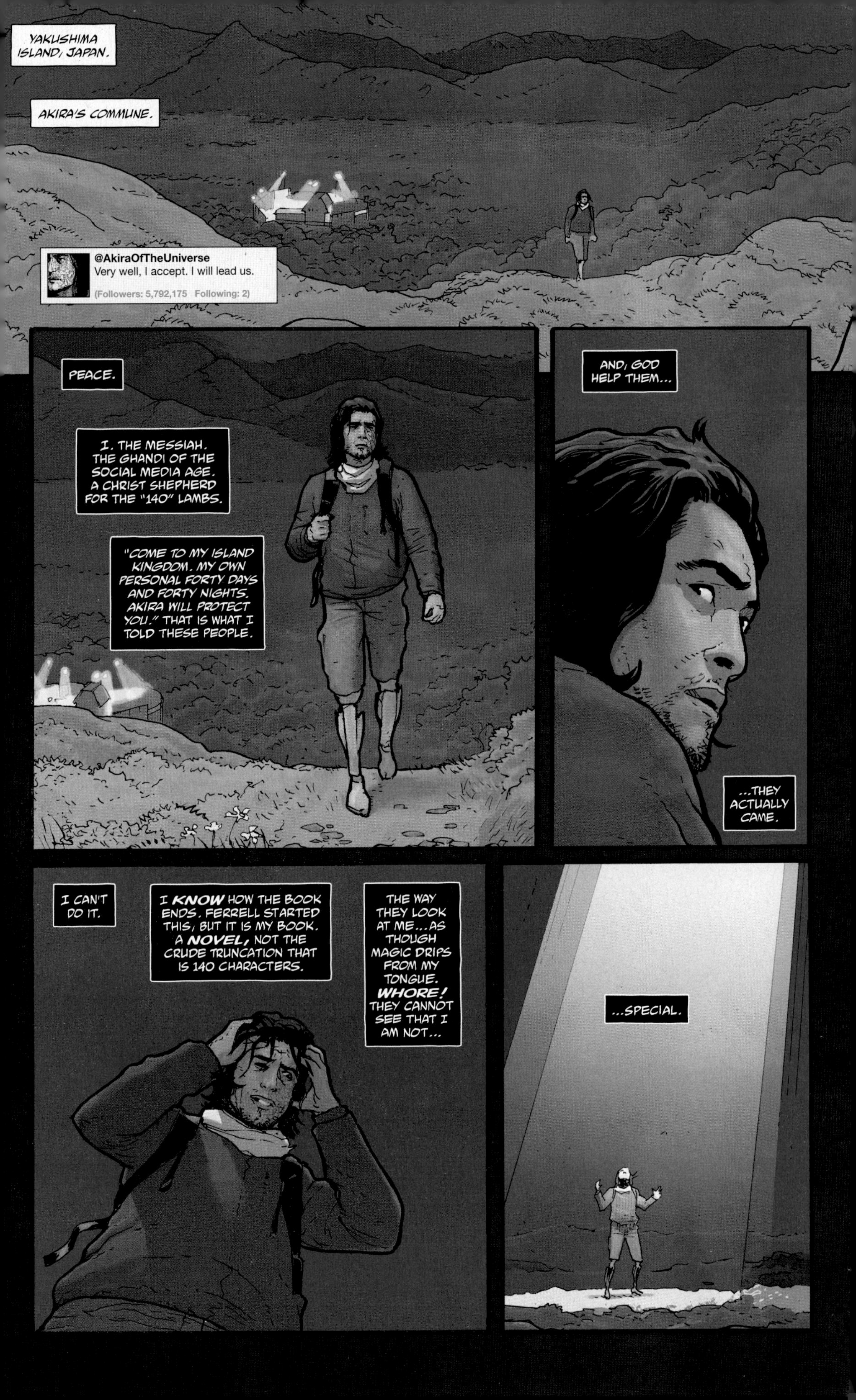
YAKUSHIMA ISLAND, JAPAN.
AKIRA'S COMMUNE.
@AkiraOfTheUniverse
Very well, I accept. I will lead us.
(Followers: 5,792,175 Following: 2)
PEACE.
I. THE MESSIAH. THE GHANDI OF THE SOCIAL MEDIA AGE. A CHRIST SHEPHERD FOR THE "140" LAMBS.
"COME TO MY ISLAND KINGDOM. MY OWN PERSONAL FORTY DAYS AND FORTY NIGHTS. AKIRA WILL PROTECT YOU." THAT IS WHAT I TOLD THESE PEOPLE.
AND, GOD HELP THEM...
...THEY ACTUALLY CAME.
I CAN'T DO IT.
I KNOW HOW THE BOOK ENDS. FERRELL STARTED THIS, BUT IT IS MY BOOK. A NOVEL, NOT THE CRUDE TRUNCATION THAT IS 140 CHARACTERS.
THE WAY THEY LOOK AT ME...AS THOUGH MAGIC DRIPS FROM MY TONGUE. WHORE! THEY CANNOT SEE THAT I AM NOT...
...SPECIAL.

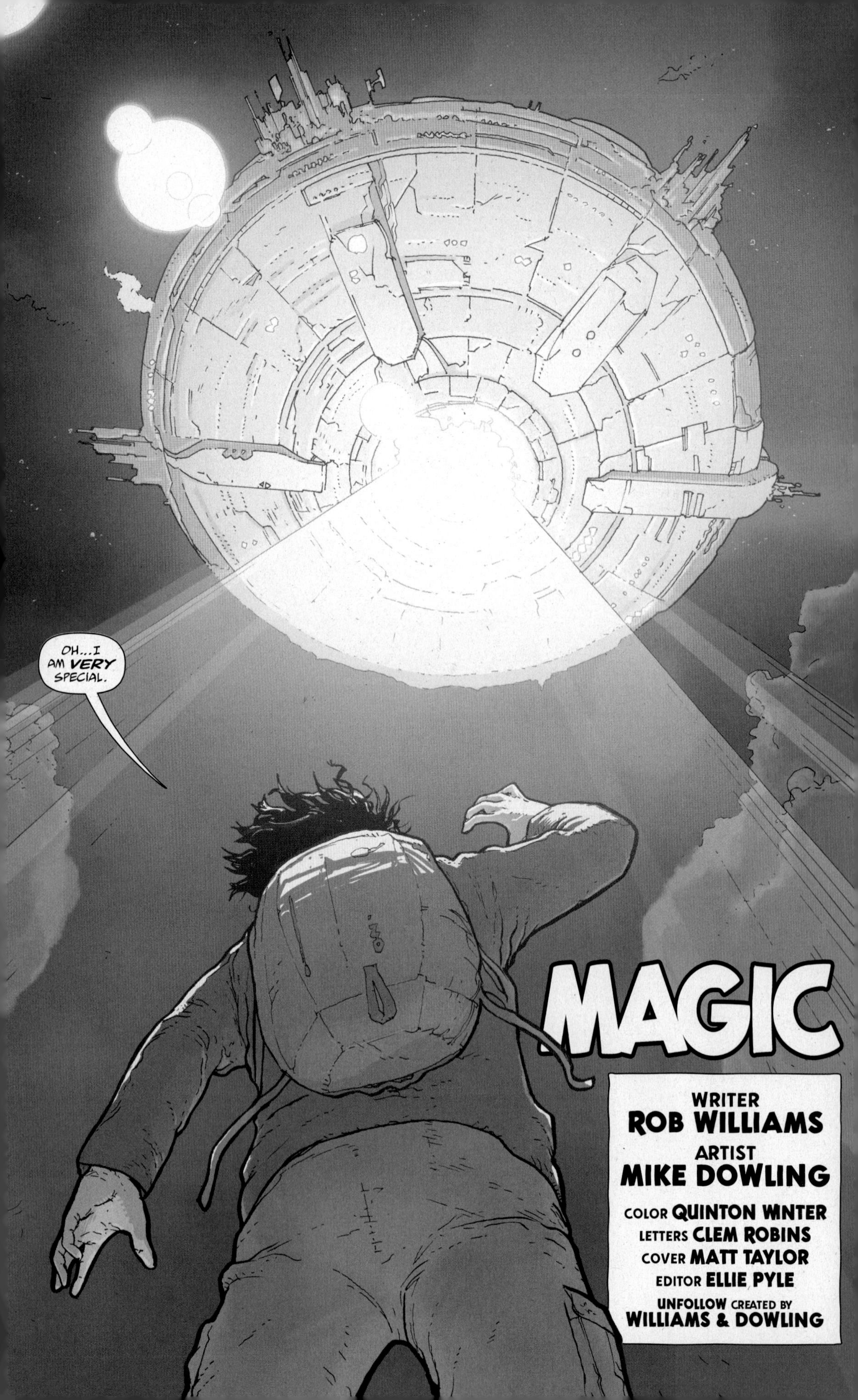
OH...I AM VERY SPECIAL.
MAGIC
WRITER ROB WILLIAMS
ARTIST MIKE DOWLING
COLOR QUINTON WINTER
LETTERS CLEM ROBINS
COVER MATT TAYLOR
EDITOR ELLIE PYLE
UNFOLLOW CREATED BY WILLIAMS & DOWLING

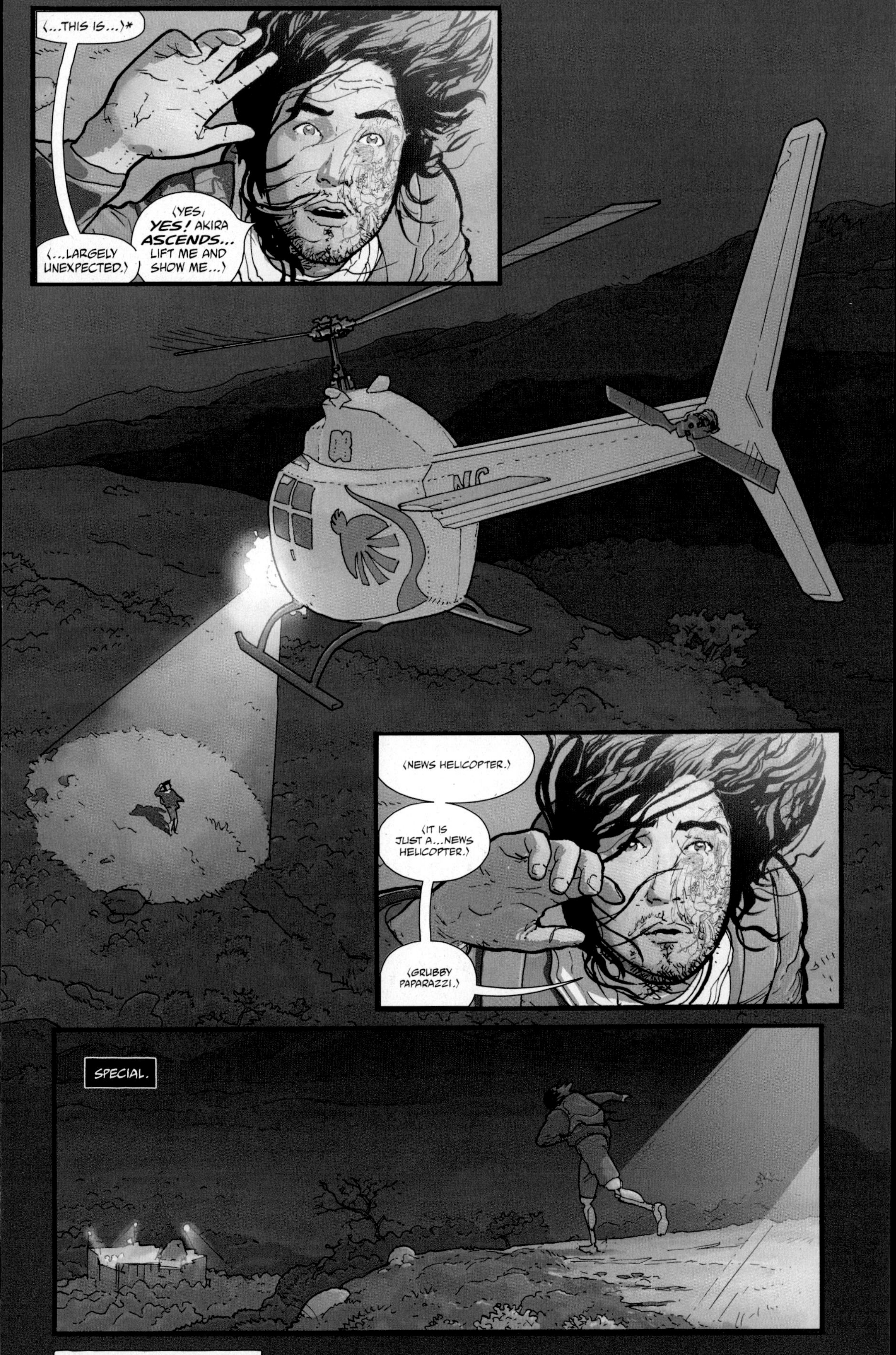

⟨...THIS IS...⟩*
⟨...LARGELY UNEXPECTED.⟩
⟨YES, YES! AKIRA ASCENDS... LIFT ME AND SHOW ME...⟩
⟨NEWS HELICOPTER.⟩
⟨IT IS JUST A...NEWS HELICOPTER.⟩
⟨GRUBBY PAPARAZZI.⟩
SPECIAL.

*TRANSLATED FROM JAPANESE.

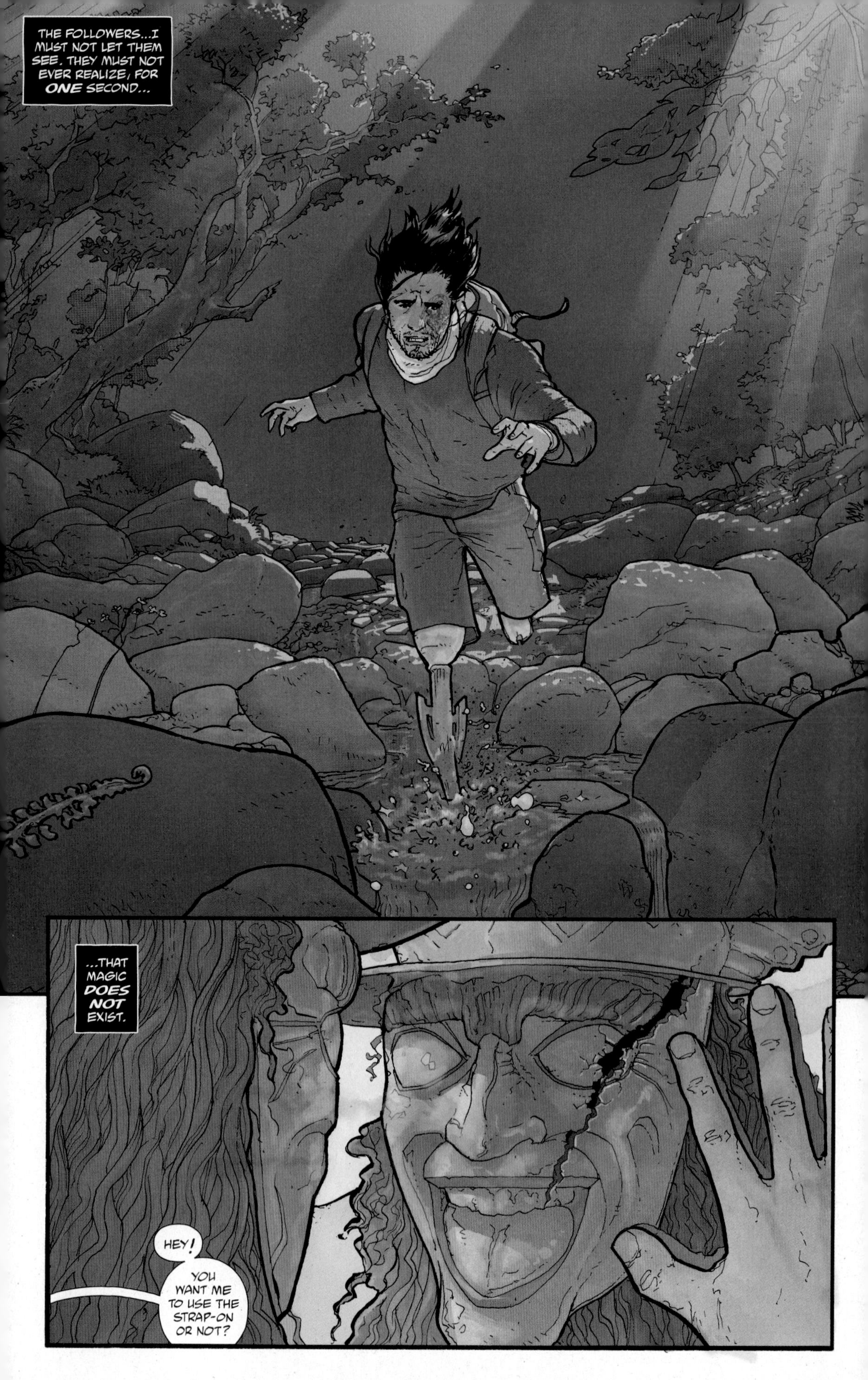
THE FOLLOWERS...I MUST NOT LET THEM SEE. THEY MUST NOT EVER REALIZE, FOR ONE SECOND...
...THAT MAGIC DOES NOT EXIST.
HEY!
YOU WANT ME TO USE THE STRAP-ON OR NOT?

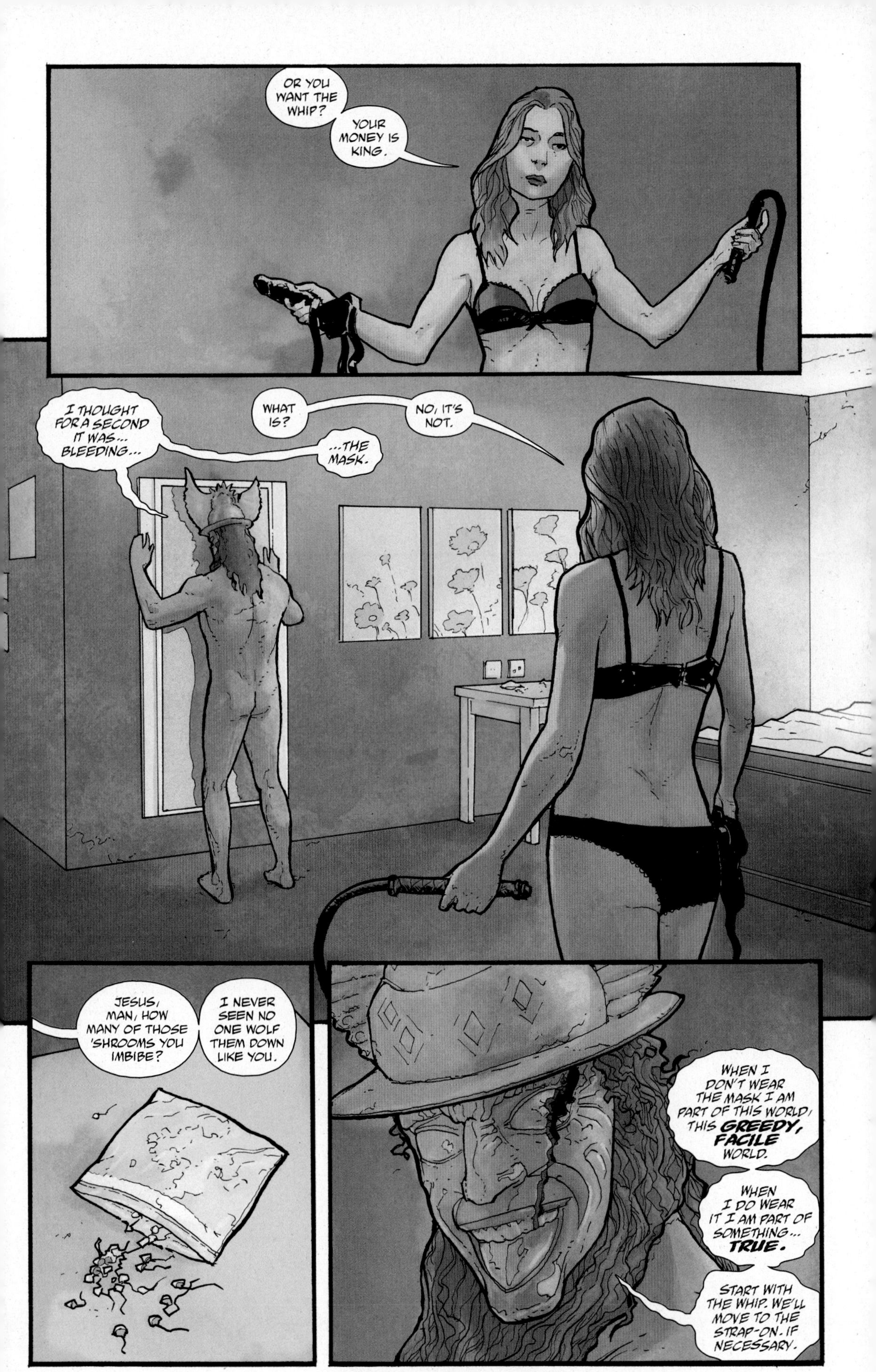
OR YOU WANT THE WHIP?
YOUR MONEY IS KING.
I THOUGHT FOR A SECOND IT WAS... BLEEDING...
WHAT IS?
...THE MASK.
NO, IT'S NOT.
JESUS, MAN, HOW MANY OF THOSE 'SHROOMS YOU IMBIBE?
I NEVER SEEN NO ONE WOLF THEM DOWN LIKE YOU.
WHEN I DON'T WEAR THE MASK I AM PART OF THIS WORLD, THIS GREEDY, FACILE WORLD.
WHEN I DO WEAR IT I AM PART OF SOMETHING... TRUE.
START WITH THE WHIP. WE'LL MOVE TO THE STRAP-ON. IF NECESSARY.

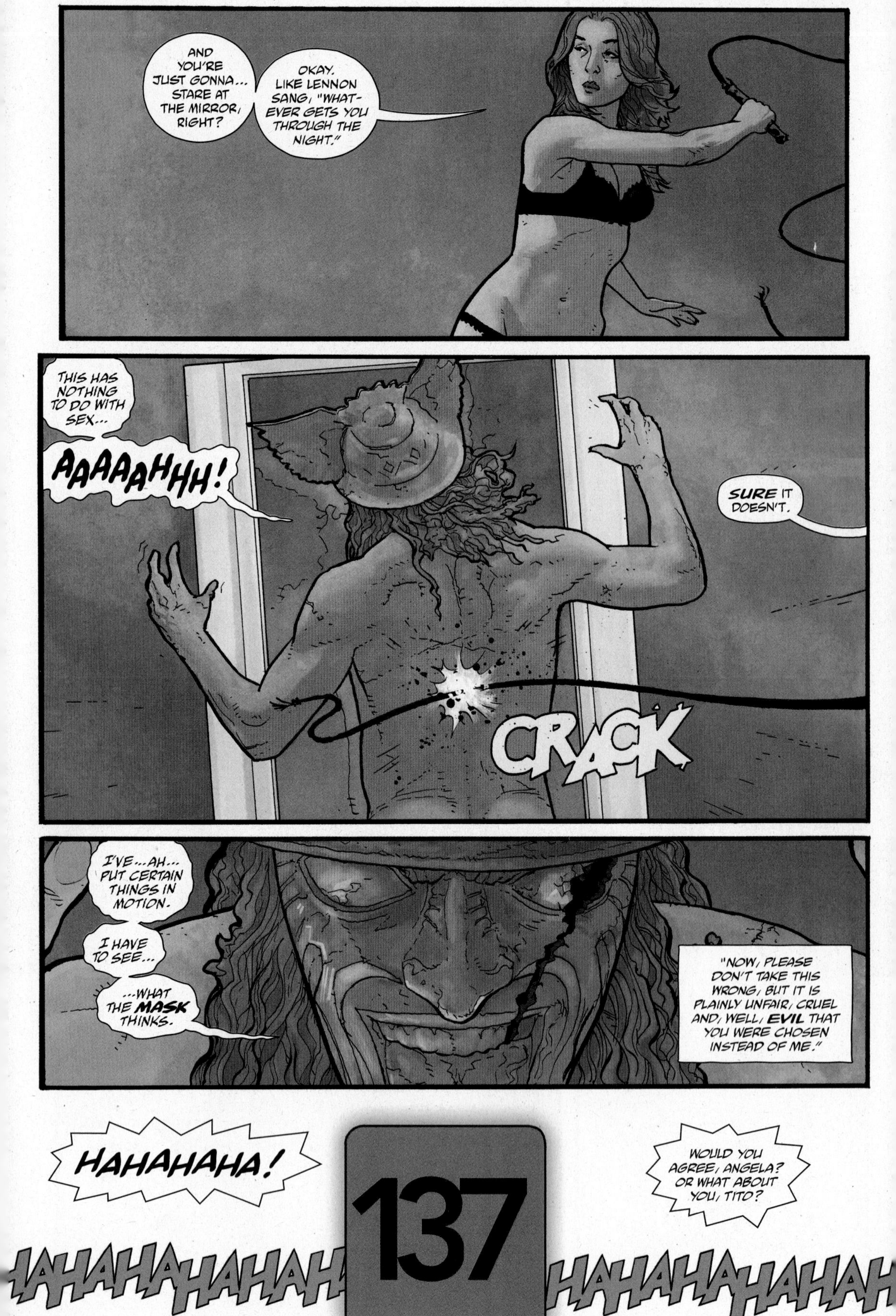

AND YOU'RE JUST GONNA... STARE AT THE MIRROR, RIGHT?
OKAY. LIKE LENNON SANG, "WHATEVER GETS YOU THROUGH THE NIGHT."
THIS HAS NOTHING TO DO WITH SEX...
AAAAAHHH!
SURE IT DOESN'T.
CRACK
I'VE...AH... PUT CERTAIN THINGS IN MOTION.
I HAVE TO SEE...
...WHAT THE MASK THINKS.
"NOW, PLEASE DON'T TAKE THIS WRONG, BUT IT IS PLAINLY UNFAIR, CRUEL AND, WELL, EVIL THAT YOU WERE CHOSEN INSTEAD OF ME."
HAHAHAHA!
WOULD YOU AGREE, ANGELA? OR WHAT ABOUT YOU, TITO?
HAHAHAHAHAHAH
HAHAHAHAHAHAH

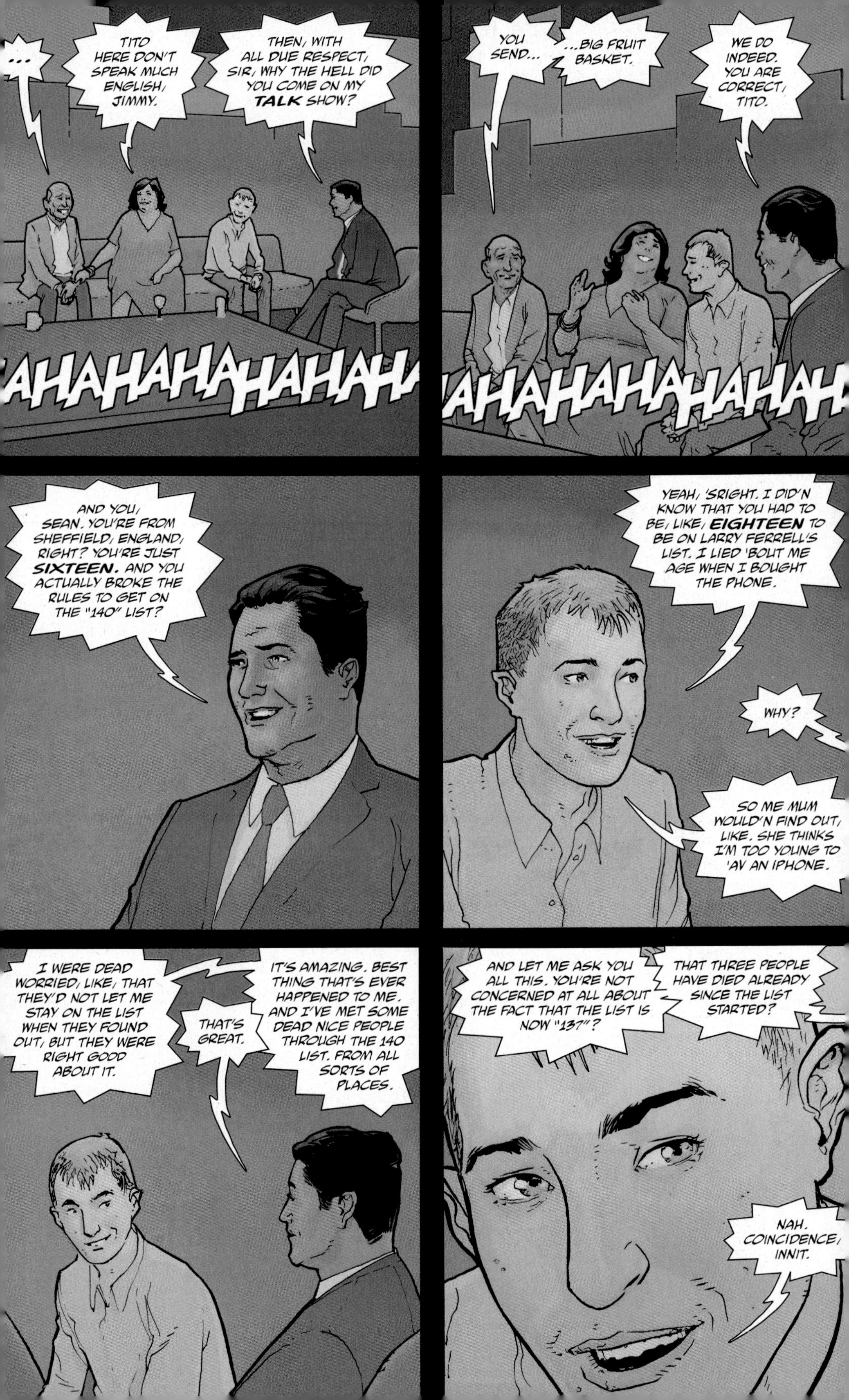
...
TITO HERE DON'T SPEAK MUCH ENGLISH, JIMMY.
THEN, WITH ALL DUE RESPECT, SIR, WHY THE HELL DID YOU COME ON MY TALK SHOW?
AHAHAHAHAHAHAH
YOU SEND...
...BIG FRUIT BASKET.
WE DO INDEED. YOU ARE CORRECT, TITO.
AHAHAHAHAHAHAH
AND YOU, SEAN. YOU'RE FROM SHEFFIELD, ENGLAND, RIGHT? YOU'RE JUST SIXTEEN. AND YOU ACTUALLY BROKE THE RULES TO GET ON THE "140" LIST?
YEAH, 'SRIGHT. I DID'N KNOW THAT YOU HAD TO BE, LIKE, EIGHTEEN TO BE ON LARRY FERRELL'S LIST. I LIED 'BOUT ME AGE WHEN I BOUGHT THE PHONE.
WHY?
SO ME MUM WOULD'N FIND OUT, LIKE. SHE THINKS I'M TOO YOUNG TO 'AV AN IPHONE.
I WERE DEAD WORRIED, LIKE, THAT THEY'D NOT LET ME STAY ON THE LIST WHEN THEY FOUND OUT, BUT THEY WERE RIGHT GOOD ABOUT IT.
THAT'S GREAT.
IT'S AMAZING. BEST THING THAT'S EVER HAPPENED TO ME. AND I'VE MET SOME DEAD NICE PEOPLE THROUGH THE 140 LIST. FROM ALL SORTS OF PLACES.
AND LET ME ASK YOU ALL THIS. YOU'RE NOT CONCERNED AT ALL ABOUT THE FACT THAT THE LIST IS NOW "137"?
THAT THREE PEOPLE HAVE DIED ALREADY SINCE THE LIST STARTED?
NAH. COINCIDENCE, INNIT.

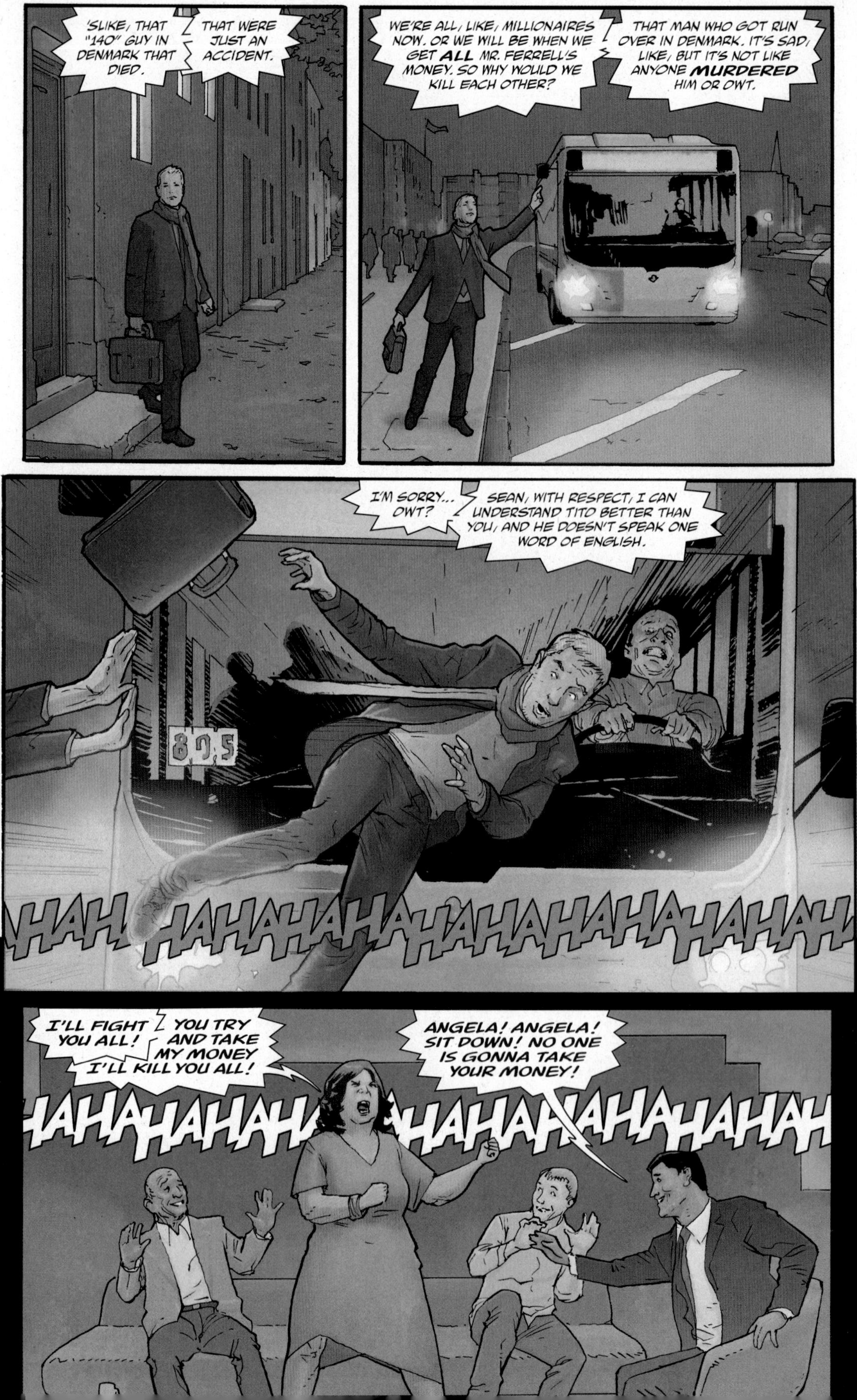
'SLIKE, THAT "140" GUY IN DENMARK THAT DIED.
THAT WERE JUST AN ACCIDENT.
WE'RE ALL, LIKE, MILLIONAIRES NOW. OR WE WILL BE WHEN WE GET ALL MR. FERRELL'S MONEY. SO WHY WOULD WE KILL EACH OTHER?
THAT MAN WHO GOT RUN OVER IN DENMARK. IT'S SAD, LIKE, BUT IT'S NOT LIKE ANYONE MURDERED HIM OR OWT.
I'M SORRY... OWT?
SEAN, WITH RESPECT, I CAN UNDERSTAND TITO BETTER THAN YOU, AND HE DOESN'T SPEAK ONE WORD OF ENGLISH.
805
HAHAHAHAHAHAHAHAHAHAHAHAHAH
I'LL FIGHT YOU ALL!
YOU TRY AND TAKE MY MONEY I'LL KILL YOU ALL!
ANGELA! ANGELA! SIT DOWN! NO ONE IS GONNA TAKE YOUR MONEY!
HAHAHAHAHAHAHAHAHAHAHAHAH

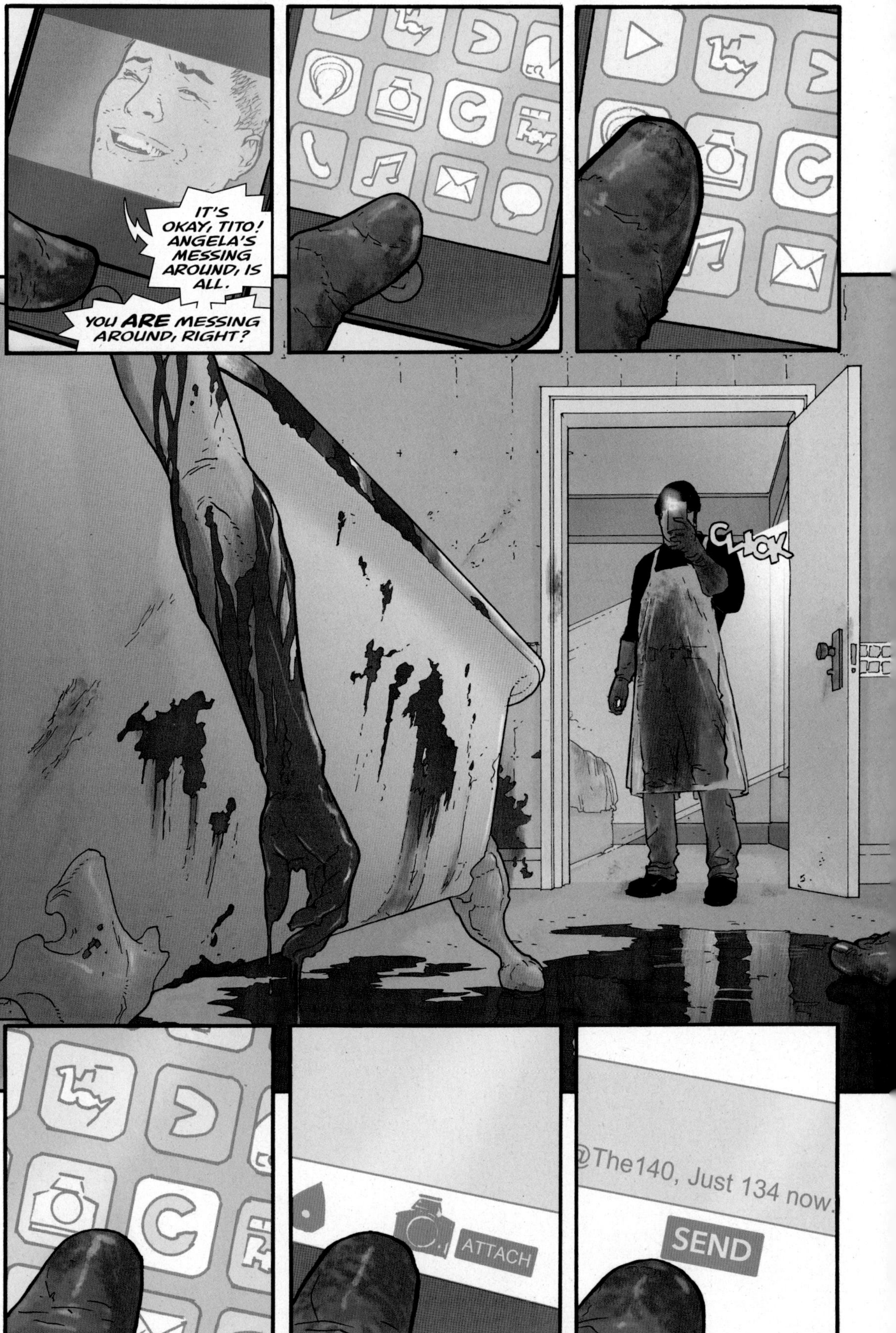
IT'S OKAY, TITO! ANGELA'S MESSING AROUND, IS ALL.
YOU ARE MESSING AROUND, RIGHT?
CLICK
ATTACH
@The140, Just 134 now.
SEND

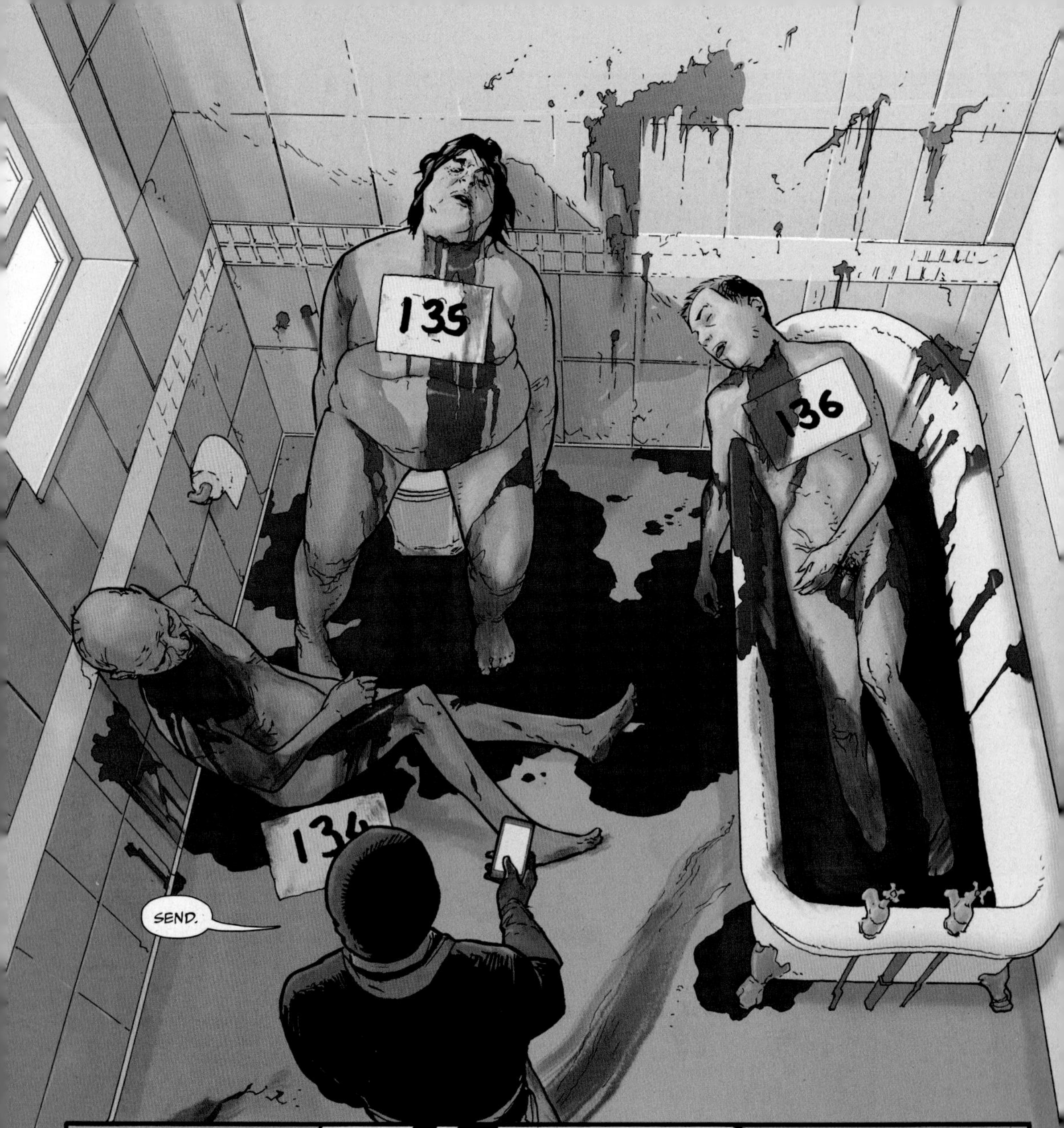
135
136
134
SEND.

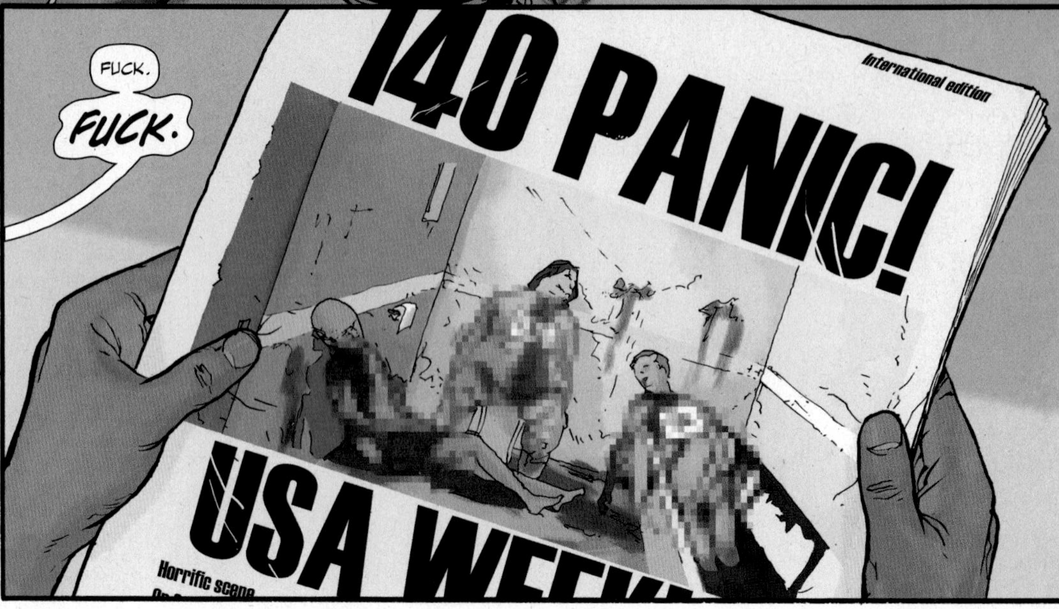
FUCK.
FUCK.
140 PANIC!
International edition
USA WEEK
Horrific scene

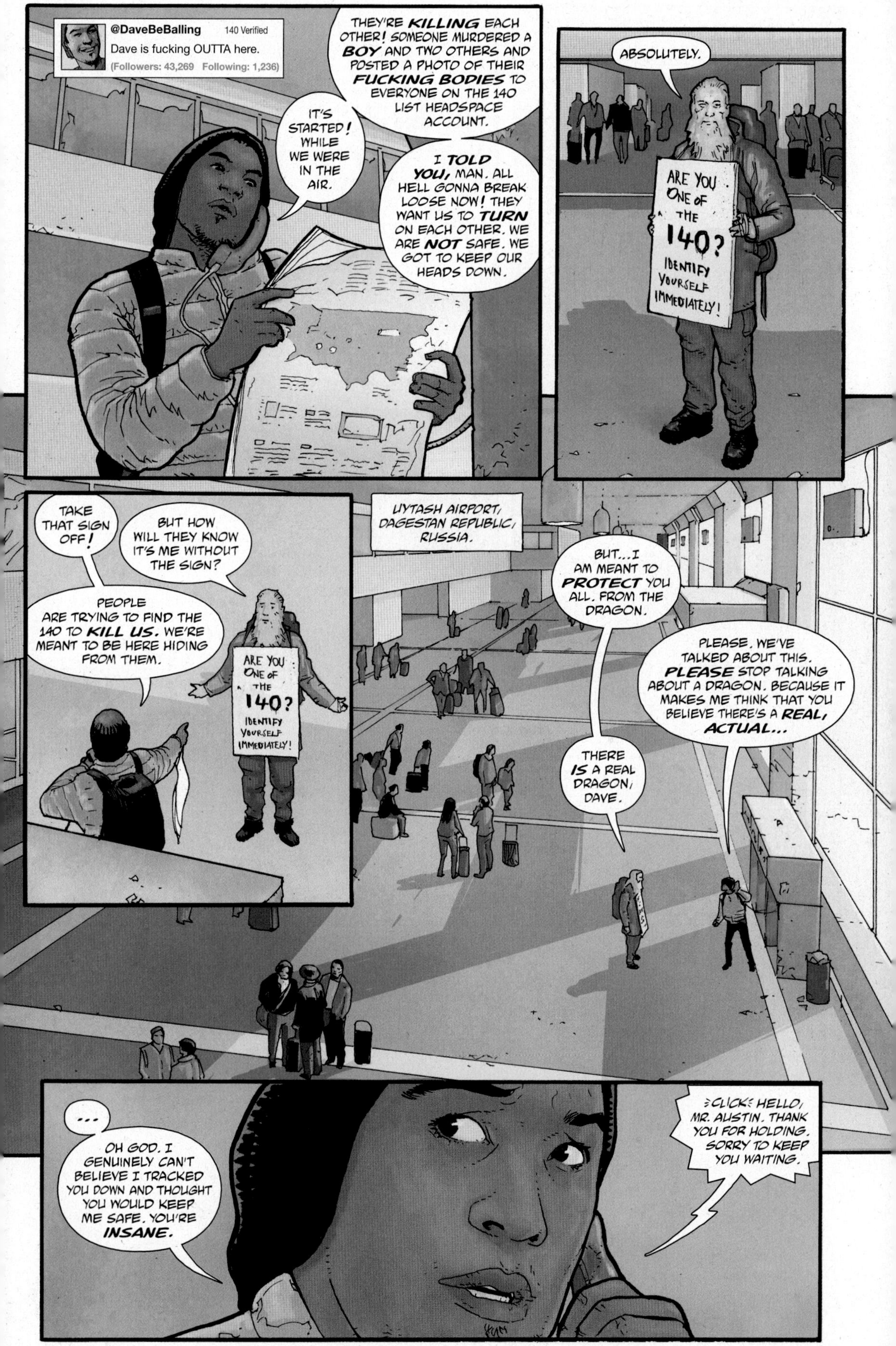
@DaveBeBalling 140 Verified
Dave is fucking OUTTA here.
(Followers: 43,269 Following: 1,236)
IT'S STARTED! WHILE WE WERE IN THE AIR.
THEY'RE KILLING EACH OTHER! SOMEONE MURDERED A BOY AND TWO OTHERS AND POSTED A PHOTO OF THEIR FUCKING BODIES TO EVERYONE ON THE 140 LIST HEADSPACE ACCOUNT.
I TOLD YOU, MAN. ALL HELL GONNA BREAK LOOSE NOW! THEY WANT US TO TURN ON EACH OTHER. WE ARE NOT SAFE. WE GOT TO KEEP OUR HEADS DOWN.
ABSOLUTELY.
ARE YOU ONE OF THE 140? IDENTIFY YOURSELF IMMEDIATELY!
UYTASH AIRPORT, DAGESTAN REPUBLIC, RUSSIA.
TAKE THAT SIGN OFF!
BUT HOW WILL THEY KNOW IT'S ME WITHOUT THE SIGN?
PEOPLE ARE TRYING TO FIND THE 140 TO KILL US. WE'RE MEANT TO BE HERE HIDING FROM THEM.
ARE YOU ONE OF THE 140? IDENTIFY YOURSELF IMMEDIATELY!
BUT...I AM MEANT TO PROTECT YOU ALL. FROM THE DRAGON.
PLEASE. WE'VE TALKED ABOUT THIS. PLEASE STOP TALKING ABOUT A DRAGON. BECAUSE IT MAKES ME THINK THAT YOU BELIEVE THERE'S A REAL, ACTUAL...
THERE IS A REAL DRAGON, DAVE.
...
OH GOD. I GENUINELY CAN'T BELIEVE I TRACKED YOU DOWN AND THOUGHT YOU WOULD KEEP ME SAFE. YOU'RE INSANE.
CLICK HELLO, MR. AUSTIN. THANK YOU FOR HOLDING. SORRY TO KEEP YOU WAITING.

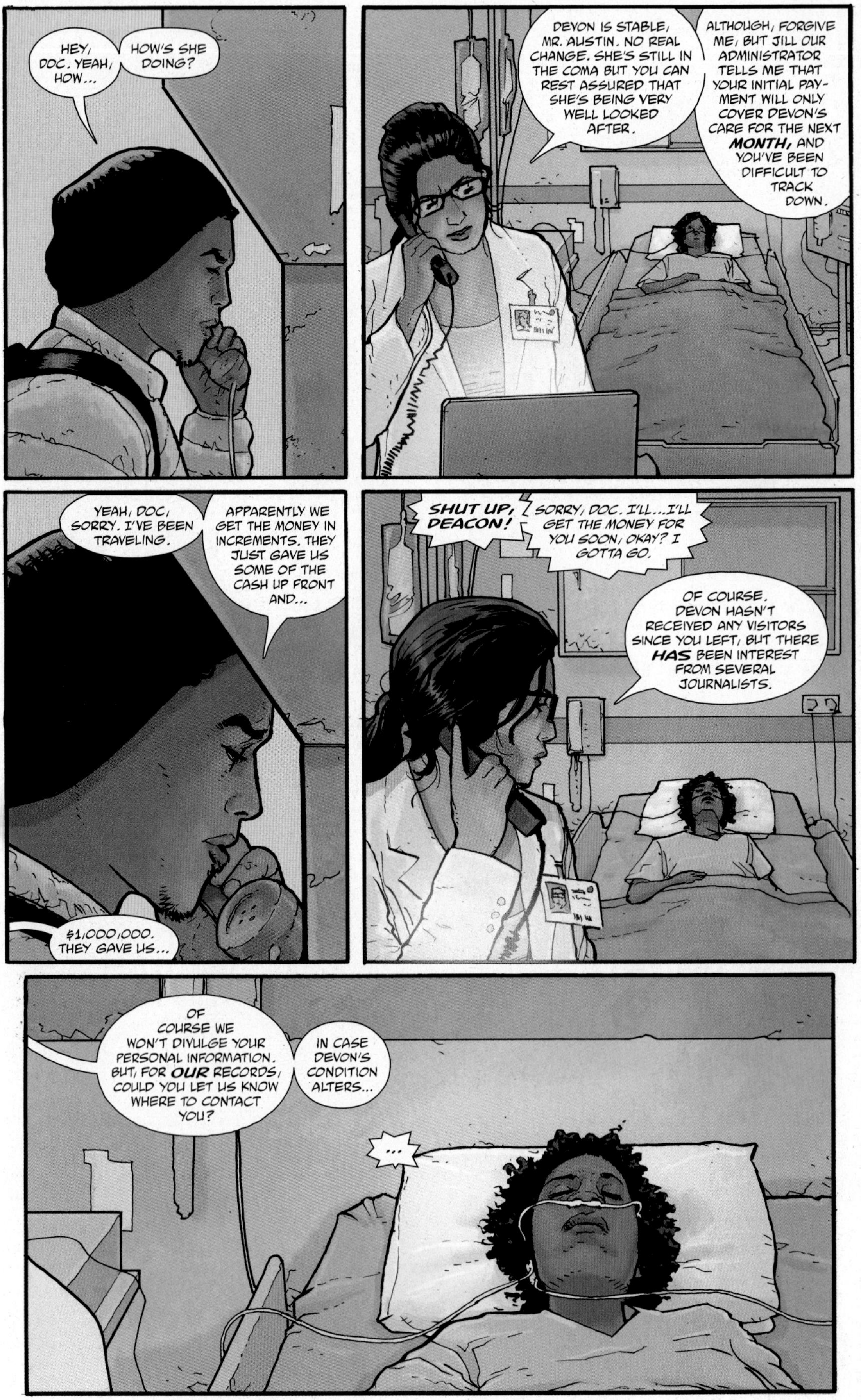
HEY, DOC. YEAH, HOW...
HOW'S SHE DOING?
DEVON IS STABLE, MR. AUSTIN. NO REAL CHANGE. SHE'S STILL IN THE COMA BUT YOU CAN REST ASSURED THAT SHE'S BEING VERY WELL LOOKED AFTER.
ALTHOUGH, FORGIVE ME, BUT JILL OUR ADMINISTRATOR TELLS ME THAT YOUR INITIAL PAYMENT WILL ONLY COVER DEVON'S CARE FOR THE NEXT MONTH, AND YOU'VE BEEN DIFFICULT TO TRACK DOWN.
YEAH, DOC, SORRY. I'VE BEEN TRAVELING.
APPARENTLY WE GET THE MONEY IN INCREMENTS. THEY JUST GAVE US SOME OF THE CASH UP FRONT AND...
$1,000,000. THEY GAVE US...
SHUT UP, DEACON!
SORRY, DOC. I'LL...I'LL GET THE MONEY FOR YOU SOON, OKAY? I GOTTA GO.
OF COURSE. DEVON HASN'T RECEIVED ANY VISITORS SINCE YOU LEFT, BUT THERE HAS BEEN INTEREST FROM SEVERAL JOURNALISTS.
OF COURSE WE WON'T DIVULGE YOUR PERSONAL INFORMATION. BUT, FOR OUR RECORDS, COULD YOU LET US KNOW WHERE TO CONTACT YOU?
IN CASE DEVON'S CONDITION ALTERS...
...

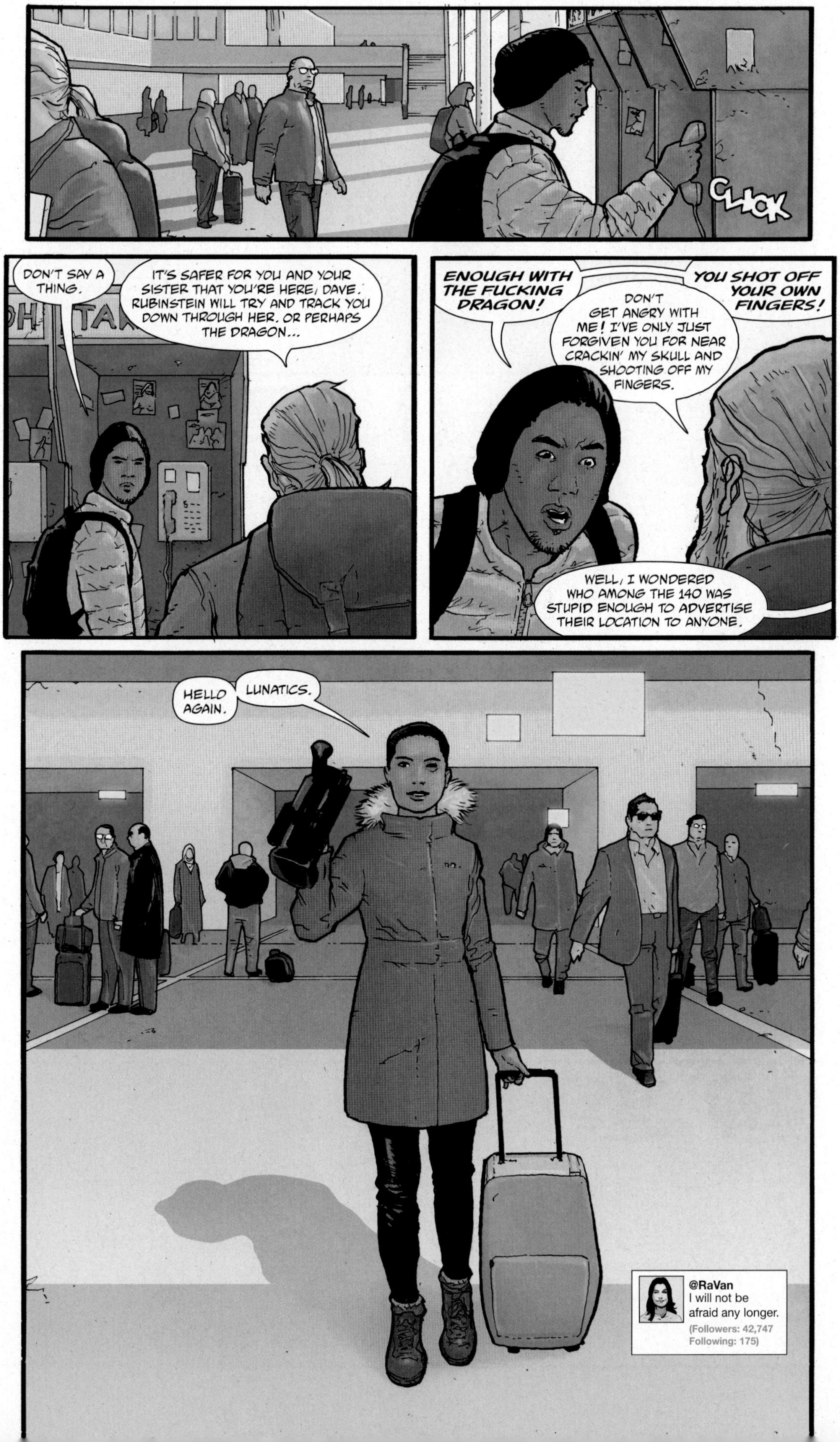
CLICK
DON'T SAY A THING.
IT'S SAFER FOR YOU AND YOUR SISTER THAT YOU'RE HERE, DAVE. RUBINSTEIN WILL TRY AND TRACK YOU DOWN THROUGH HER. OR PERHAPS THE DRAGON...
ENOUGH WITH THE FUCKING DRAGON!
YOU SHOT OFF YOUR OWN FINGERS!
DON'T GET ANGRY WITH ME! I'VE ONLY JUST FORGIVEN YOU FOR NEAR CRACKIN' MY SKULL AND SHOOTING OFF MY FINGERS.
WELL, I WONDERED WHO AMONG THE 140 WAS STUPID ENOUGH TO ADVERTISE THEIR LOCATION TO ANYONE.
HELLO AGAIN.
LUNATICS.
@RaVan
I will not be afraid any longer.
(Followers: 42,747
Following: 175)

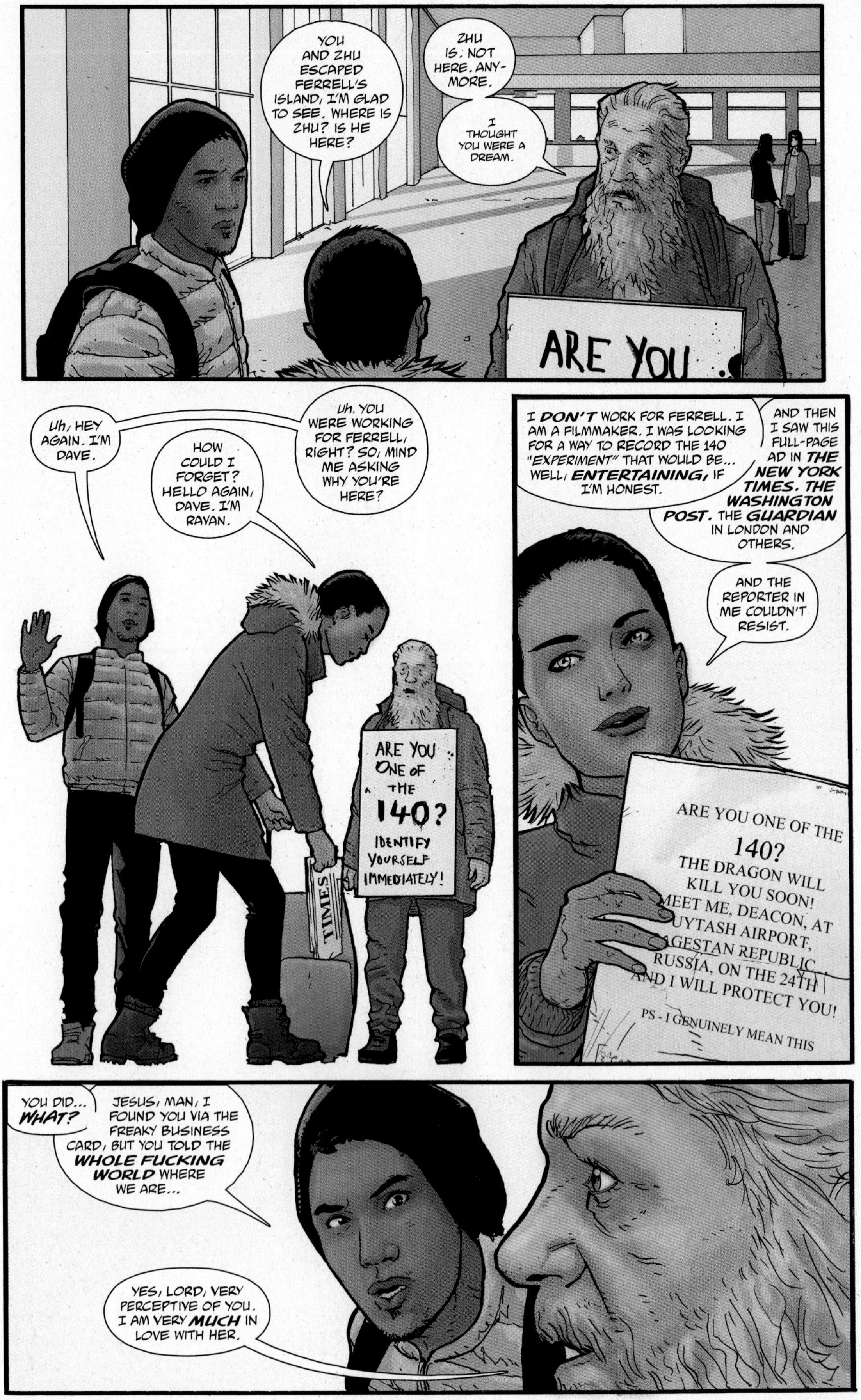

YOU AND ZHU ESCAPED FERRELL'S ISLAND, I'M GLAD TO SEE. WHERE IS ZHU? IS HE HERE?
ZHU IS. NOT HERE. ANY-MORE.
I THOUGHT YOU WERE A DREAM.
ARE YOU
UH, HEY AGAIN. I'M DAVE.
HOW COULD I FORGET? HELLO AGAIN, DAVE. I'M RAYAN.
UH, YOU WERE WORKING FOR FERRELL, RIGHT? SO, MIND ME ASKING WHY YOU'RE HERE?
ARE YOU ONE OF THE 140? IDENTIFY YOURSELF IMMEDIATELY!
TIMES
I DON'T WORK FOR FERRELL. I AM A FILMMAKER. I WAS LOOKING FOR A WAY TO RECORD THE 140 "EXPERIMENT" THAT WOULD BE... WELL, ENTERTAINING, IF I'M HONEST.
AND THEN I SAW THIS FULL-PAGE AD IN THE NEW YORK TIMES. THE WASHINGTON POST. THE GUARDIAN IN LONDON AND OTHERS.
AND THE REPORTER IN ME COULDN'T RESIST.
ARE YOU ONE OF THE 140?
THE DRAGON WILL KILL YOU SOON!
EET ME, DEACON, AT
UYTASH AIRPORT,
AGESTAN REPUBLIC
RUSSIA, ON THE 24TH
AND I WILL PROTECT YOU!
PS - I GENUINELY MEAN THIS
YOU DID... WHAT?
JESUS, MAN, I FOUND YOU VIA THE FREAKY BUSINESS CARD, BUT YOU TOLD THE WHOLE FUCKING WORLD WHERE WE ARE...
YES, LORD, VERY PERCEPTIVE OF YOU. I AM VERY MUCH IN LOVE WITH HER.

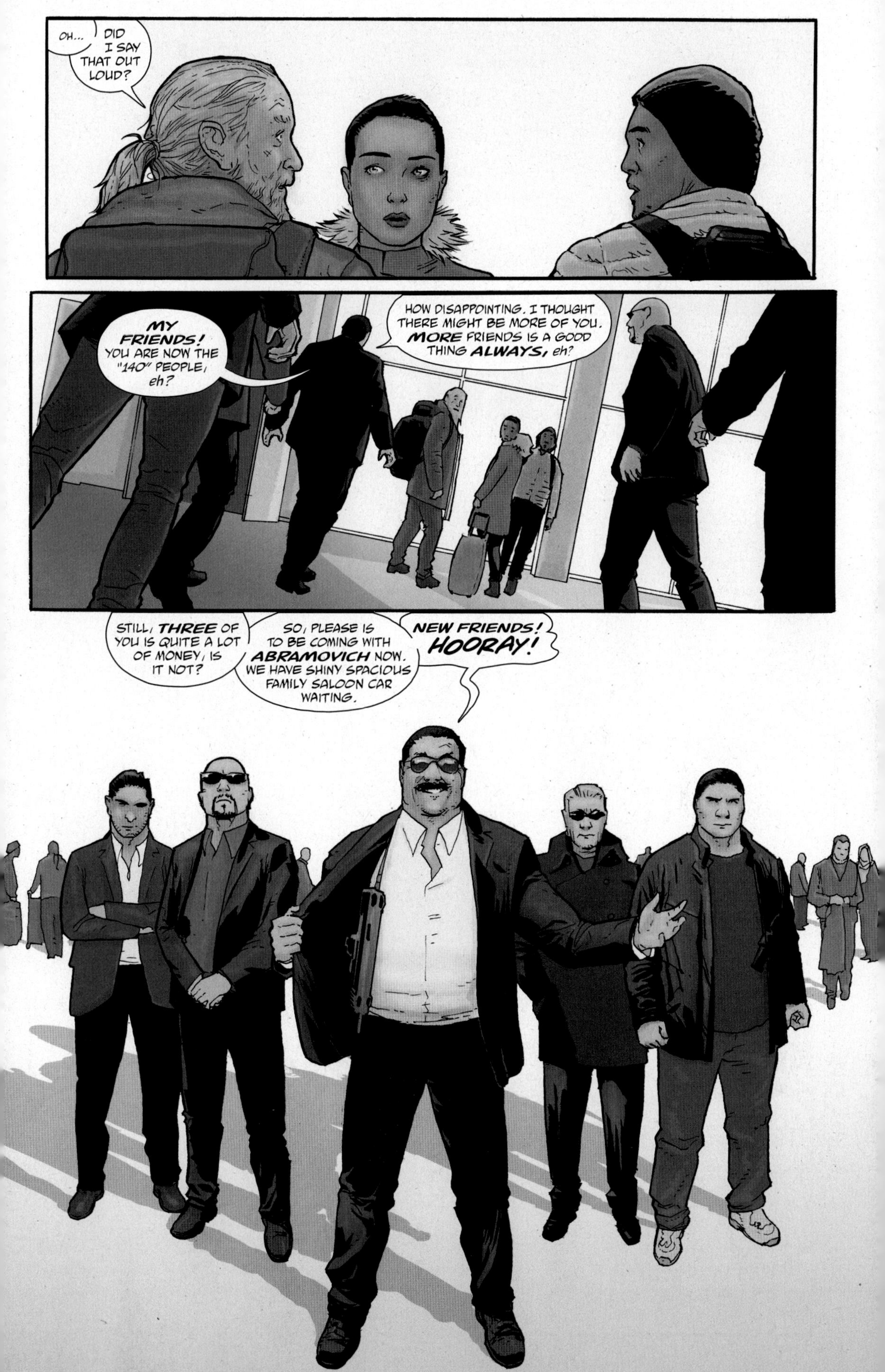
OH...
DID I SAY THAT OUT LOUD?
MY FRIENDS! YOU ARE NOW THE "140" PEOPLE, eh?
HOW DISAPPOINTING. I THOUGHT THERE MIGHT BE MORE OF YOU. MORE FRIENDS IS A GOOD THING ALWAYS, eh?
STILL, THREE OF YOU IS QUITE A LOT OF MONEY, IS IT NOT?
SO, PLEASE IS TO BE COMING WITH ABRAMOVICH NOW. WE HAVE SHINY SPACIOUS FAMILY SALOON CAR WAITING.
NEW FRIENDS! HOORAY!

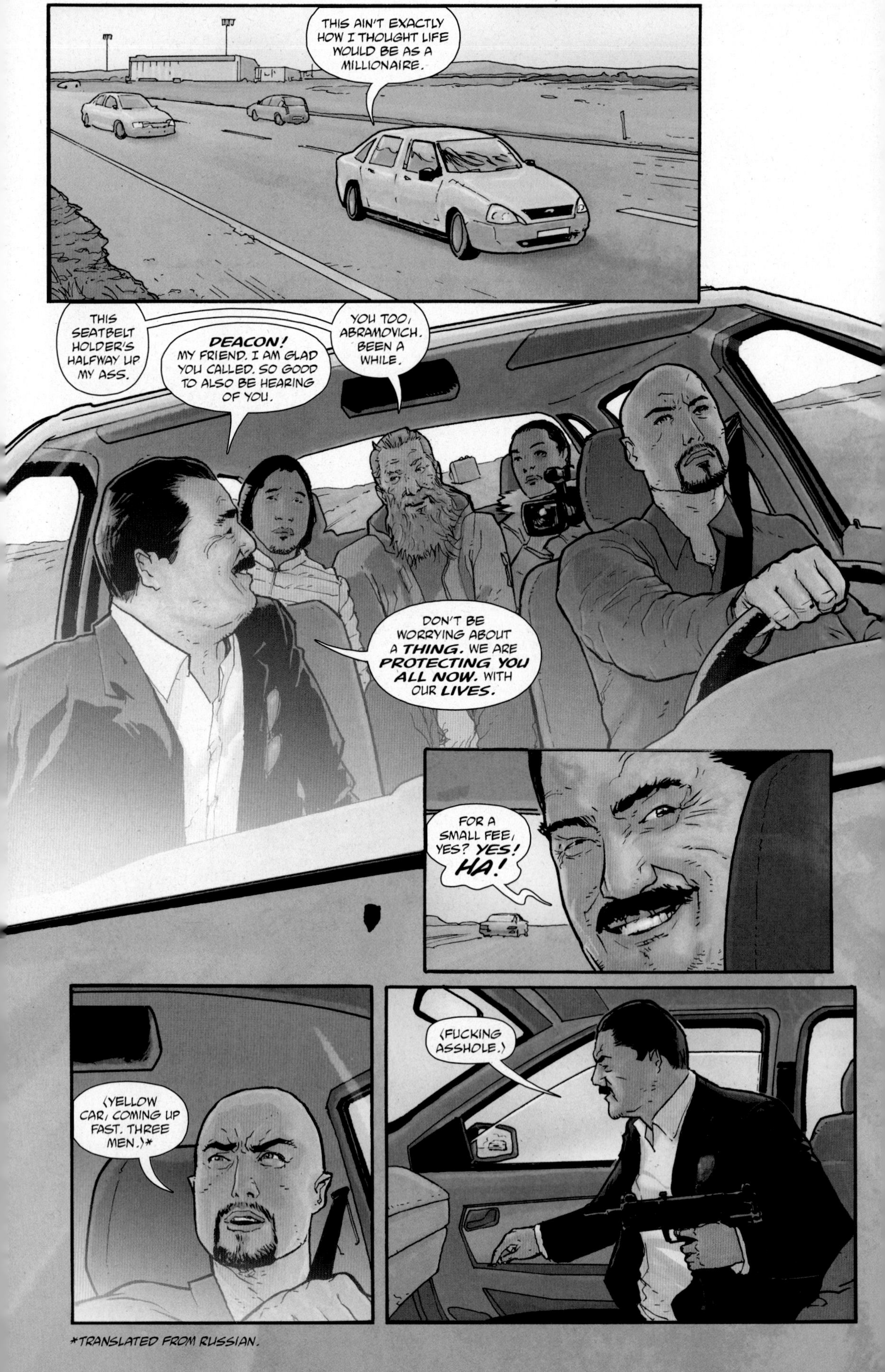
THIS AIN'T EXACTLY HOW I THOUGHT LIFE WOULD BE AS A MILLIONAIRE.
THIS SEATBELT HOLDER'S HALFWAY UP MY ASS.
DEACON! MY FRIEND. I AM GLAD YOU CALLED. SO GOOD TO ALSO BE HEARING OF YOU.
YOU TOO, ABRAMOVICH. BEEN A WHILE.
DON'T BE WORRYING ABOUT A THING. WE ARE PROTECTING YOU ALL NOW. WITH OUR LIVES.
FOR A SMALL FEE, YES? YES! HA!
‹YELLOW CAR, COMING UP FAST. THREE MEN.›*
‹FUCKING ASSHOLE.›
*TRANSLATED FROM RUSSIAN.

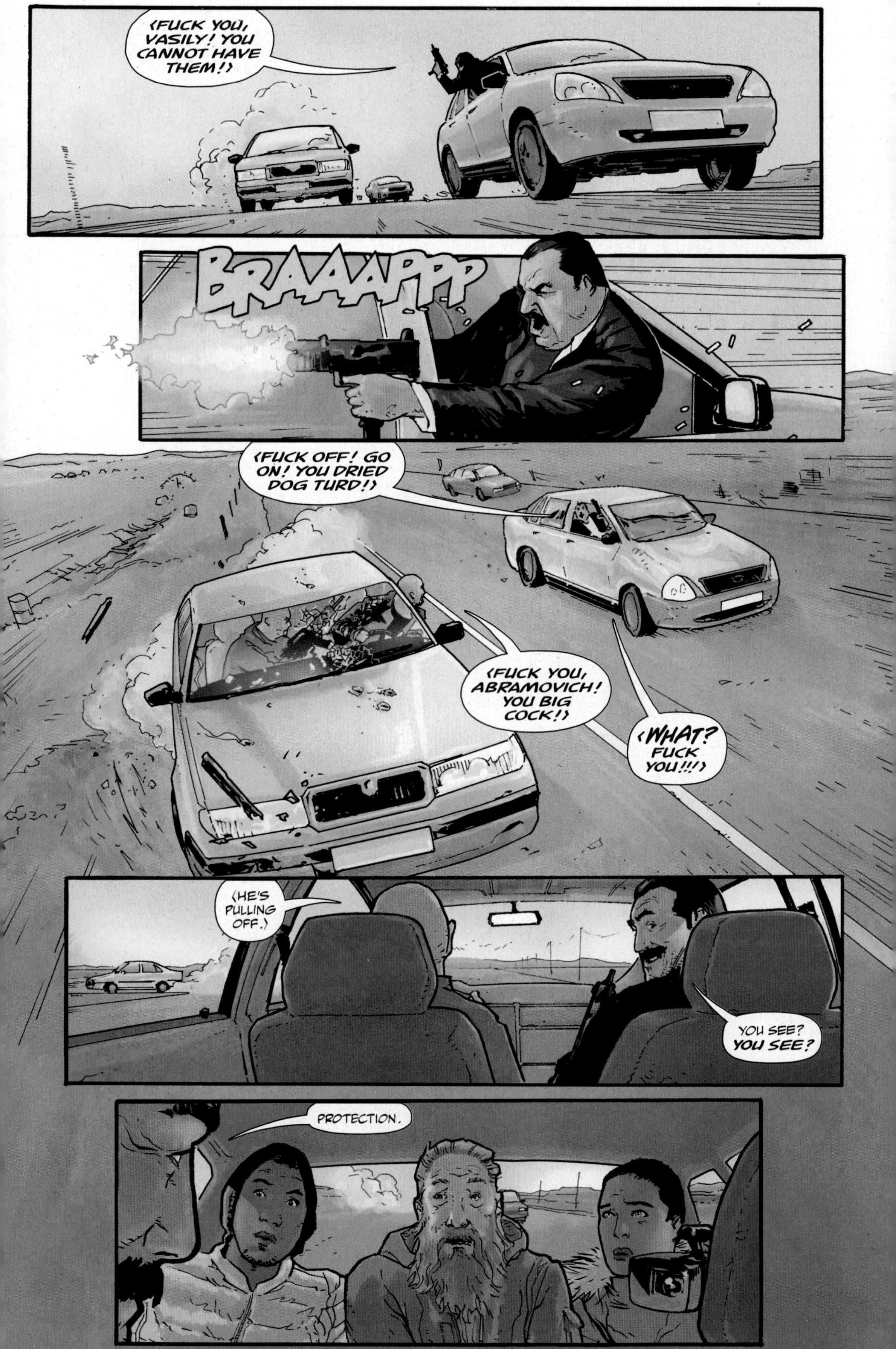
‹FUCK YOU, VASILY! YOU CANNOT HAVE THEM!›
BRAAAPPP
‹FUCK OFF! GO ON! YOU DRIED DOG TURD!›
‹FUCK YOU, ABRAMOVICH! YOU BIG COCK!›
‹WHAT? FUCK YOU!!!›
‹HE'S PULLING OFF.›
YOU SEE? YOU SEE?
PROTECTION.

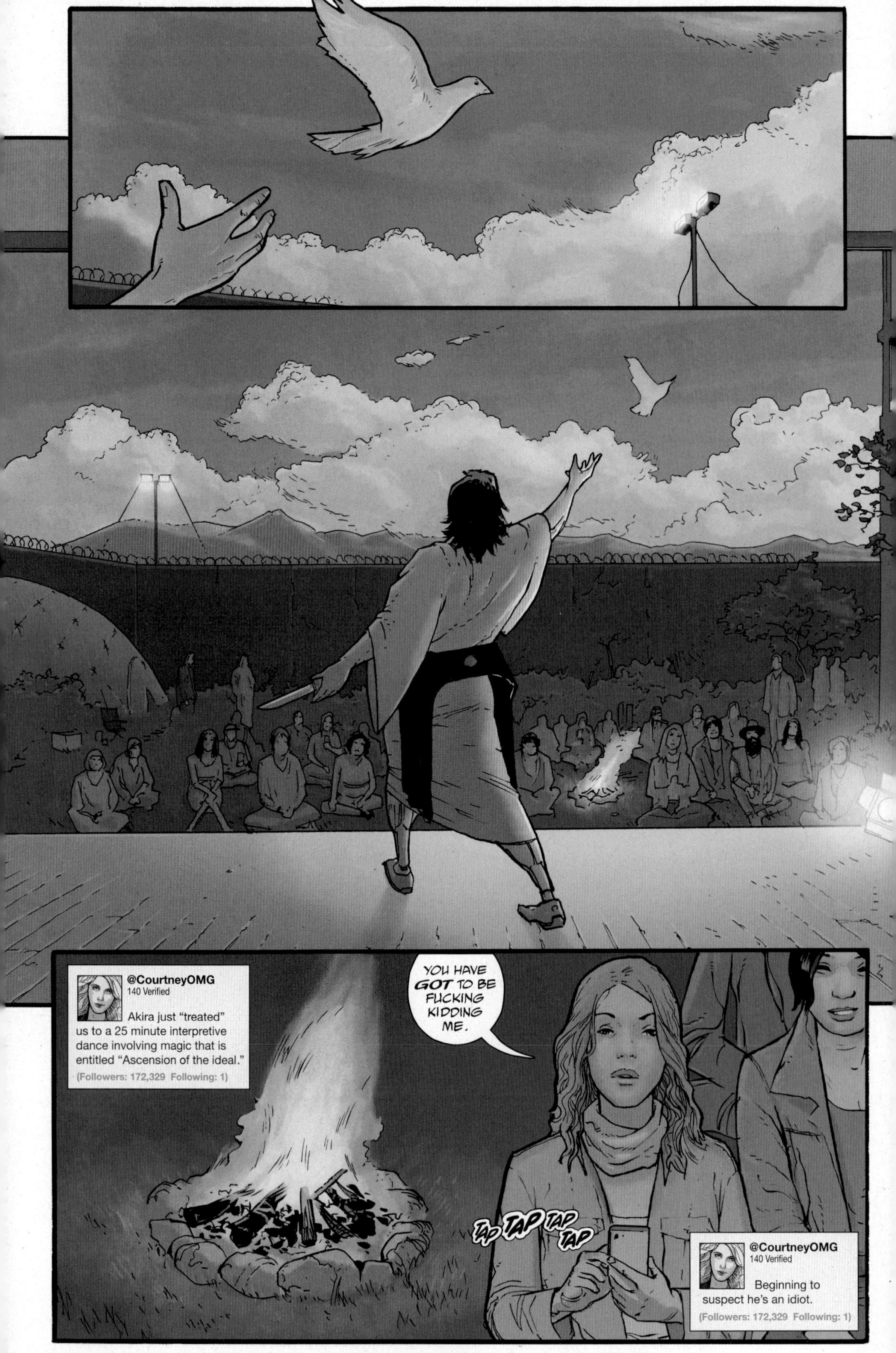
@CourtneyOMG
140 Verified
Akira just "treated" us to a 25 minute interpretive dance involving magic that is entitled "Ascension of the ideal."
(Followers: 172,329 Following: 1)
YOU HAVE GOT TO BE FUCKING KIDDING ME.
TAP TAP TAP TAP
@CourtneyOMG
140 Verified
Beginning to suspect he's an idiot.
(Followers: 172,329 Following: 1)

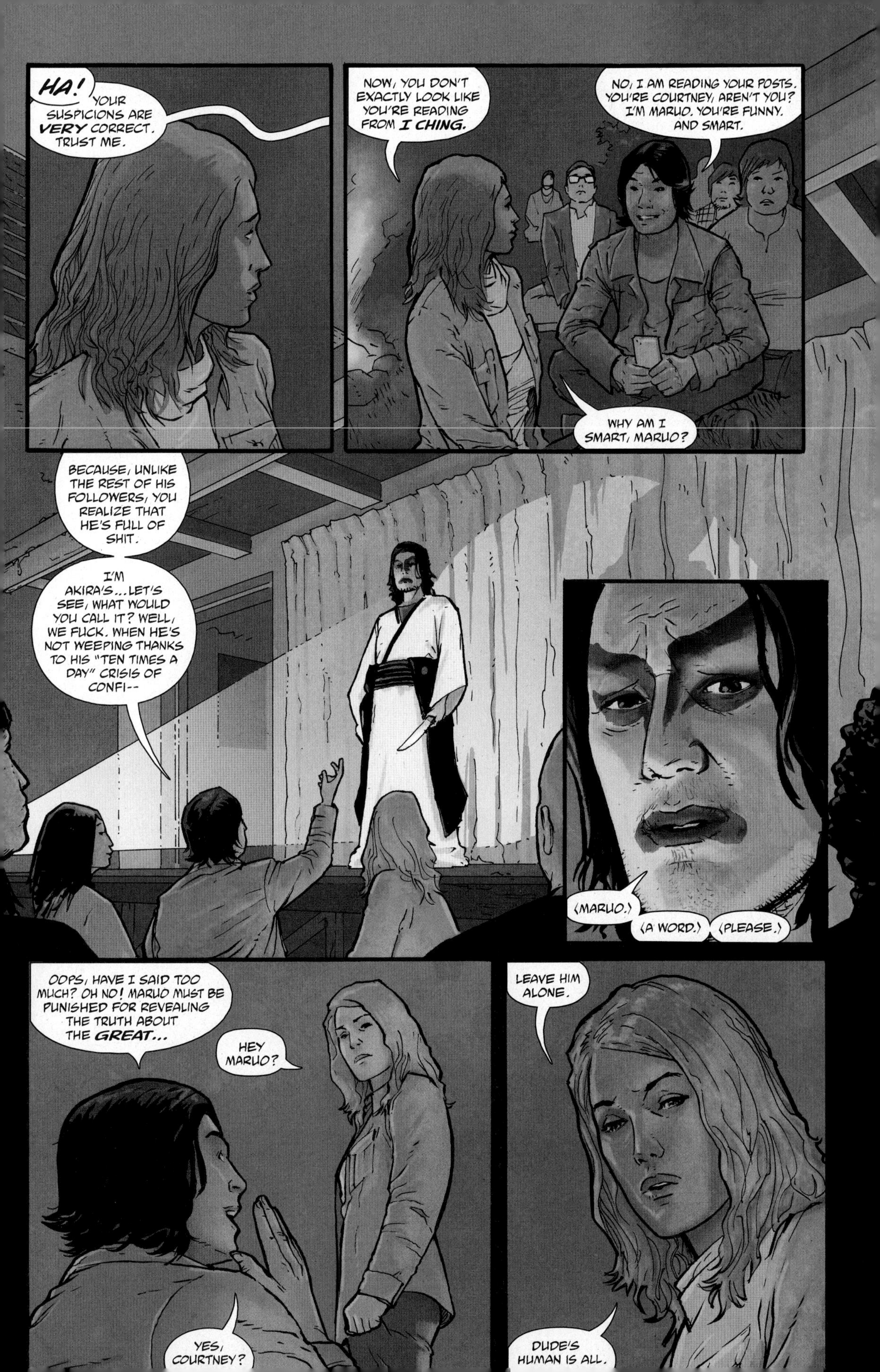
HA! YOUR SUSPICIONS ARE VERY CORRECT. TRUST ME.
NOW, YOU DON'T EXACTLY LOOK LIKE YOU'RE READING FROM I CHING.
NO, I AM READING YOUR POSTS. YOU'RE COURTNEY, AREN'T YOU? I'M MARUO. YOU'RE FUNNY. AND SMART.
WHY AM I SMART, MARUO?
BECAUSE, UNLIKE THE REST OF HIS FOLLOWERS, YOU REALIZE THAT HE'S FULL OF SHIT.
I'M AKIRA'S... LET'S SEE, WHAT WOULD YOU CALL IT? WELL, WE FUCK. WHEN HE'S NOT WEEPING THANKS TO HIS "TEN TIMES A DAY" CRISIS OF CONFI--
⟨MARUO.⟩
⟨A WORD.⟩
⟨PLEASE.⟩
OOPS, HAVE I SAID TOO MUCH? OH NO! MARUO MUST BE PUNISHED FOR REVEALING THE TRUTH ABOUT THE GREAT...
HEY MARUO?
YES, COURTNEY?
LEAVE HIM ALONE.
DUDE'S HUMAN IS ALL.

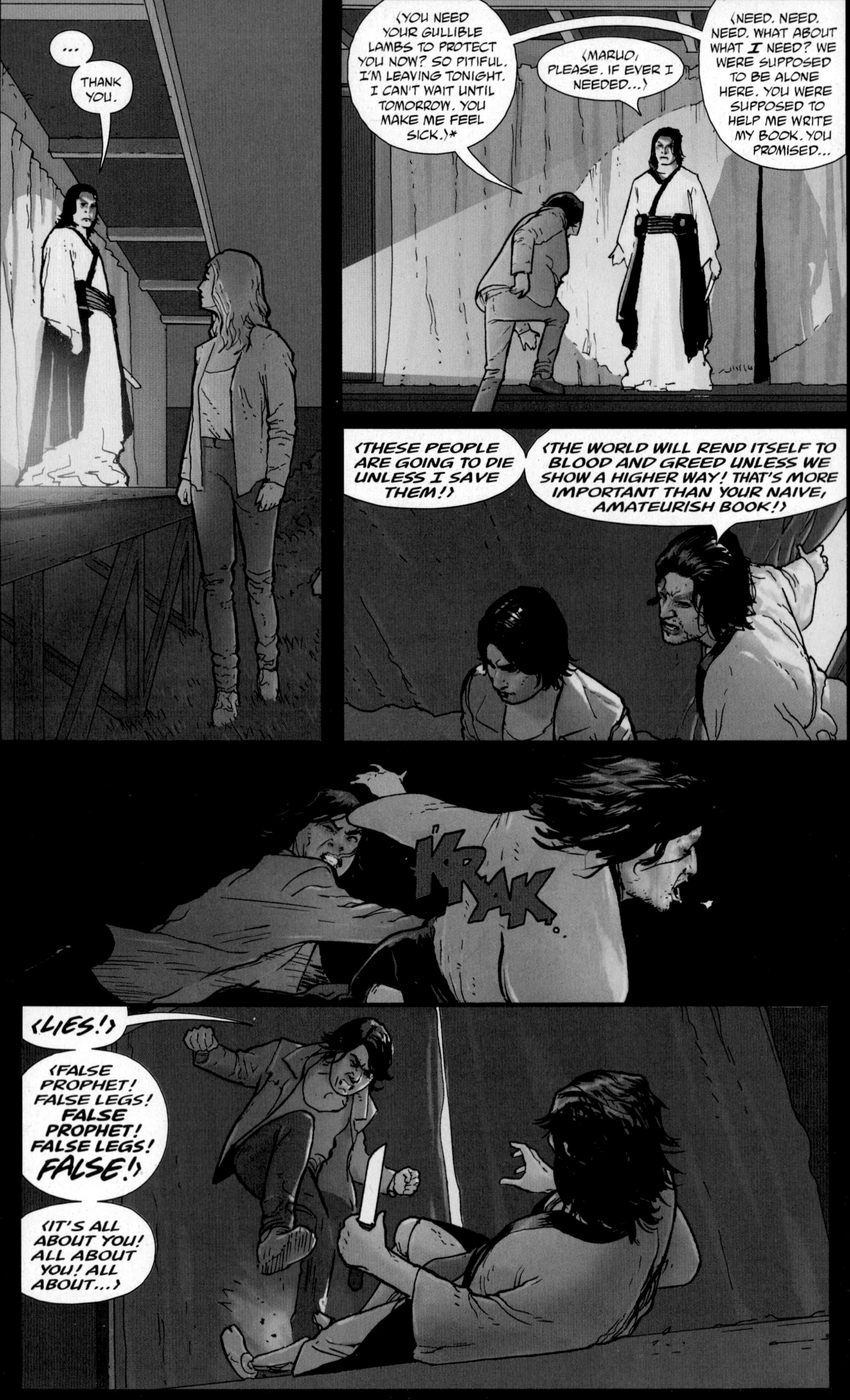
...
THANK YOU.
‹YOU NEED YOUR GULLIBLE LAMBS TO PROTECT YOU NOW? SO PITIFUL. I'M LEAVING TONIGHT. I CAN'T WAIT UNTIL TOMORROW. YOU MAKE ME FEEL SICK.›*
‹MARUO, PLEASE. IF EVER I NEEDED...›
‹NEED. NEED. NEED. WHAT ABOUT WHAT I NEED? WE WERE SUPPOSED TO BE ALONE HERE. YOU WERE SUPPOSED TO HELP ME WRITE MY BOOK. YOU PROMISED...
‹THESE PEOPLE ARE GOING TO DIE UNLESS I SAVE THEM!›
‹THE WORLD WILL REND ITSELF TO BLOOD AND GREED UNLESS WE SHOW A HIGHER WAY! THAT'S MORE IMPORTANT THAN YOUR NAIVE, AMATEURISH BOOK!›
KRAK
‹LIES!›
‹FALSE PROPHET! FALSE LEGS! FALSE PROPHET! FALSE LEGS! FALSE!›
‹IT'S ALL ABOUT YOU! ALL ABOUT YOU! ALL ABOUT...›

*TRANSLATED FROM JAPANESE.

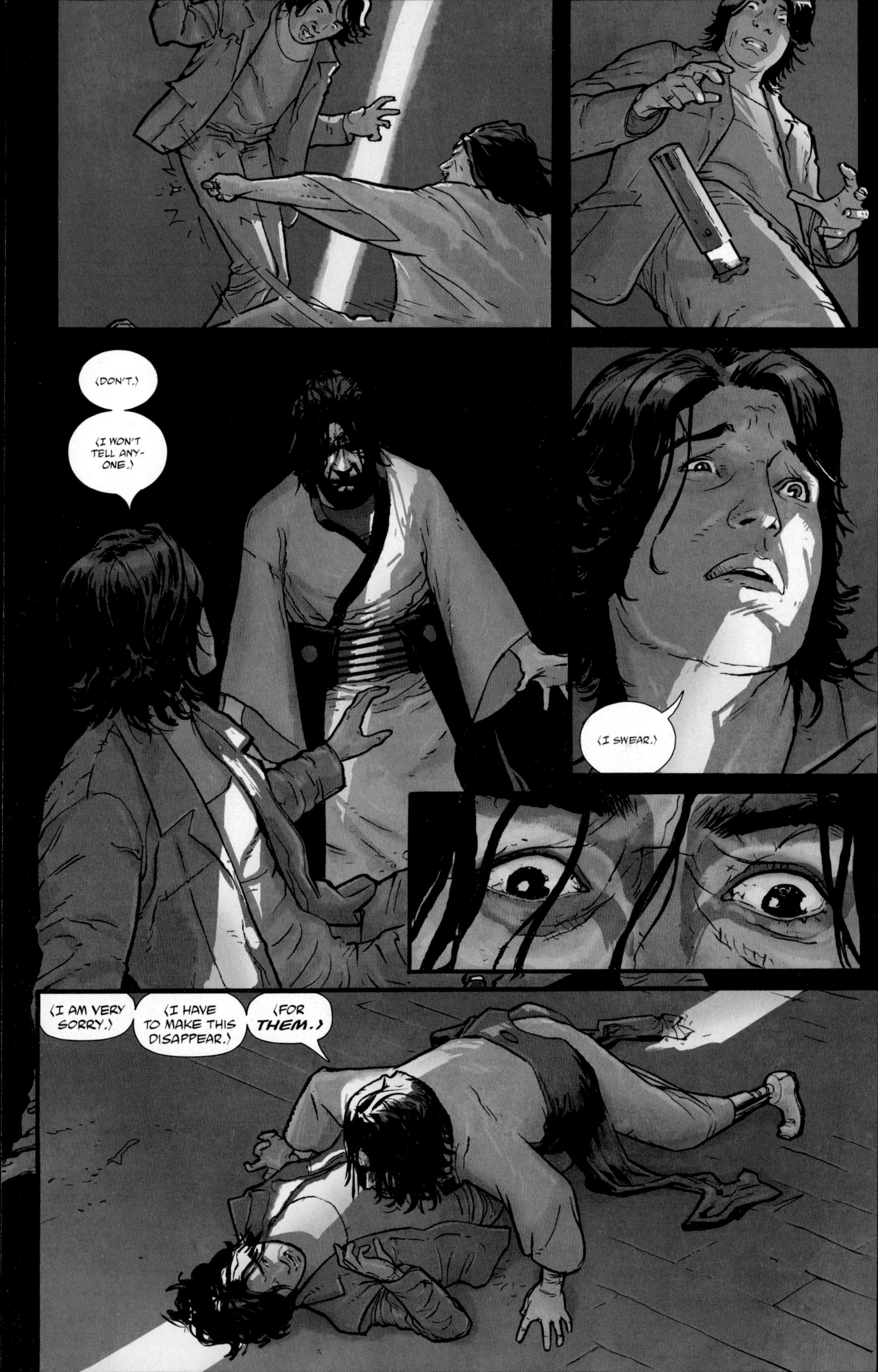
‹DON'T.›
‹I WON'T TELL ANY-ONE.›
‹I SWEAR.›
‹I AM VERY SORRY.›
‹I HAVE TO MAKE THIS DISAPPEAR.›
‹FOR *THEM*.›

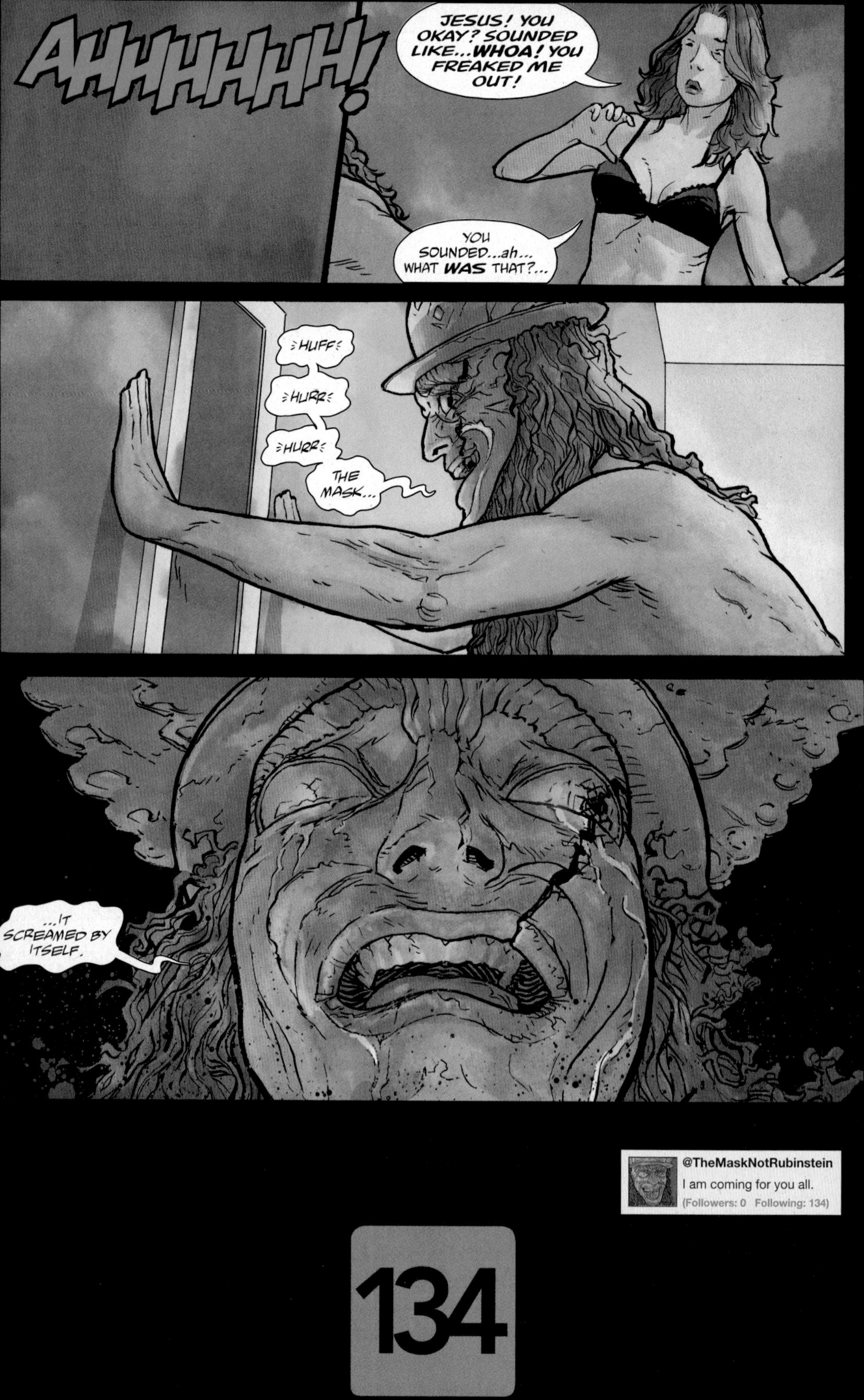
AHHHHHH!
JESUS! YOU OKAY? SOUNDED LIKE...WHOA! YOU FREAKED ME OUT!
YOU SOUNDED...ah... WHAT WAS THAT?...
HUFF
HURR
HURR
THE MASK...
...IT SCREAMED BY ITSELF.

@TheMaskNotRubinstein
I am coming for you all.
(Followers: 0 Following: 134)

134

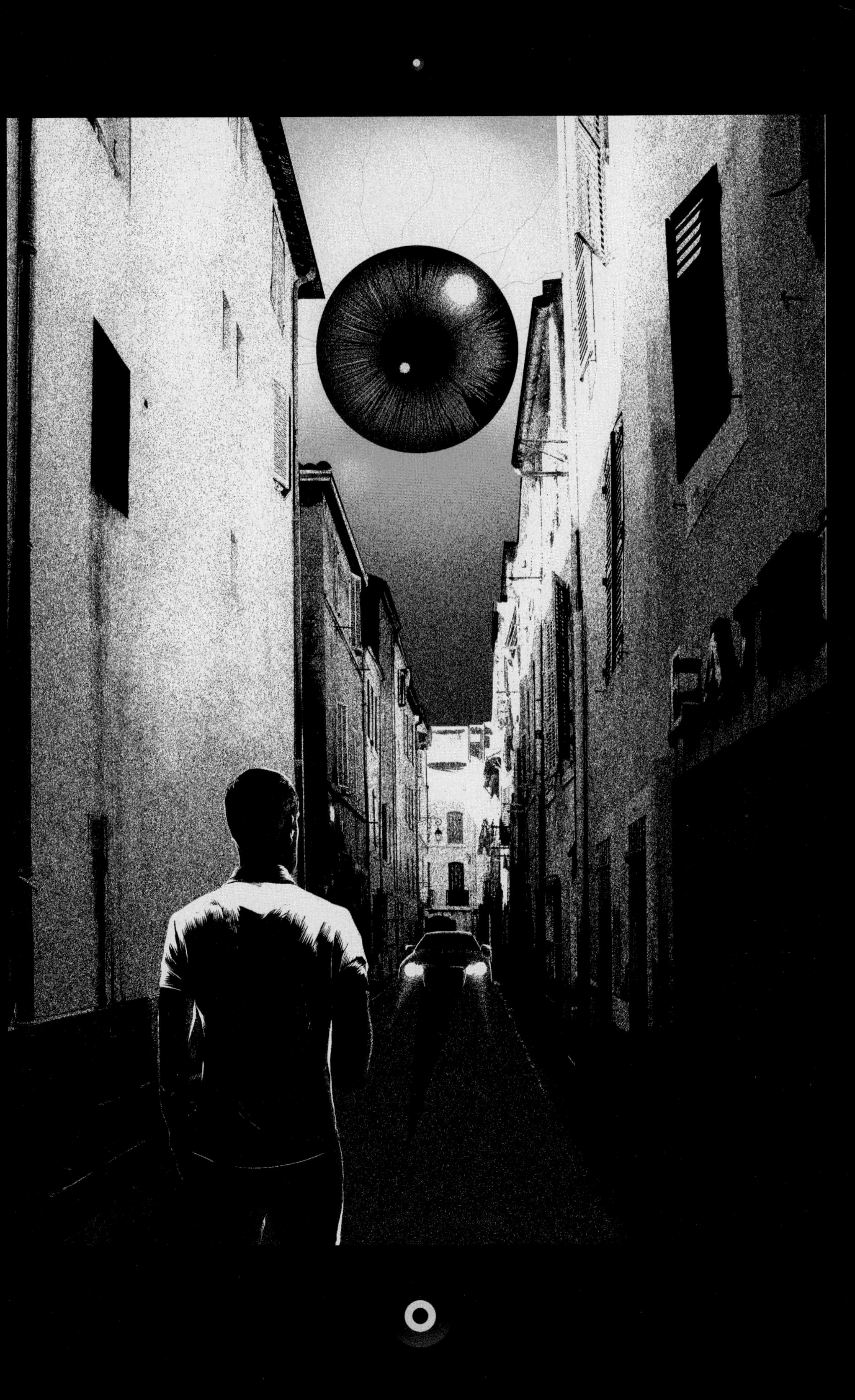

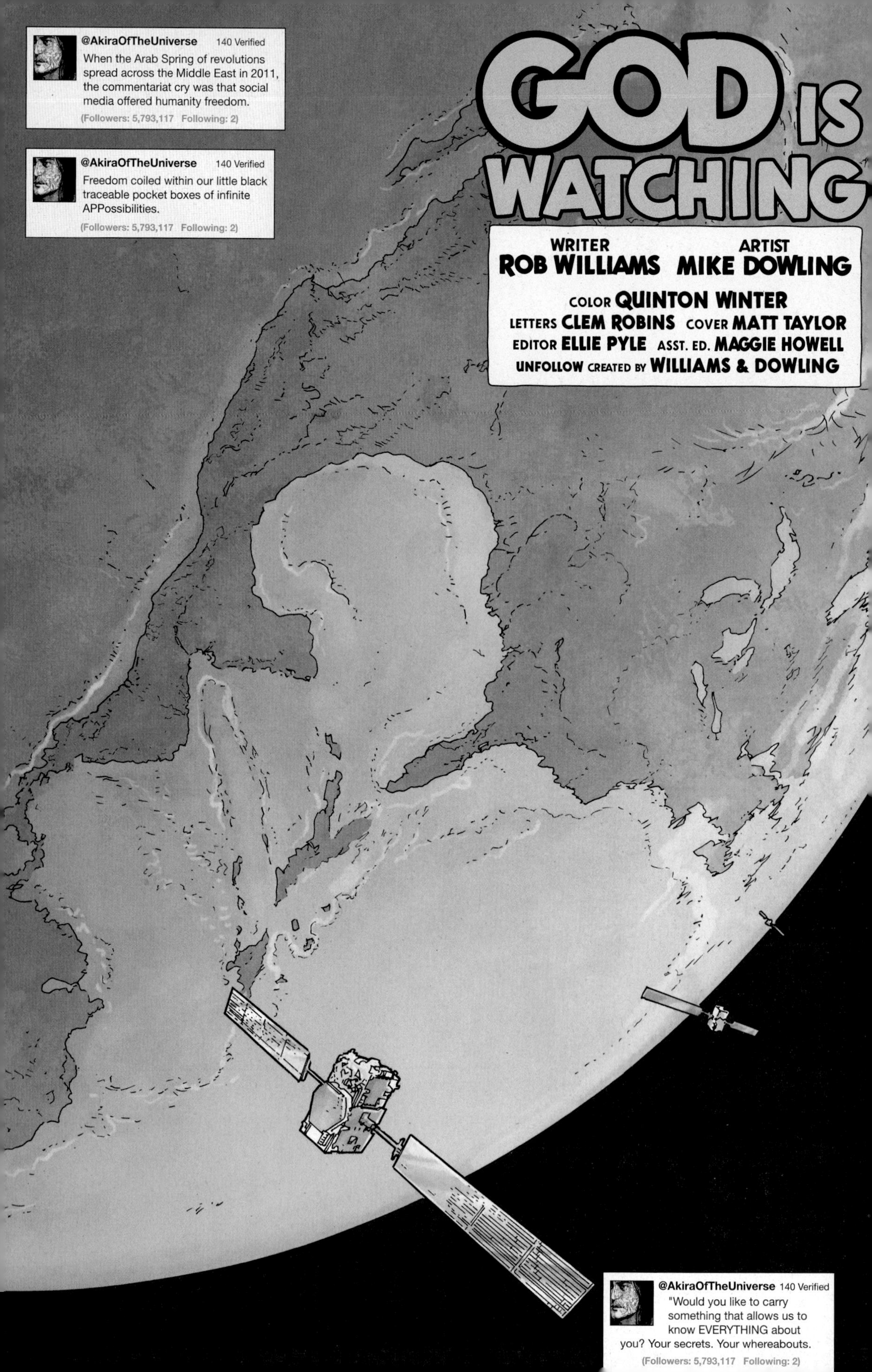

@AkiraOfTheUniverse 140 Verified
When the Arab Spring of revolutions spread across the Middle East in 2011, the commentariat cry was that social media offered humanity freedom.
(Followers: 5,793,117 Following: 2)
@AkiraOfTheUniverse 140 Verified
Freedom coiled within our little black traceable pocket boxes of infinite APPossibilities.
(Followers: 5,793,117 Following: 2)
GOD IS WATCHING
WRITER ROB WILLIAMS ARTIST MIKE DOWLING
COLOR QUINTON WINTER
LETTERS CLEM ROBINS COVER MATT TAYLOR
EDITOR ELLIE PYLE ASST. ED. MAGGIE HOWELL
UNFOLLOW CREATED BY WILLIAMS & DOWLING
@AkiraOfTheUniverse 140 Verified
"Would you like to carry something that allows us to know EVERYTHING about you? Your secrets. Your whereabouts.
(Followers: 5,793,117 Following: 2)

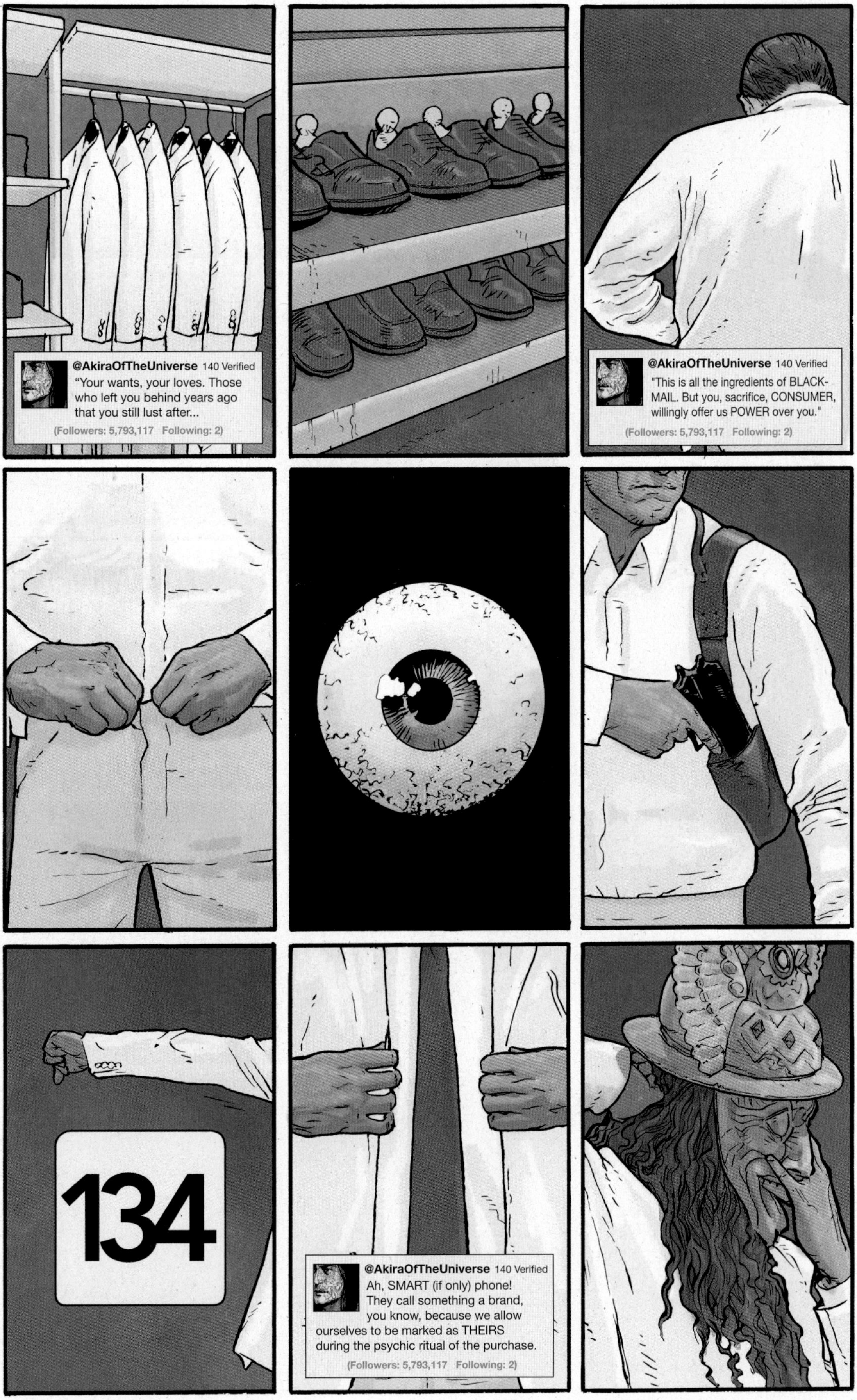
@AkiraOfTheUniverse 140 Verified
“Your wants, your loves. Those who left you behind years ago that you still lust after...
(Followers: 5,793,117 Following: 2)
@AkiraOfTheUniverse 140 Verified
"This is all the ingredients of BLACK-MAIL. But you, sacrifice, CONSUMER, willingly offer us POWER over you."
(Followers: 5,793,117 Following: 2)
134
@AkiraOfTheUniverse 140 Verified
Ah, SMART (if only) phone! They call something a brand, you know, because we allow ourselves to be marked as THEIRS during the psychic ritual of the purchase.
(Followers: 5,793,117 Following: 2)

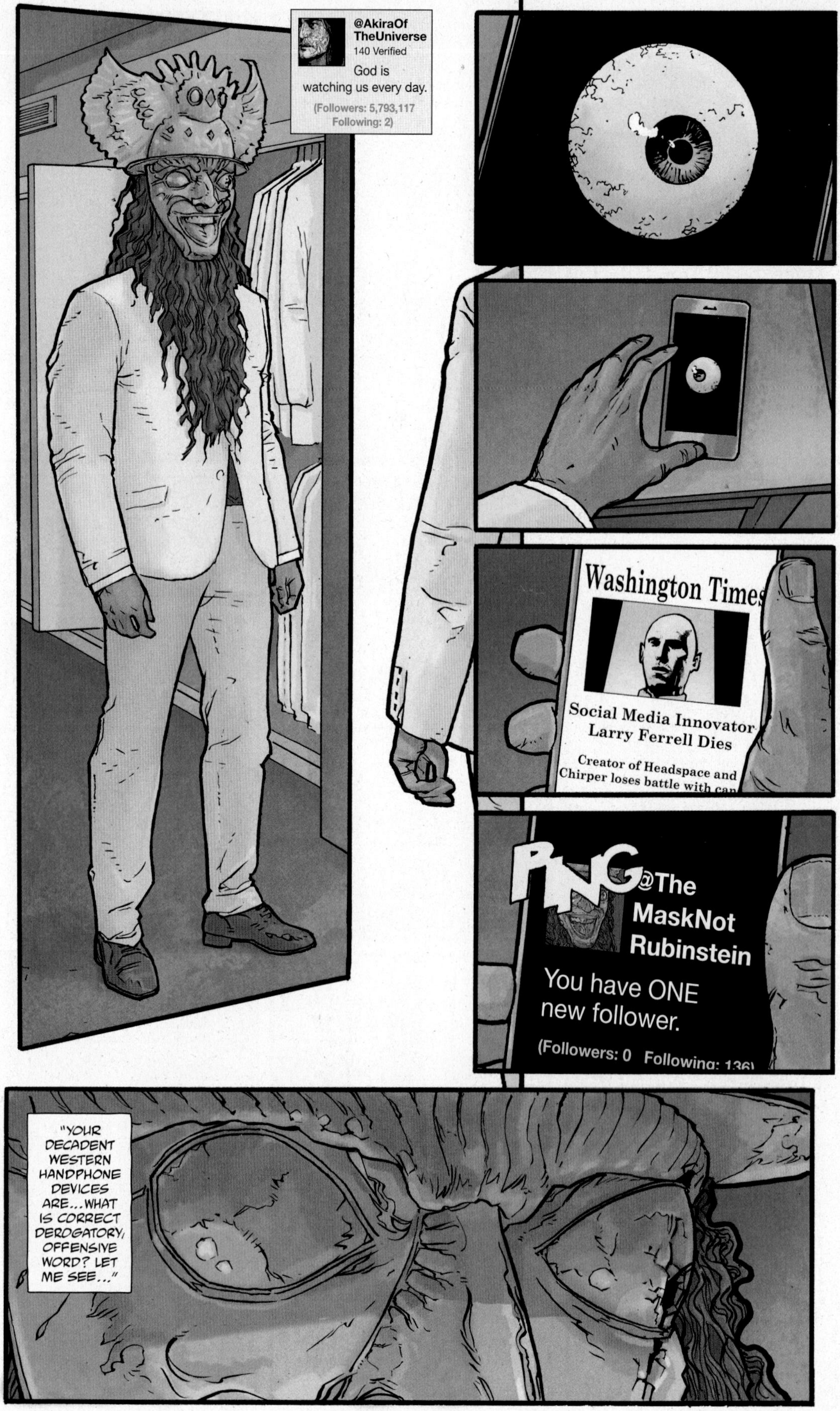
@AkiraOf TheUniverse
140 Verified
God is watching us every day.
(Followers: 5,793,117 Following: 2)
Washington Times
Social Media Innovator Larry Ferrell Dies
Creator of Headspace and Chirper loses battle with can
PING
@The MaskNot Rubinstein
You have ONE new follower.
(Followers: 0 Following: 136)
"YOUR DECADENT WESTERN HANDPHONE DEVICES ARE... WHAT IS CORRECT DEROGATORY, OFFENSIVE WORD? LET ME SEE..."

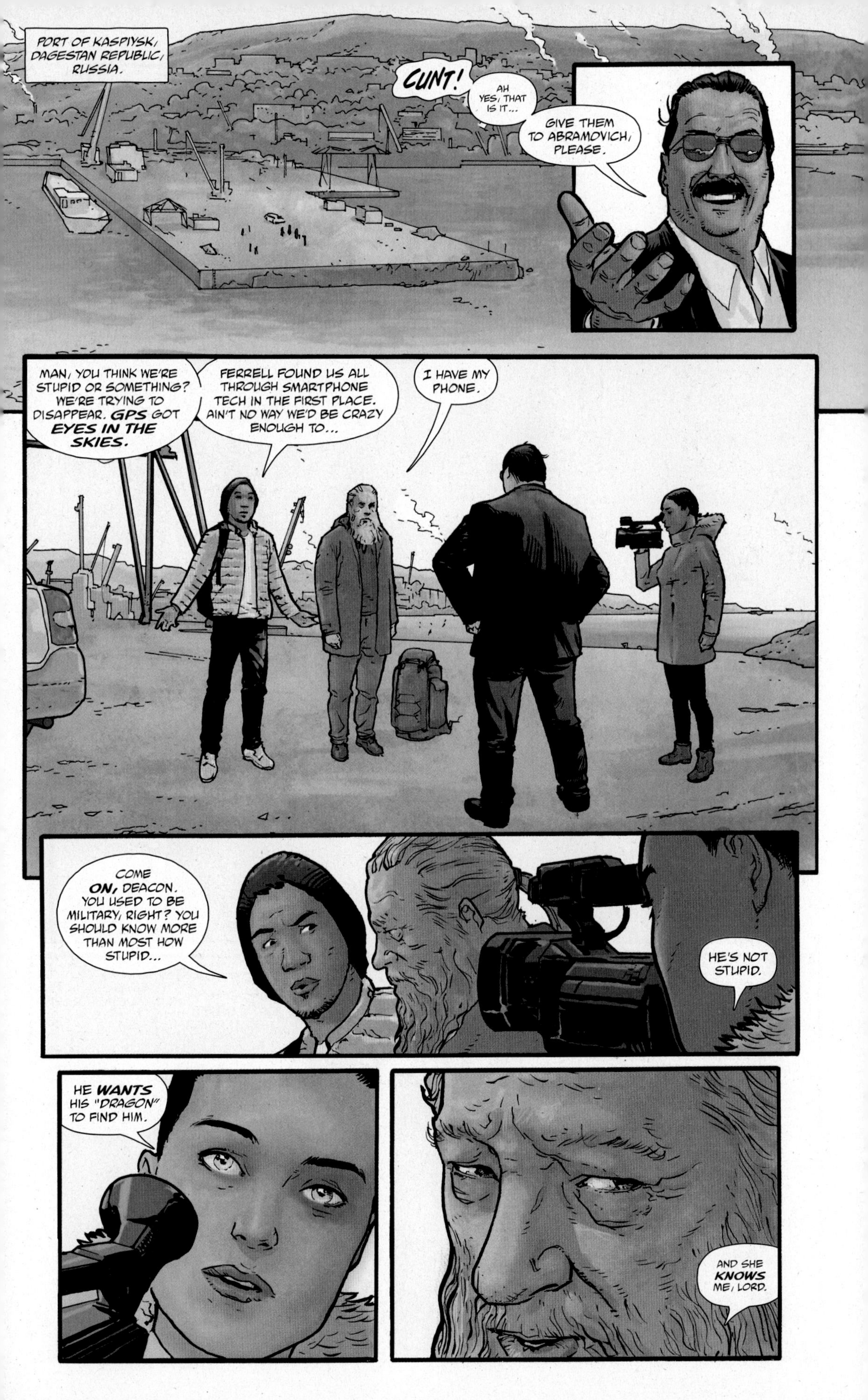
PORT OF KASPIYSK, DAGESTAN REPUBLIC, RUSSIA.
CUNT!
AH YES, THAT IS IT...
GIVE THEM TO ABRAMOVICH, PLEASE.
MAN, YOU THINK WE'RE STUPID OR SOMETHING? WE'RE TRYING TO DISAPPEAR. GPS GOT EYES IN THE SKIES.
FERRELL FOUND US ALL THROUGH SMARTPHONE TECH IN THE FIRST PLACE. AIN'T NO WAY WE'D BE CRAZY ENOUGH TO...
I HAVE MY PHONE.
COME ON, DEACON. YOU USED TO BE MILITARY, RIGHT? YOU SHOULD KNOW MORE THAN MOST HOW STUPID...
HE'S NOT STUPID.
HE WANTS HIS "DRAGON" TO FIND HIM.
AND SHE KNOWS ME, LORD.

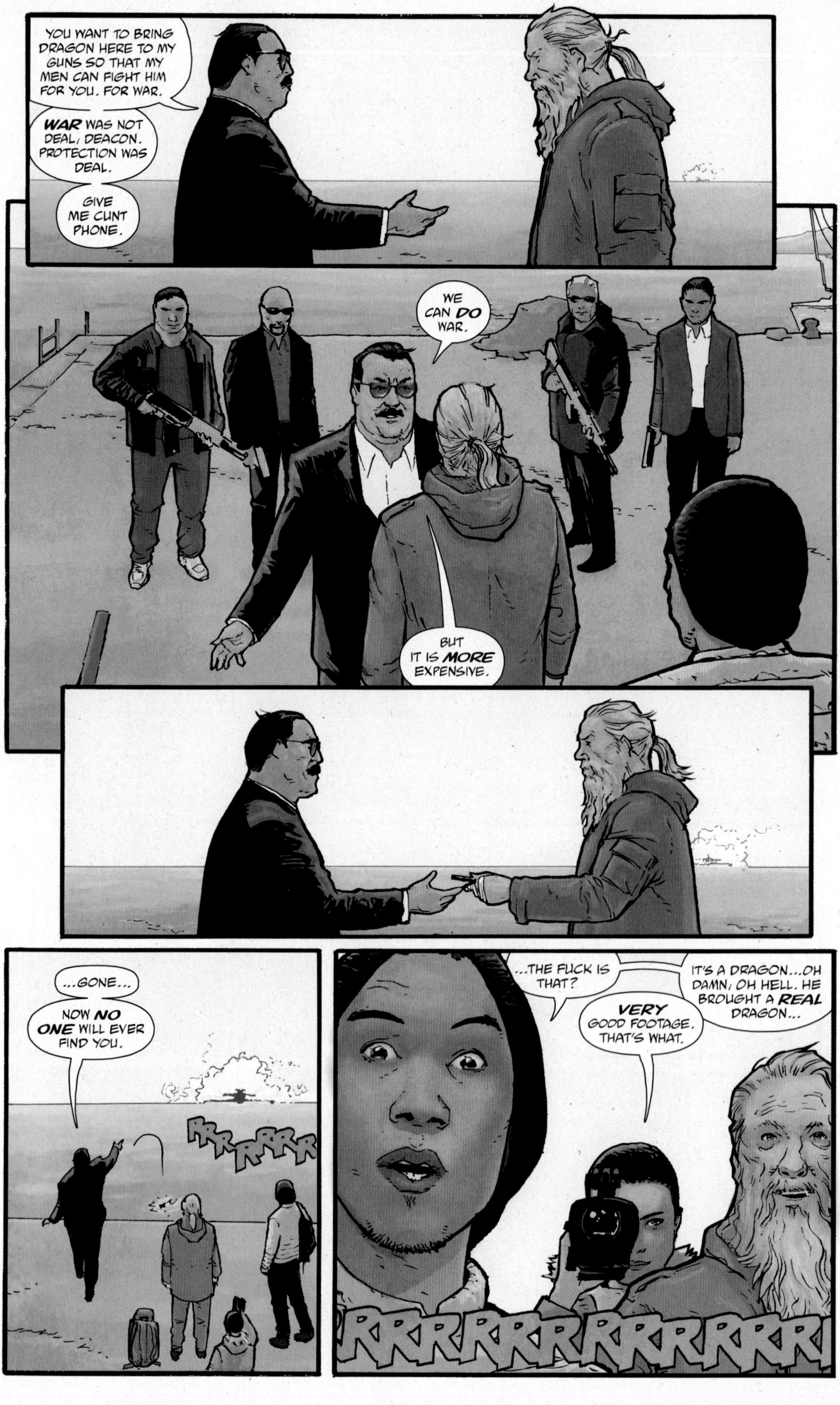
YOU WANT TO BRING DRAGON HERE TO MY GUNS SO THAT MY MEN CAN FIGHT HIM FOR YOU. FOR WAR.
WAR WAS NOT DEAL, DEACON. PROTECTION WAS DEAL.
GIVE ME CUNT PHONE.
WE CAN DO WAR.
BUT IT IS MORE EXPENSIVE.
...GONE...
NOW NO ONE WILL EVER FIND YOU.
RRRRRRRR
...THE FUCK IS THAT?
IT'S A DRAGON...OH DAMN, OH HELL. HE BROUGHT A REAL DRAGON...
VERY GOOD FOOTAGE. THAT'S WHAT.
RRRRRRRRRRRRRRRRR

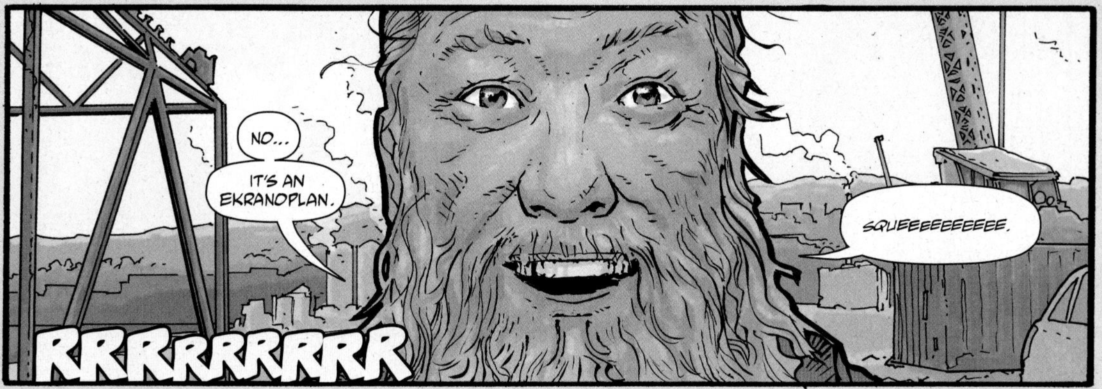
NO...
IT'S AN EKRANOPLAN.
SQUEEEEEEEEEE.
RRRRRRRRRR

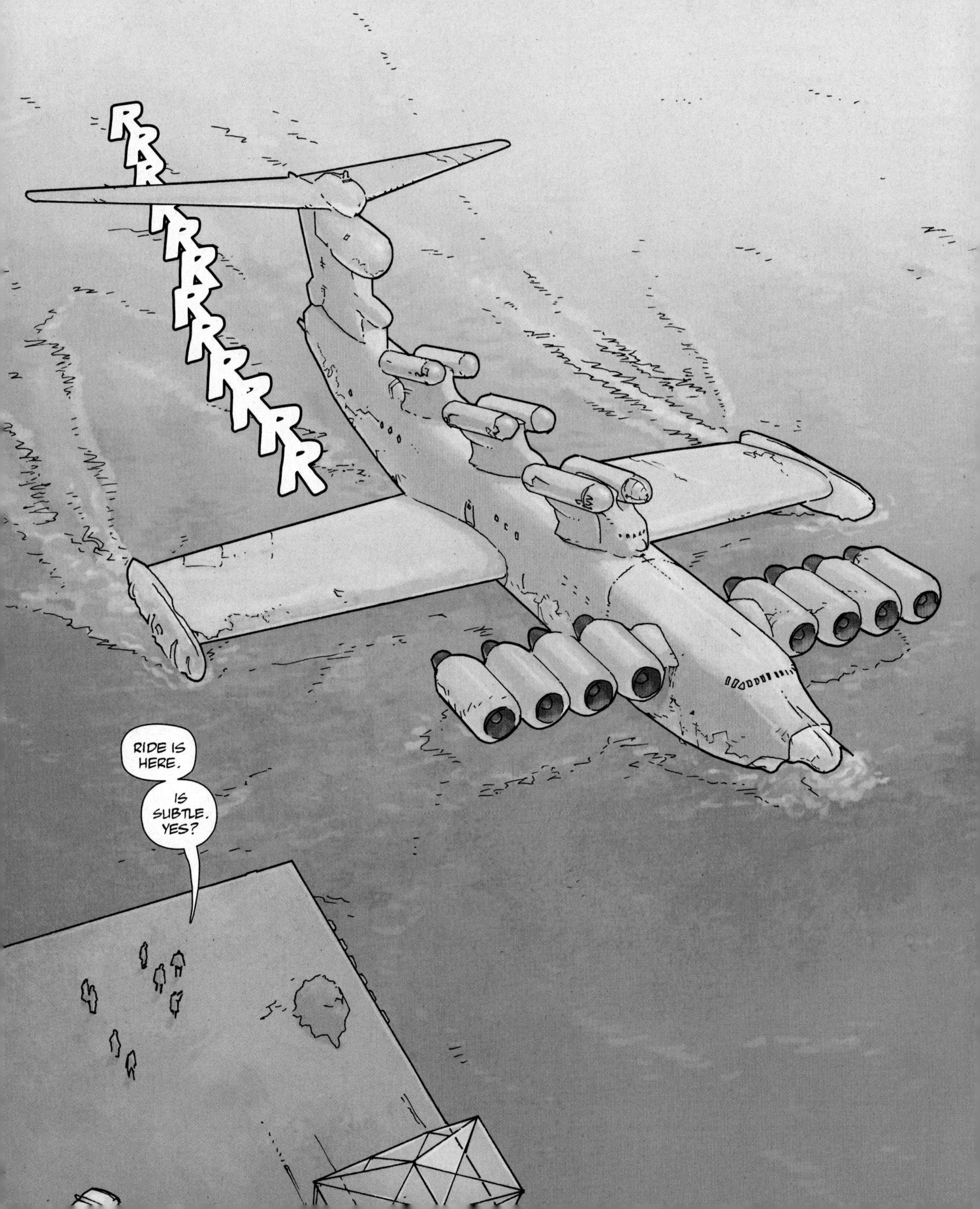
RRRRRRRRRRRR
RIDE IS HERE.
IS SUBTLE. YES?

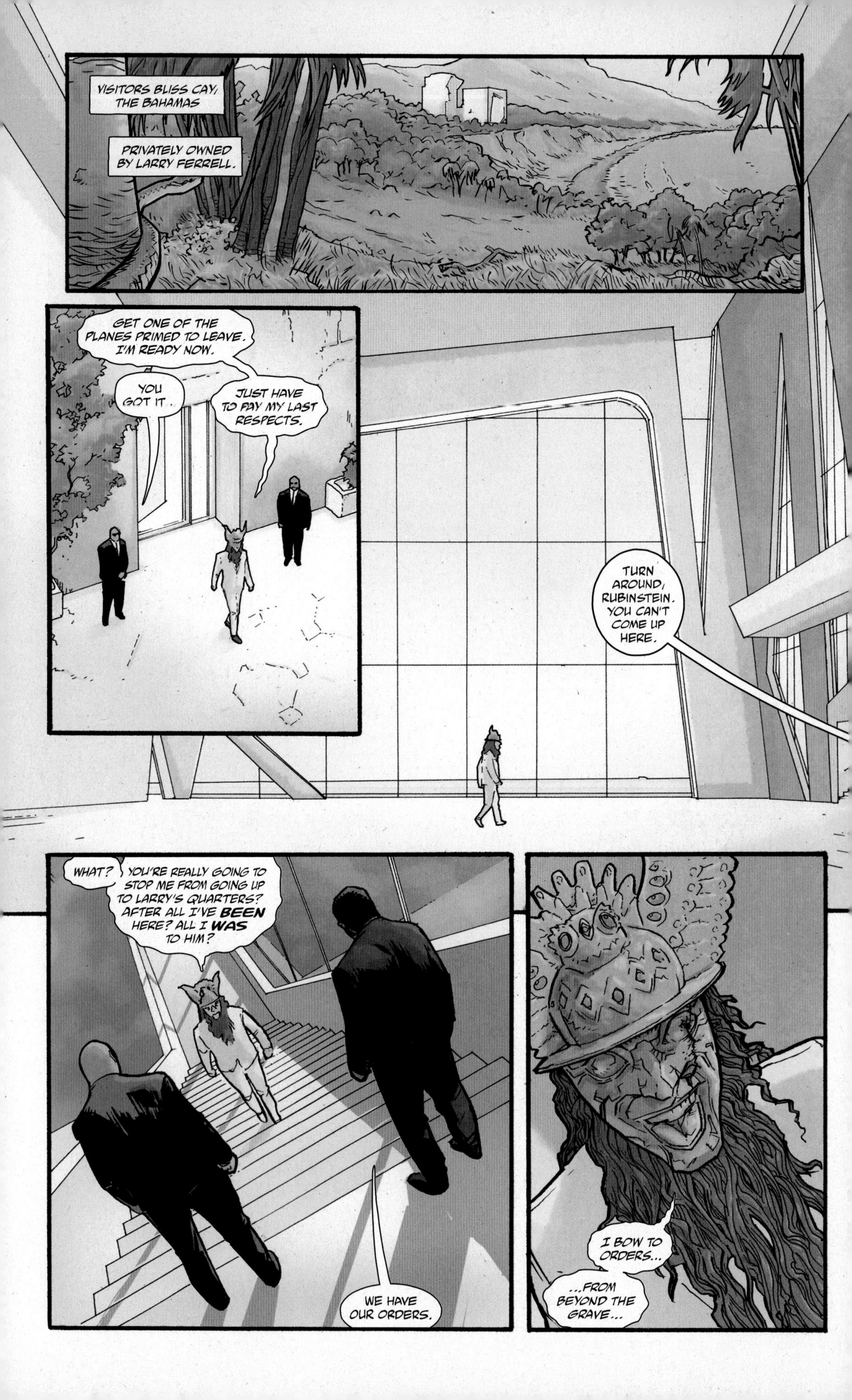
VISITORS BLISS CAY, THE BAHAMAS
PRIVATELY OWNED BY LARRY FERRELL.
GET ONE OF THE PLANES PRIMED TO LEAVE. I'M READY NOW.
YOU GOT IT.
JUST HAVE TO PAY MY LAST RESPECTS.
TURN AROUND, RUBINSTEIN. YOU CAN'T COME UP HERE.
WHAT?
YOU'RE REALLY GOING TO STOP ME FROM GOING UP TO LARRY'S QUARTERS? AFTER ALL I'VE BEEN HERE? ALL I WAS TO HIM?
WE HAVE OUR ORDERS.
I BOW TO ORDERS...
...FROM BEYOND THE GRAVE...

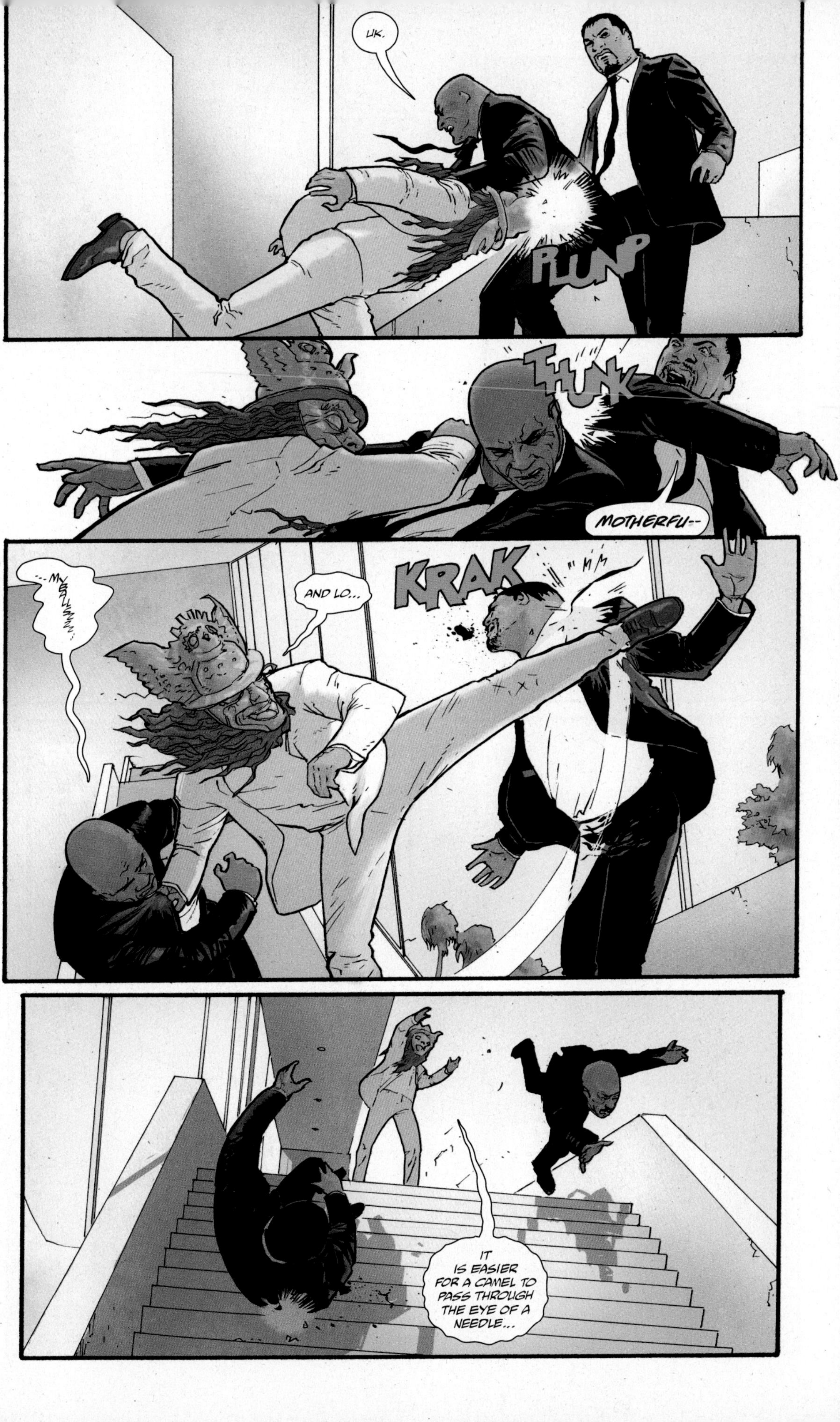
UK.
PLUNP
THUNK
MOTHERFU--
...MY BALLSZZZ...
AND LO...
KRAK
IT IS EASIER FOR A CAMEL TO PASS THROUGH THE EYE OF A NEEDLE...

...THAN FOR A RICH MAN TO ENTER HEAVEN...

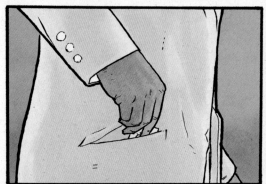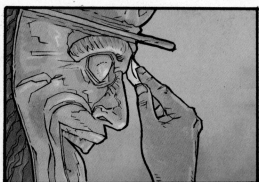

I AM READY.

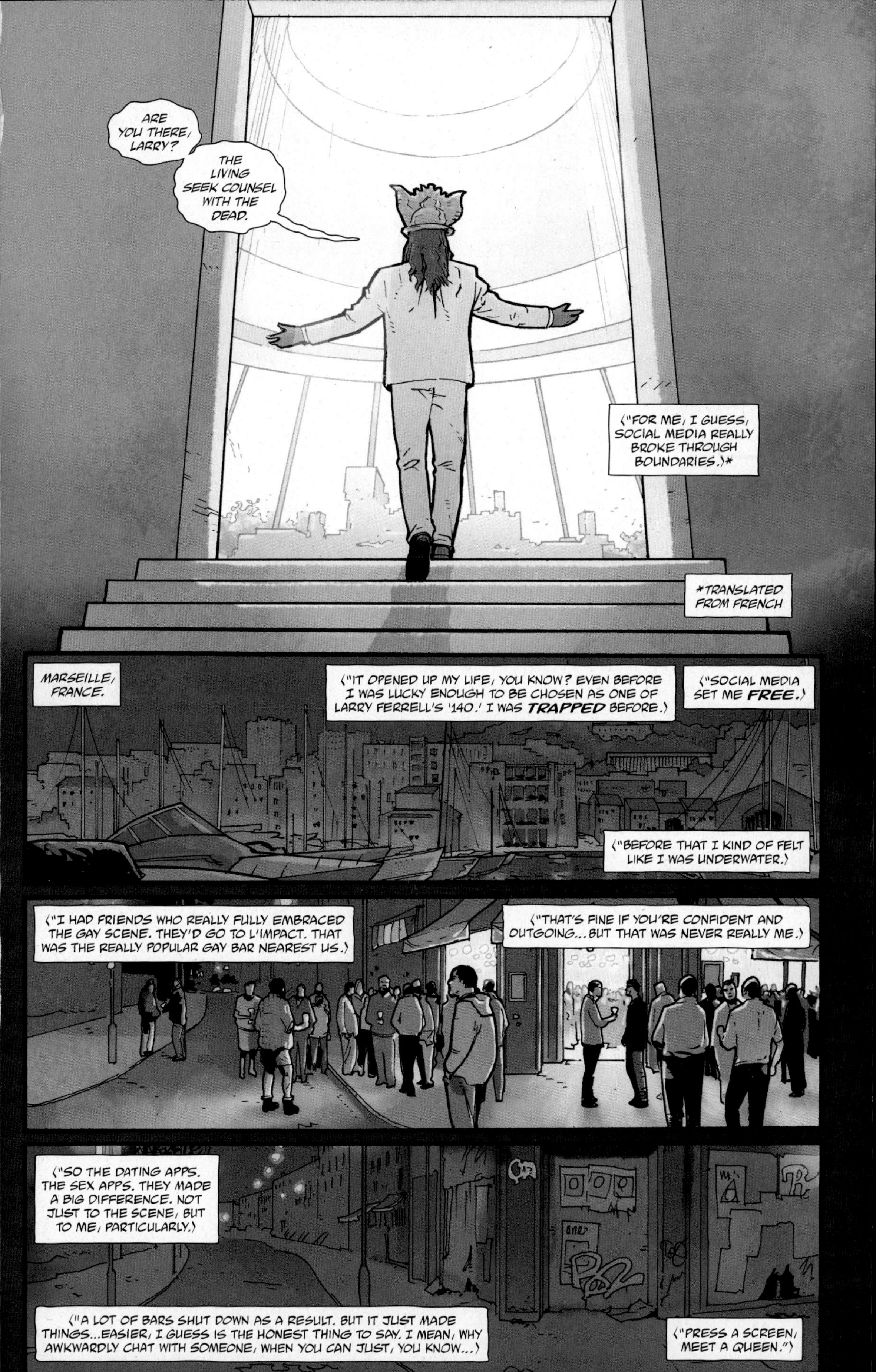
ARE YOU THERE, LARRY?
THE LIVING SEEK COUNSEL WITH THE DEAD.
‹"FOR ME, I GUESS, SOCIAL MEDIA REALLY BROKE THROUGH BOUNDARIES.›*
*TRANSLATED FROM FRENCH
MARSEILLE, FRANCE.
‹"IT OPENED UP MY LIFE, YOU KNOW? EVEN BEFORE I WAS LUCKY ENOUGH TO BE CHOSEN AS ONE OF LARRY FERRELL'S '140,' I WAS **TRAPPED** BEFORE.›
‹"SOCIAL MEDIA SET ME **FREE.**›
‹"BEFORE THAT I KIND OF FELT LIKE I WAS UNDERWATER.›
‹"I HAD FRIENDS WHO REALLY FULLY EMBRACED THE GAY SCENE. THEY'D GO TO L'IMPACT. THAT WAS THE REALLY POPULAR GAY BAR NEAREST US.›
‹"THAT'S FINE IF YOU'RE CONFIDENT AND OUTGOING... BUT THAT WAS NEVER REALLY ME.›
‹"SO THE DATING APPS. THE SEX APPS. THEY MADE A BIG DIFFERENCE. NOT JUST TO THE SCENE, BUT TO ME, PARTICULARLY.›
‹"A LOT OF BARS SHUT DOWN AS A RESULT. BUT IT JUST MADE THINGS...EASIER, I GUESS IS THE HONEST THING TO SAY. I MEAN, WHY AWKWARDLY CHAT WITH SOMEONE, WHEN YOU CAN JUST, YOU KNOW...›
‹"PRESS A SCREEN, MEET A QUEEN."›

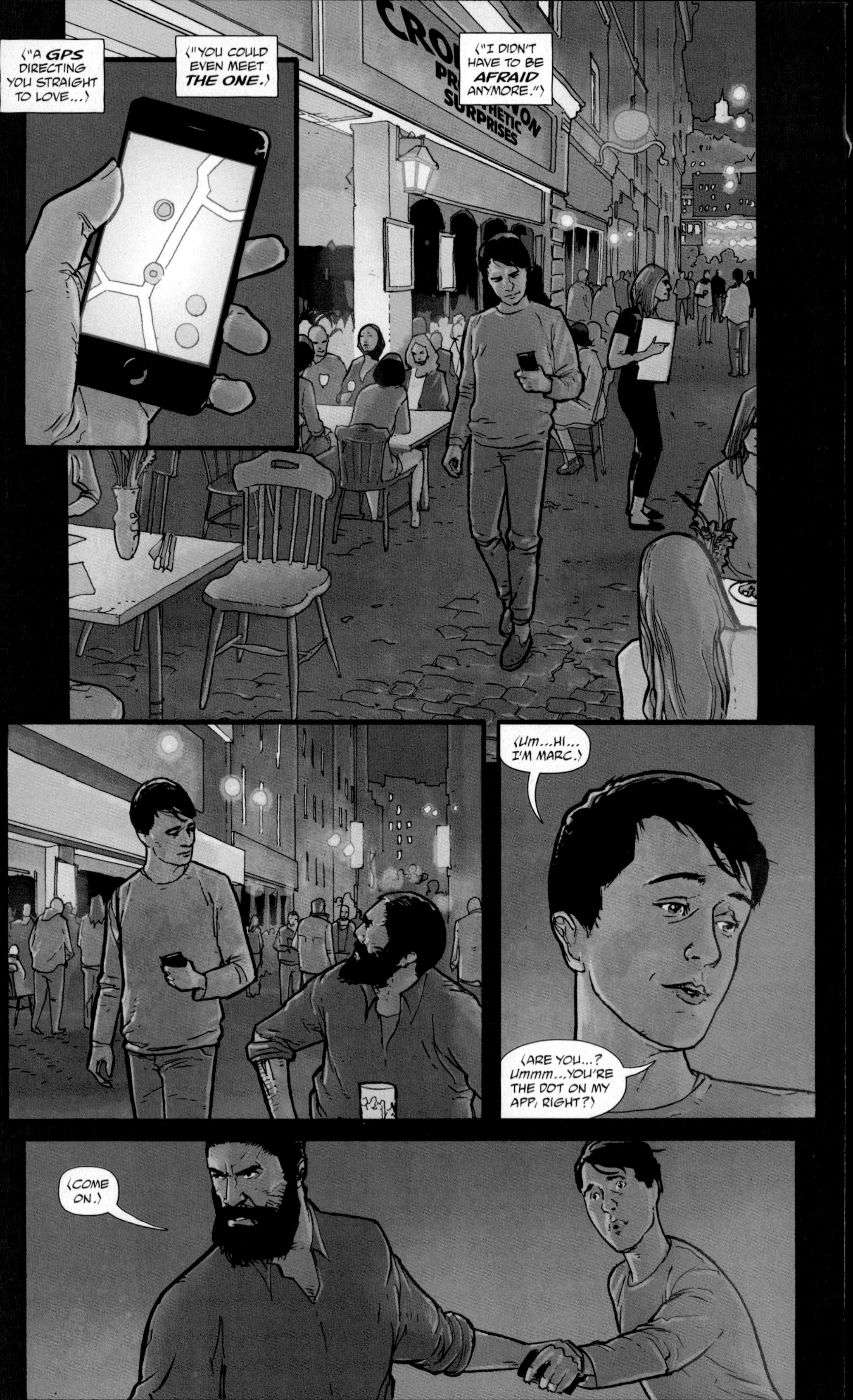

⟨"A GPS DIRECTING YOU STRAIGHT TO LOVE...⟩
⟨"YOU COULD EVEN MEET THE ONE.⟩
⟨"I DIDN'T HAVE TO BE AFRAID ANYMORE."⟩
PROSTHETIC SURPRISES
⟨UM...HI... I'M MARC.⟩
⟨ARE YOU...? UMMM...YOU'RE THE DOT ON MY APP, RIGHT?⟩
⟨COME ON.⟩

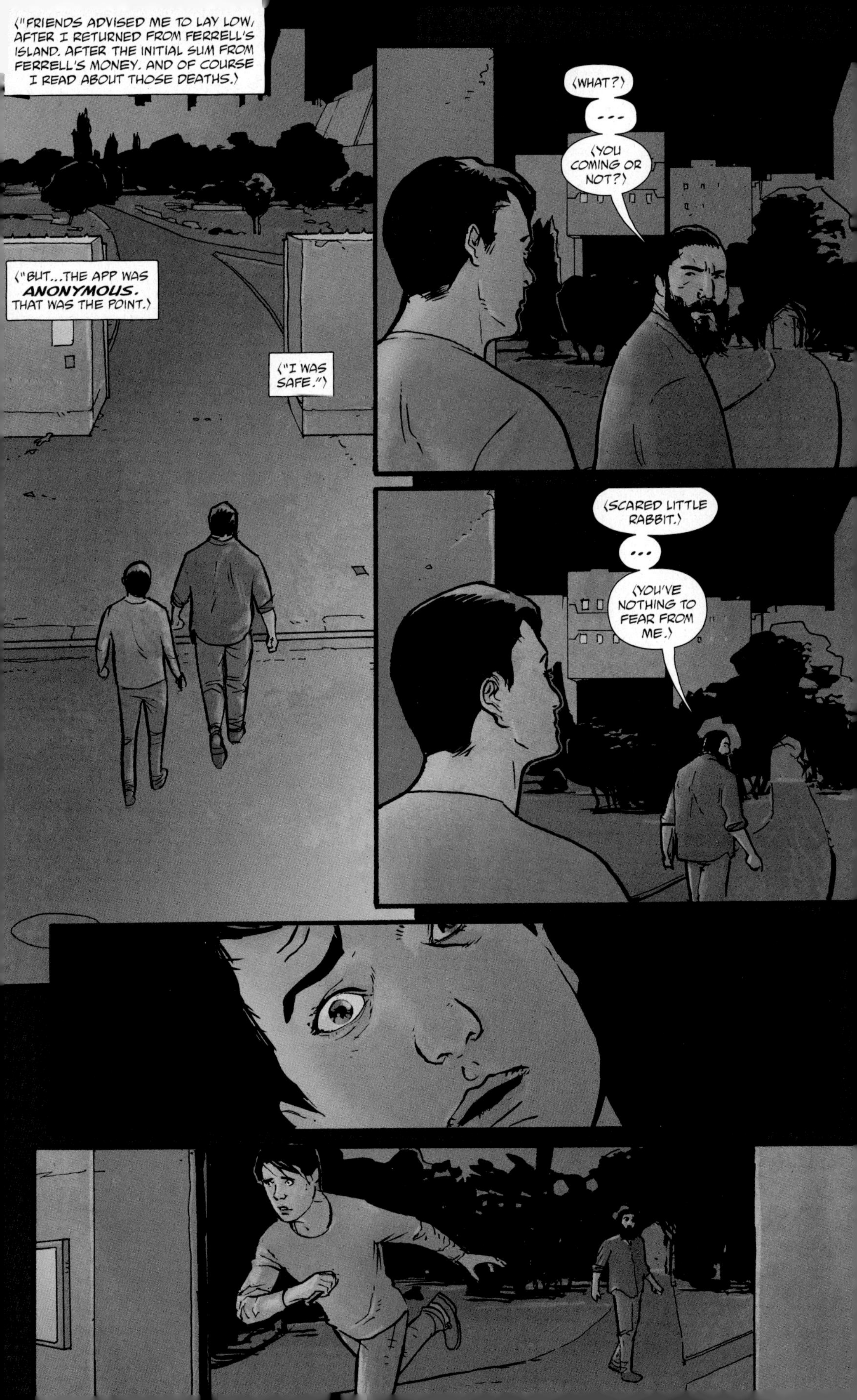
("FRIENDS ADVISED ME TO LAY LOW, AFTER I RETURNED FROM FERRELL'S ISLAND. AFTER THE INITIAL SUM FROM FERRELL'S MONEY. AND OF COURSE I READ ABOUT THOSE DEATHS.)
("BUT...THE APP WAS ANONYMOUS. THAT WAS THE POINT.)
("I WAS SAFE.")
(WHAT?)
...
(YOU COMING OR NOT?)
(SCARED LITTLE RABBIT.)
...
(YOU'VE NOTHING TO FEAR FROM ME.)

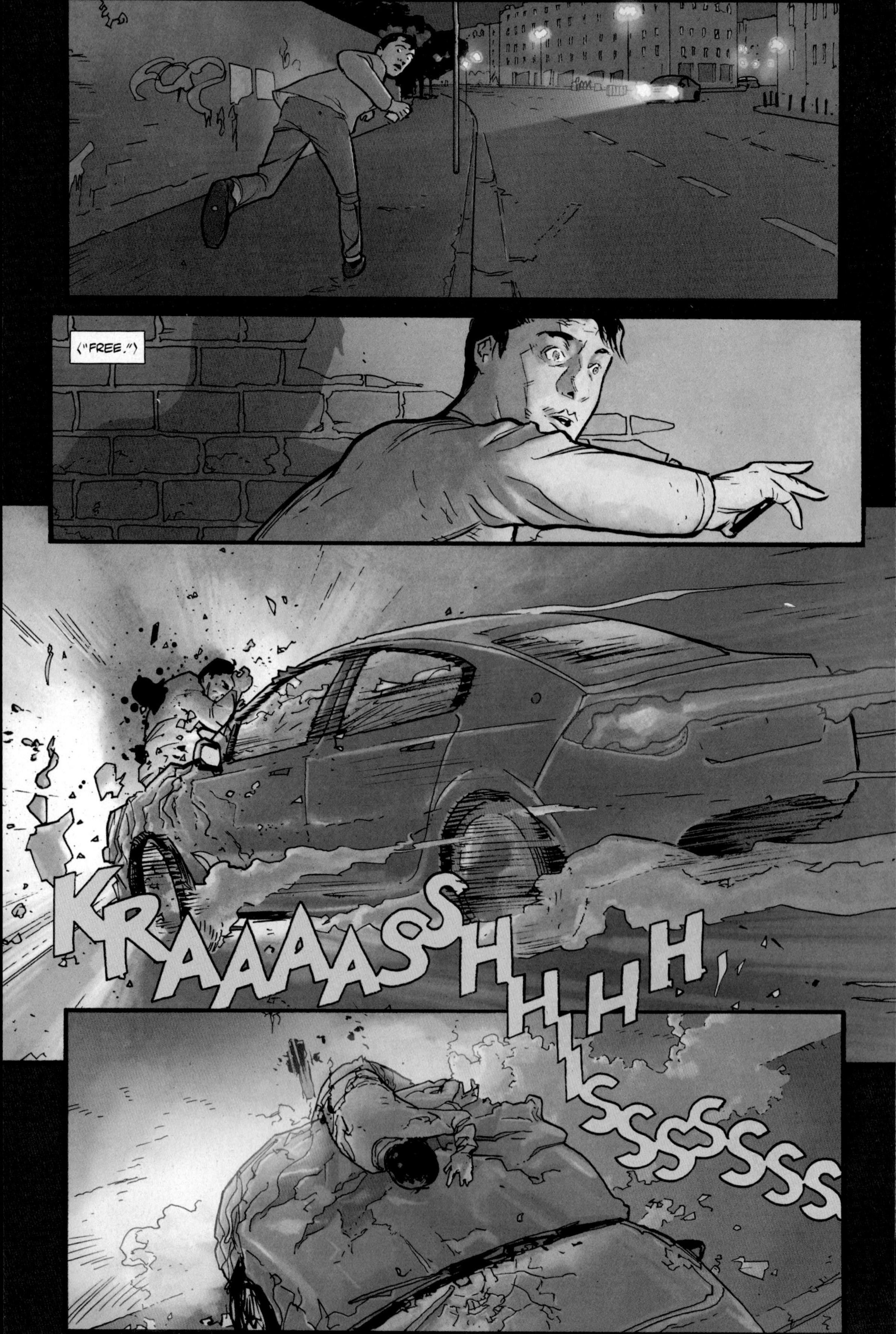
⟨"FREE."⟩
KRAAAASSHHHH
HISSSSSSSS

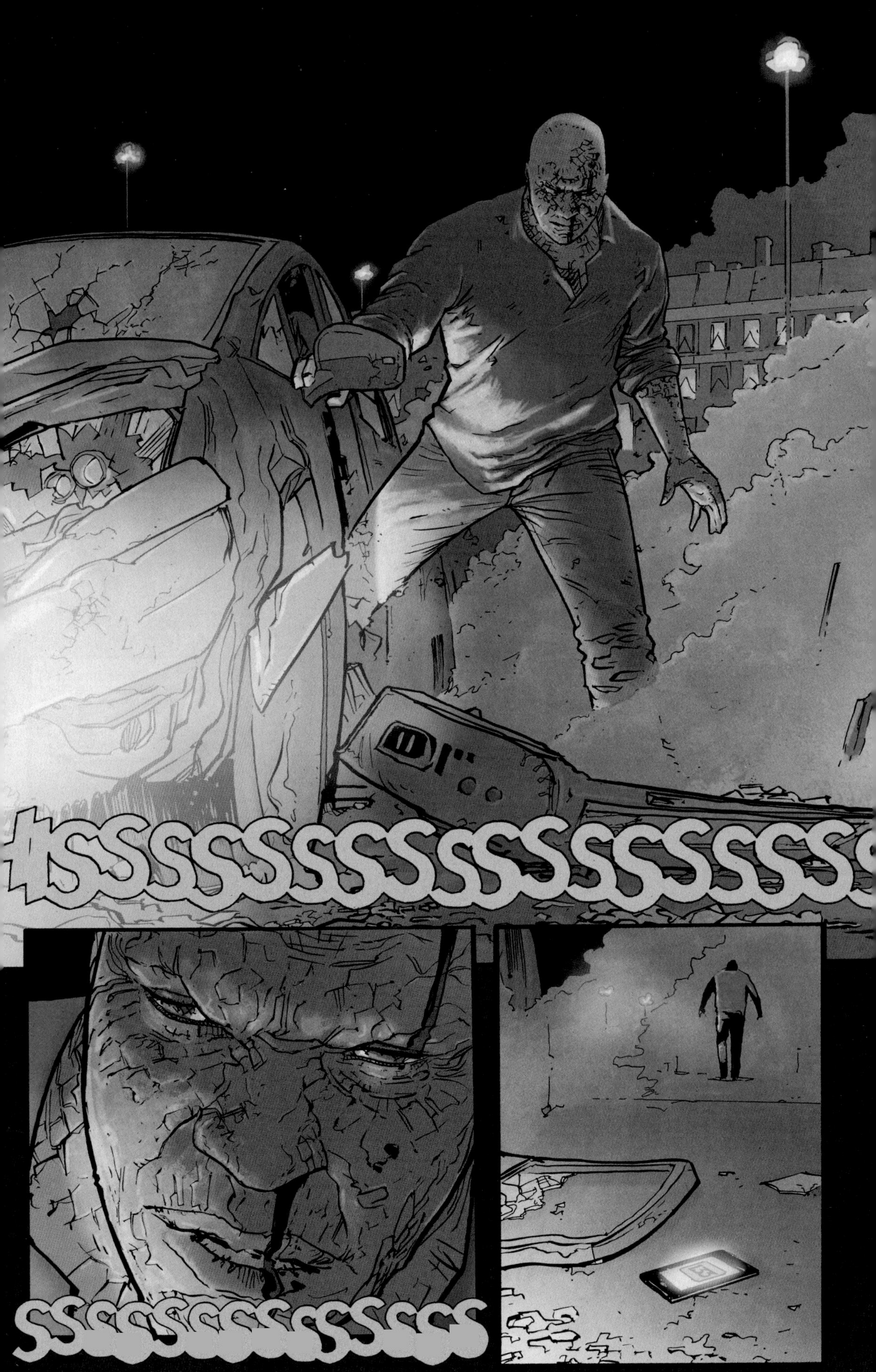

tSSSSSSSSSSSSSSSSS
SSSSSSSSSSSSSS

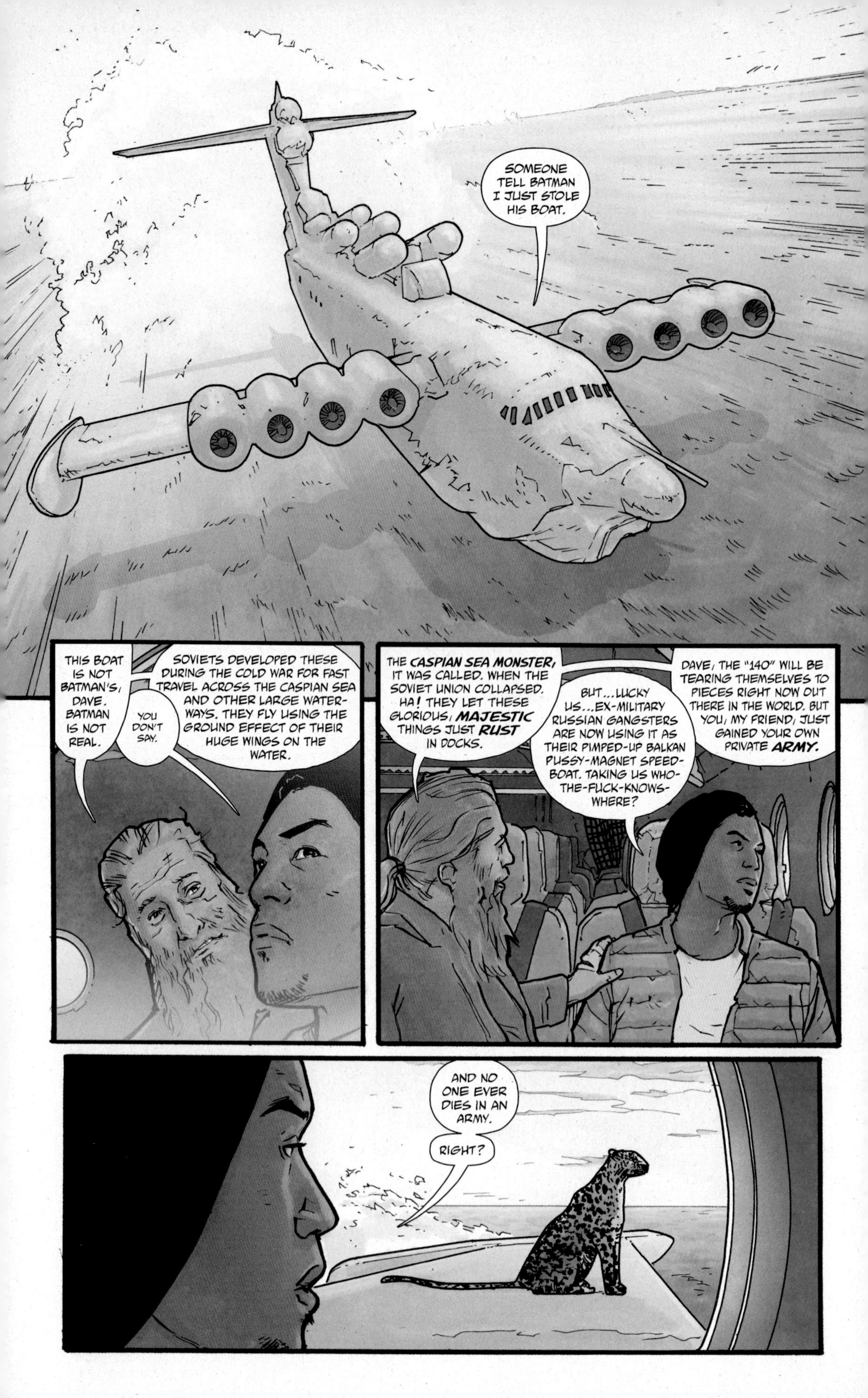
SOMEONE TELL BATMAN I JUST STOLE HIS BOAT.
THIS BOAT IS NOT BATMAN'S, DAVE. BATMAN IS NOT REAL.
YOU DON'T SAY.
SOVIETS DEVELOPED THESE DURING THE COLD WAR FOR FAST TRAVEL ACROSS THE CASPIAN SEA AND OTHER LARGE WATER-WAYS. THEY FLY USING THE GROUND EFFECT OF THEIR HUGE WINGS ON THE WATER.
THE CASPIAN SEA MONSTER, IT WAS CALLED. WHEN THE SOVIET UNION COLLAPSED. HA! THEY LET THESE GLORIOUS, MAJESTIC THINGS JUST RUST IN DOCKS.
BUT...LUCKY US...EX-MILITARY RUSSIAN GANGSTERS ARE NOW USING IT AS THEIR PIMPED-UP BALKAN PUSSY-MAGNET SPEED-BOAT. TAKING US WHO-THE-FUCK-KNOWS-WHERE?
DAVE, THE "140" WILL BE TEARING THEMSELVES TO PIECES RIGHT NOW OUT THERE IN THE WORLD. BUT YOU, MY FRIEND, JUST GAINED YOUR OWN PRIVATE ARMY.
AND NO ONE EVER DIES IN AN ARMY.
RIGHT?

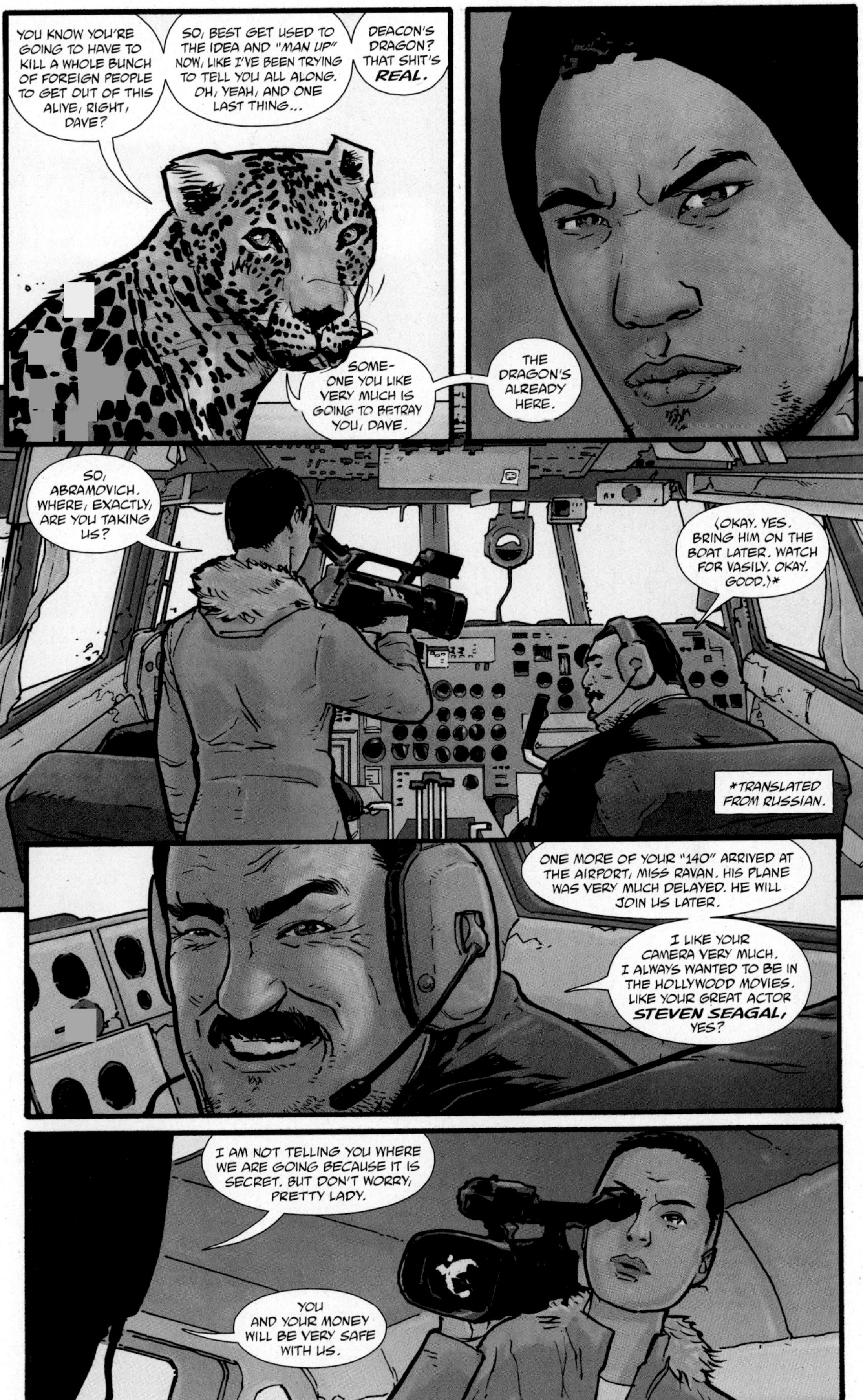
YOU KNOW YOU'RE GOING TO HAVE TO KILL A WHOLE BUNCH OF FOREIGN PEOPLE TO GET OUT OF THIS ALIVE, RIGHT, DAVE?
SO, BEST GET USED TO THE IDEA AND "MAN UP" NOW, LIKE I'VE BEEN TRYING TO TELL YOU ALL ALONG. OH, YEAH, AND ONE LAST THING...
DEACON'S DRAGON? THAT SHIT'S REAL.
SOME-ONE YOU LIKE VERY MUCH IS GOING TO BETRAY YOU, DAVE.
THE DRAGON'S ALREADY HERE.
SO, ABRAMOVICH. WHERE, EXACTLY, ARE YOU TAKING US?
(OKAY. YES. BRING HIM ON THE BOAT LATER. WATCH FOR VASILY. OKAY. GOOD.)*
*TRANSLATED FROM RUSSIAN.
ONE MORE OF YOUR "140" ARRIVED AT THE AIRPORT, MISS RAVAN. HIS PLANE WAS VERY MUCH DELAYED. HE WILL JOIN US LATER.
I LIKE YOUR CAMERA VERY MUCH. I ALWAYS WANTED TO BE IN THE HOLLYWOOD MOVIES. LIKE YOUR GREAT ACTOR STEVEN SEAGAL, YES?
I AM NOT TELLING YOU WHERE WE ARE GOING BECAUSE IT IS SECRET. BUT DON'T WORRY, PRETTY LADY.
YOU AND YOUR MONEY WILL BE VERY SAFE WITH US.

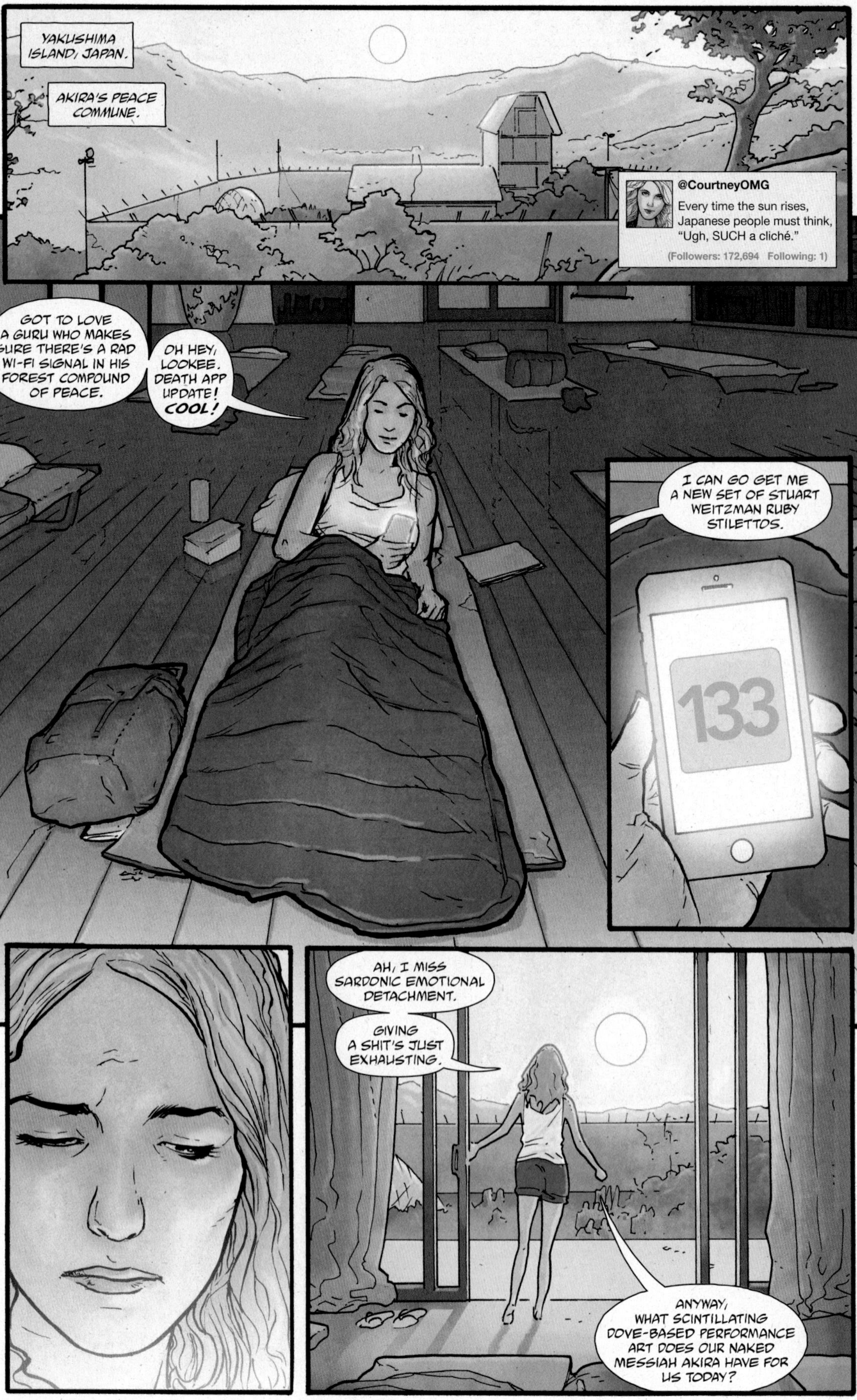
YAKUSHIMA ISLAND, JAPAN.
AKIRA'S PEACE COMMUNE.
@CourtneyOMG
Every time the sun rises, Japanese people must think, "Ugh, SUCH a cliché."
(Followers: 172,694 Following: 1)
GOT TO LOVE A GURU WHO MAKES SURE THERE'S A RAD WI-FI SIGNAL IN HIS FOREST COMPOUND OF PEACE.
OH HEY, LOOKEE. DEATH APP UPDATE! COOL!
I CAN GO GET ME A NEW SET OF STUART WEITZMAN RUBY STILETTOS.
133
AH, I MISS SARDONIC EMOTIONAL DETACHMENT.
GIVING A SHIT'S JUST EXHAUSTING.
ANYWAY, WHAT SCINTILLATING DOVE-BASED PERFORMANCE ART DOES OUR NAKED MESSIAH AKIRA HAVE FOR US TODAY?

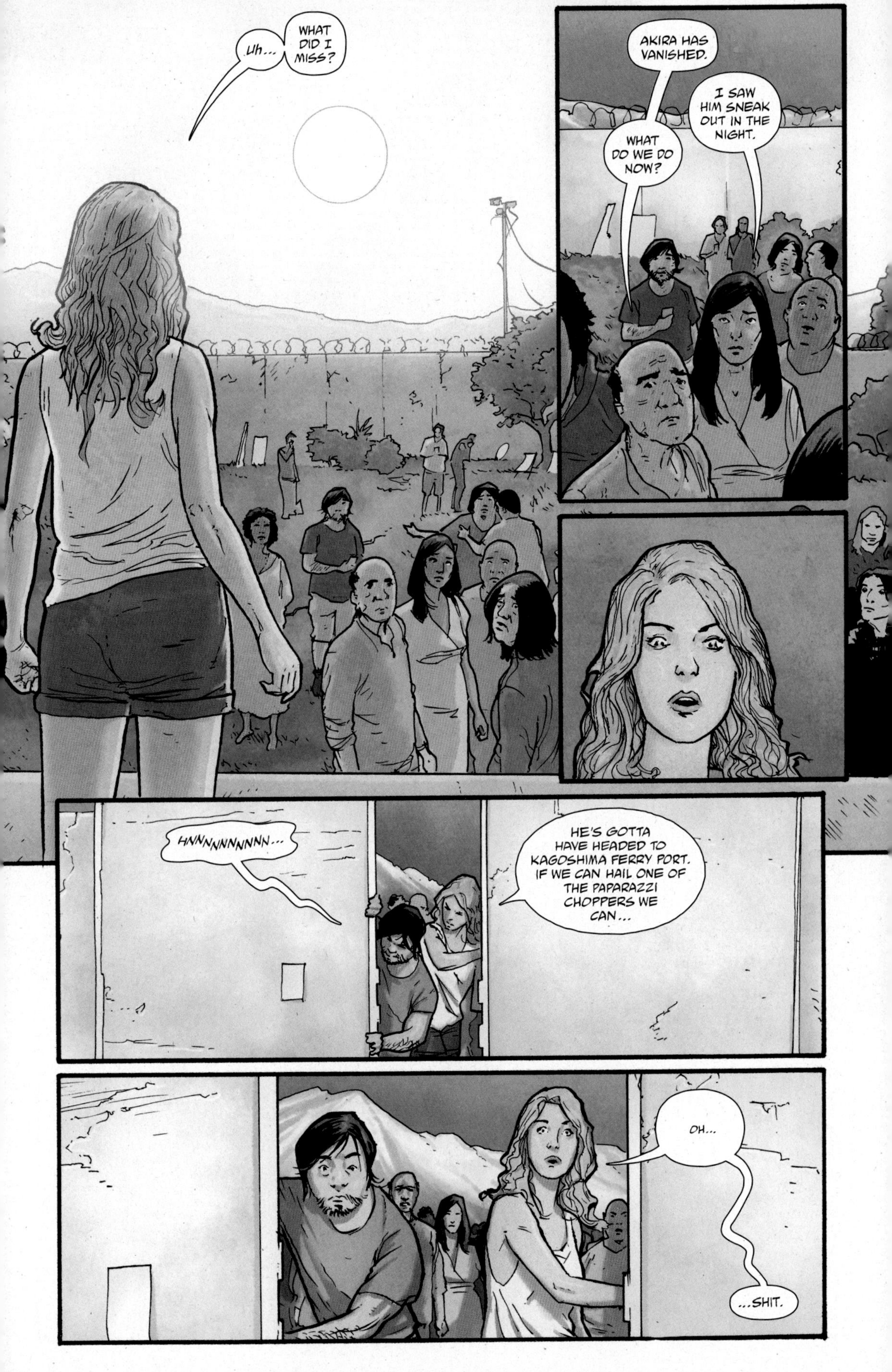
Uh...
WHAT DID I MISS?
AKIRA HAS VANISHED.
WHAT DO WE DO NOW?
I SAW HIM SNEAK OUT IN THE NIGHT.
HNNNNNNNNNN...
HE'S GOTTA HAVE HEADED TO KAGOSHIMA FERRY PORT. IF WE CAN HAIL ONE OF THE PAPARAZZI CHOPPERS WE CAN...
OH...
...SHIT.

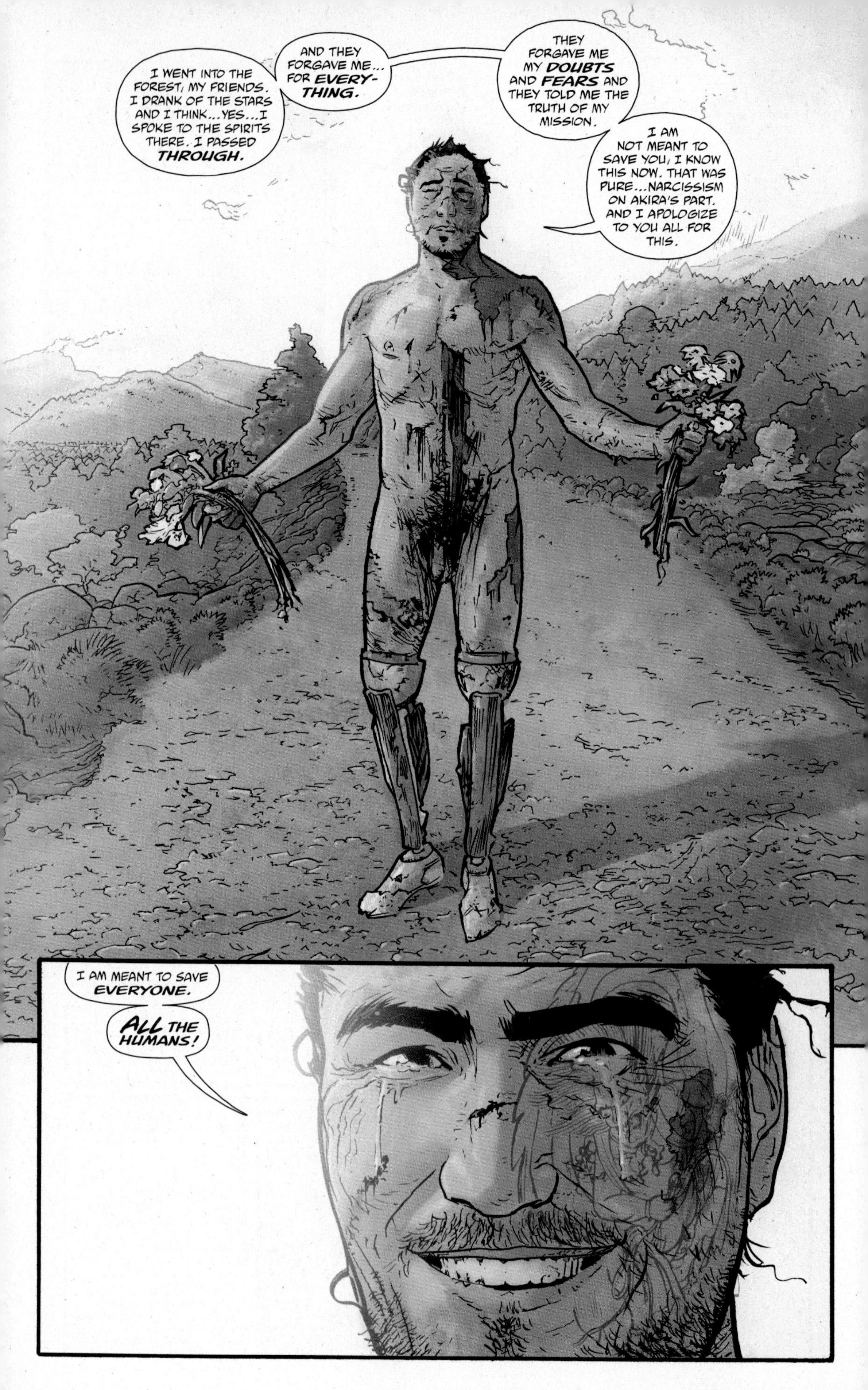
I WENT INTO THE FOREST, MY FRIENDS. I DRANK OF THE STARS AND I THINK...YES...I SPOKE TO THE SPIRITS THERE. I PASSED THROUGH.
AND THEY FORGAVE ME... FOR EVERY-THING.
THEY FORGAVE ME MY DOUBTS AND FEARS AND THEY TOLD ME THE TRUTH OF MY MISSION.
I AM NOT MEANT TO SAVE YOU, I KNOW THIS NOW. THAT WAS PURE...NARCISSISM ON AKIRA'S PART. AND I APOLOGIZE TO YOU ALL FOR THIS.
I AM MEANT TO SAVE EVERYONE.
ALL THE HUMANS!

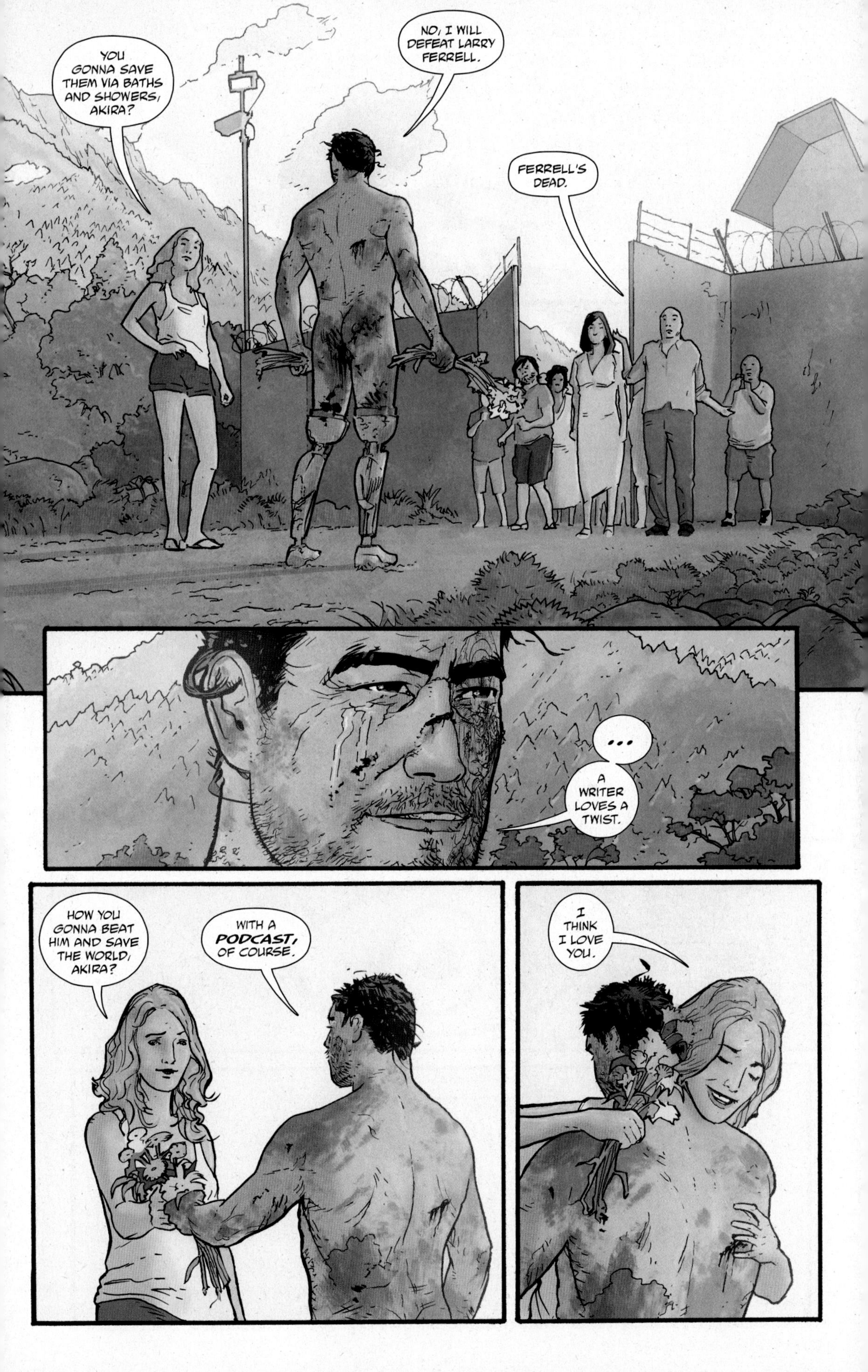
YOU GONNA SAVE THEM VIA BATHS AND SHOWERS, AKIRA?
NO, I WILL DEFEAT LARRY FERRELL.
FERRELL'S DEAD.
...
A WRITER LOVES A TWIST.
HOW YOU GONNA BEAT HIM AND SAVE THE WORLD, AKIRA?
WITH A PODCAST, OF COURSE.
I THINK I LOVE YOU.

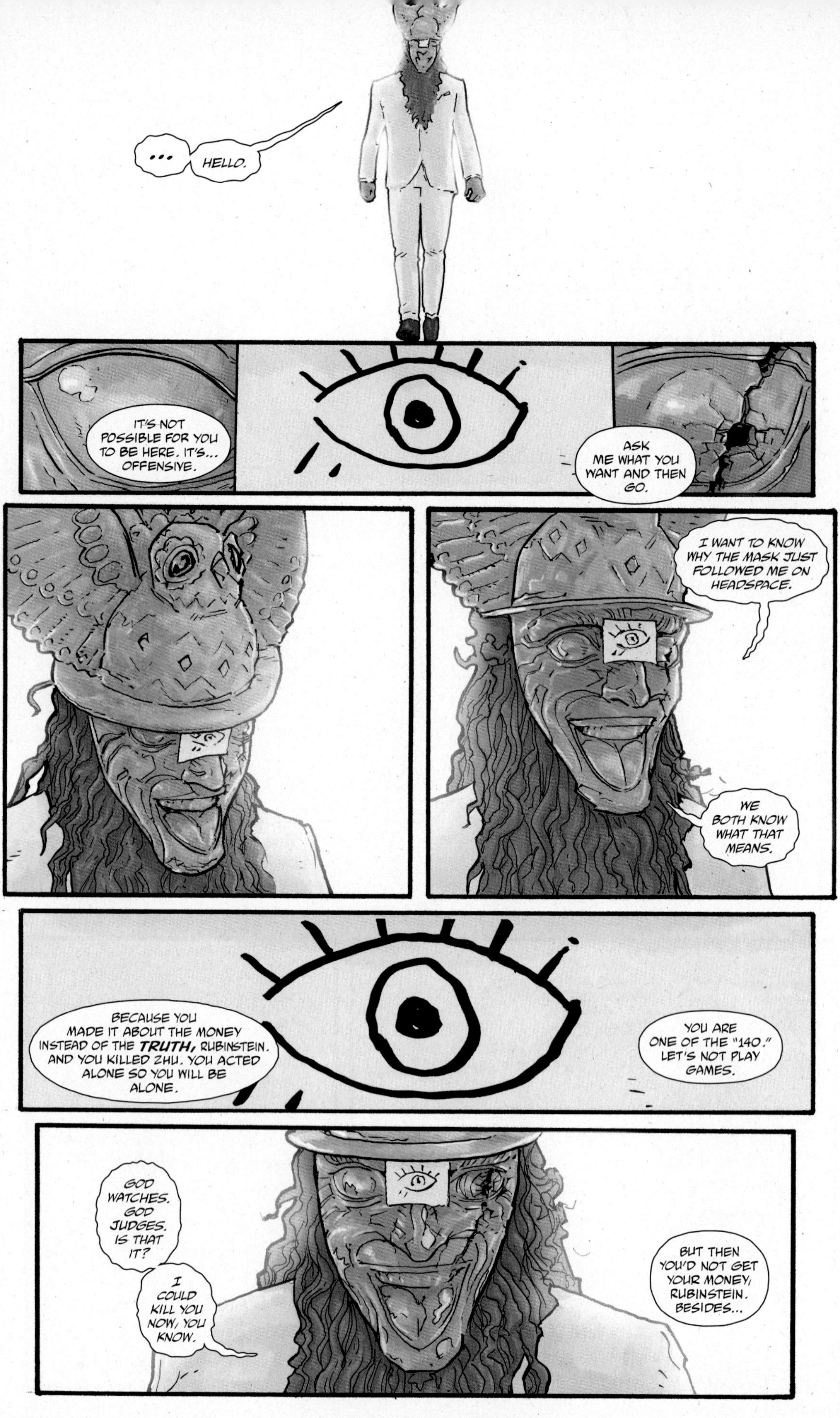
...
HELLO.
IT'S NOT POSSIBLE FOR YOU TO BE HERE. IT'S... OFFENSIVE.
ASK ME WHAT YOU WANT AND THEN GO.
I WANT TO KNOW WHY THE MASK JUST FOLLOWED ME ON HEADSPACE.
WE BOTH KNOW WHAT THAT MEANS.
BECAUSE YOU MADE IT ABOUT THE MONEY INSTEAD OF THE TRUTH, RUBINSTEIN. AND YOU KILLED ZHU. YOU ACTED ALONE SO YOU WILL BE ALONE.
YOU ARE ONE OF THE "140." LET'S NOT PLAY GAMES.
GOD WATCHES. GOD JUDGES. IS THAT IT?
I COULD KILL YOU NOW, YOU KNOW.
BUT THEN YOU'D NOT GET YOUR MONEY, RUBINSTEIN. BESIDES...

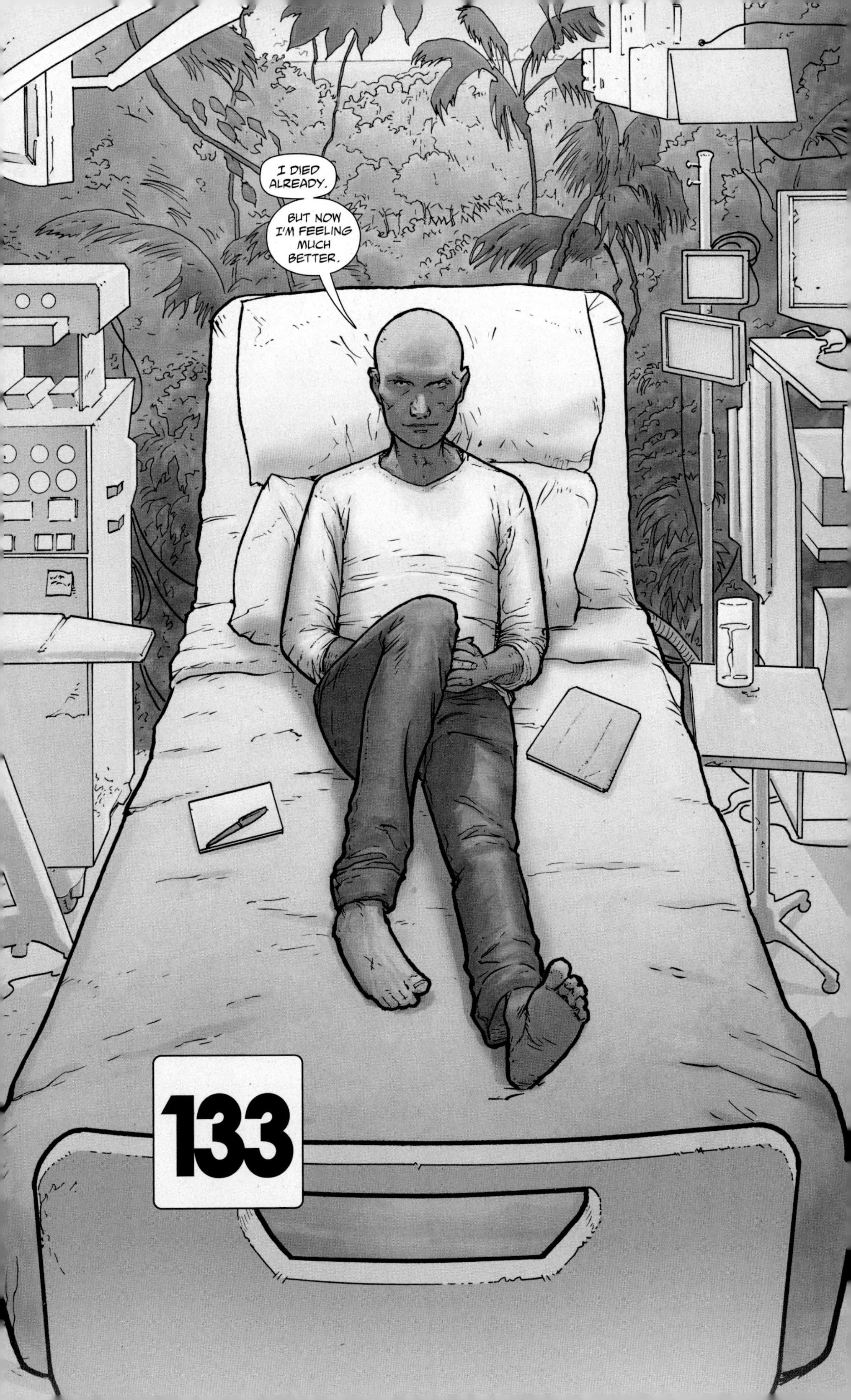
I DIED ALREADY.
BUT NOW I'M FEELING MUCH BETTER.
133

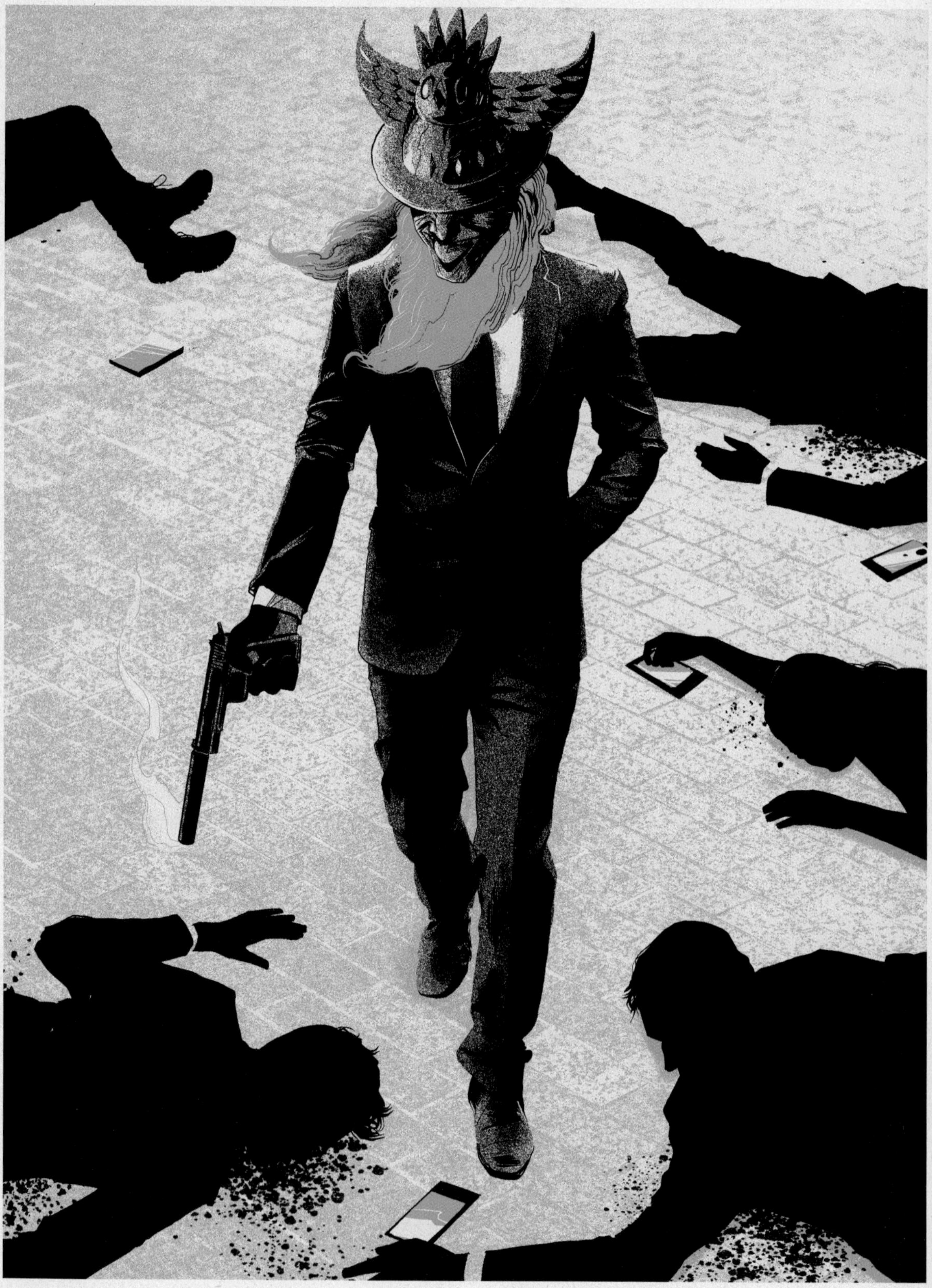

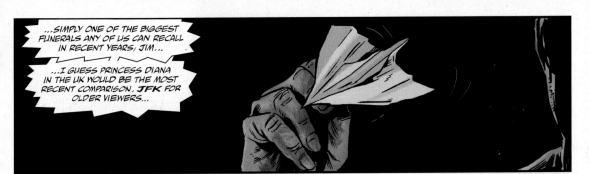

...SIMPLY ONE OF THE BIGGEST FUNERALS ANY OF US CAN RECALL IN RECENT YEARS, JIM...

...I GUESS PRINCESS DIANA IN THE UK WOULD BE THE MOST RECENT COMPARISON. *JFK* FOR OLDER VIEWERS...

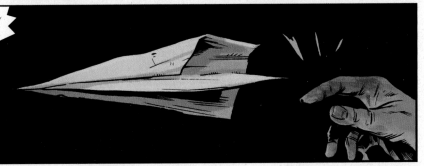

...IS IT ANY SURPRISE? I MEAN, SOCIAL MEDIA CHANGED THIS WORLD. BROUGHT US ALL CLOSER TOGETHER.

I GUESS LARRY FERRELL SAW THE FUTURE AND MOVED US TOWARDS IT. SOME HAVE CALLED HIM A PROPHET.

TO MANY OF OUR YOUNG PEOPLE, FERRELL'S SOCIAL MEDIA PLATFORMS BECAME AN EXTENSION OF THEIR OWN IDENTITY.

IT'S REALLY NO WONDER THEY'RE SO AFFECTED. THOUSANDS UPON THOUSANDS HAVE TURNED OUT IN THE STREETS OF SEATTLE TO TRY AND GAIN SIGHT OF THE COFFIN.

MANY OF HIS CELEBRATED "140 LIST" HAVE ATTENDED THE FUNERAL TODAY. SOME STAYED AWAY, HAVING GONE INTO HIDING.

PAUL DANO IS HERE, THE HOLLYWOOD ACTOR WHO IS PLAYING THE PART OF LARRY FERRELL IN THE UPCOMING AARON SORKIN-SCRIPTED BIOPIC.

IT REALLY IS A TRAGEDY FOR THE WHOLE OF HUMANITY, JIM, THAT WE'VE LOST SOMEONE THIS BRILLIANT THIS YOUNG.

TAP

R.I.P. LARRY FERRELL...

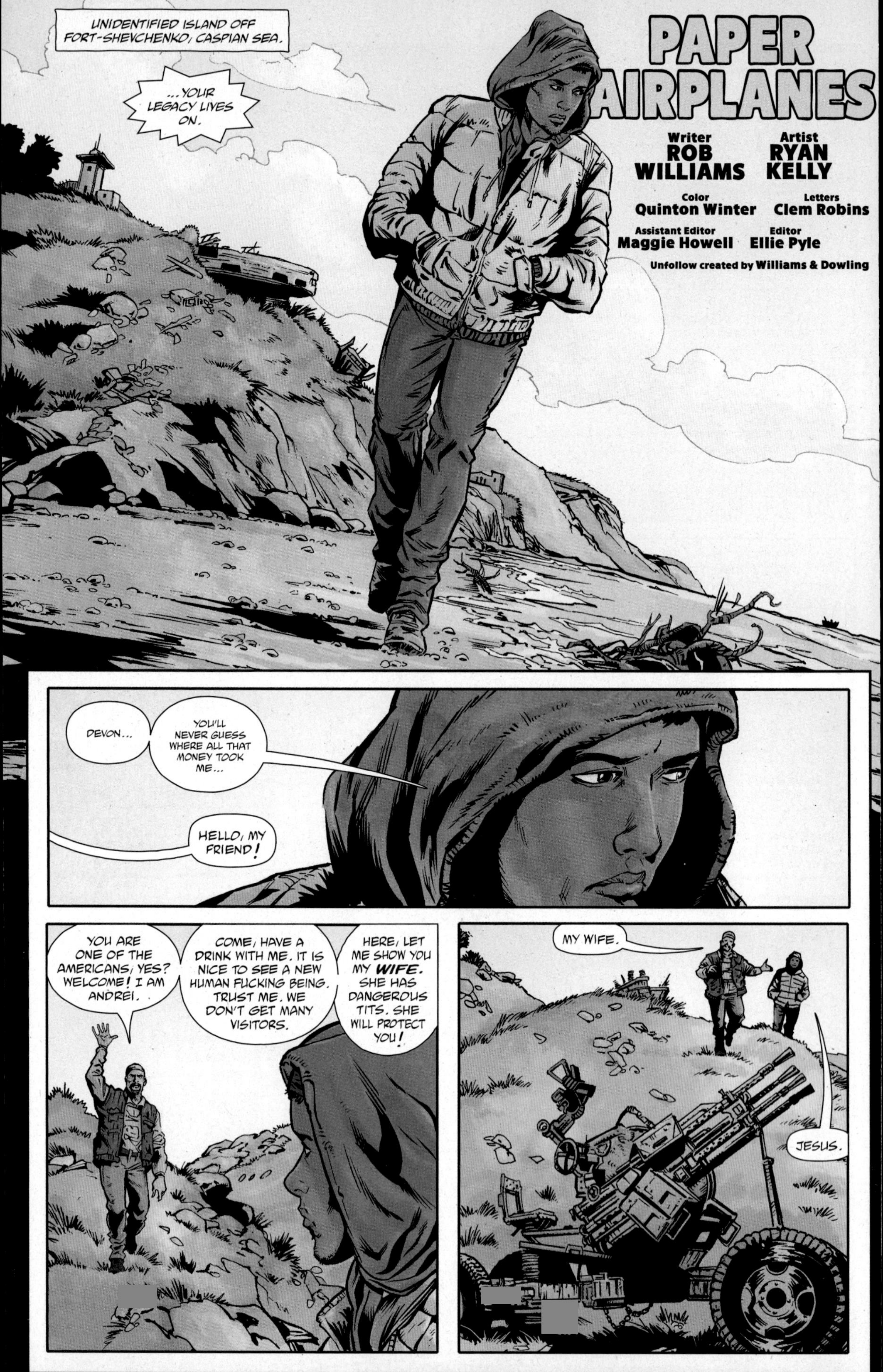
UNIDENTIFIED ISLAND OFF FORT-SHEVCHENKO, CASPIAN SEA.
...YOUR LEGACY LIVES ON.
PAPER AIRPLANES
Writer ROB WILLIAMS
Artist RYAN KELLY
Color Quinton Winter
Letters Clem Robins
Assistant Editor Maggie Howell
Editor Ellie Pyle
Unfollow created by Williams & Dowling
DEVON...
YOU'LL NEVER GUESS WHERE ALL THAT MONEY TOOK ME...
HELLO, MY FRIEND!
YOU ARE ONE OF THE AMERICANS, YES? WELCOME! I AM ANDREI.
COME, HAVE A DRINK WITH ME. IT IS NICE TO SEE A NEW HUMAN FUCKING BEING. TRUST ME. WE DON'T GET MANY VISITORS.
HERE, LET ME SHOW YOU MY WIFE. SHE HAS DANGEROUS TITS. SHE WILL PROTECT YOU!
MY WIFE.
JESUS.

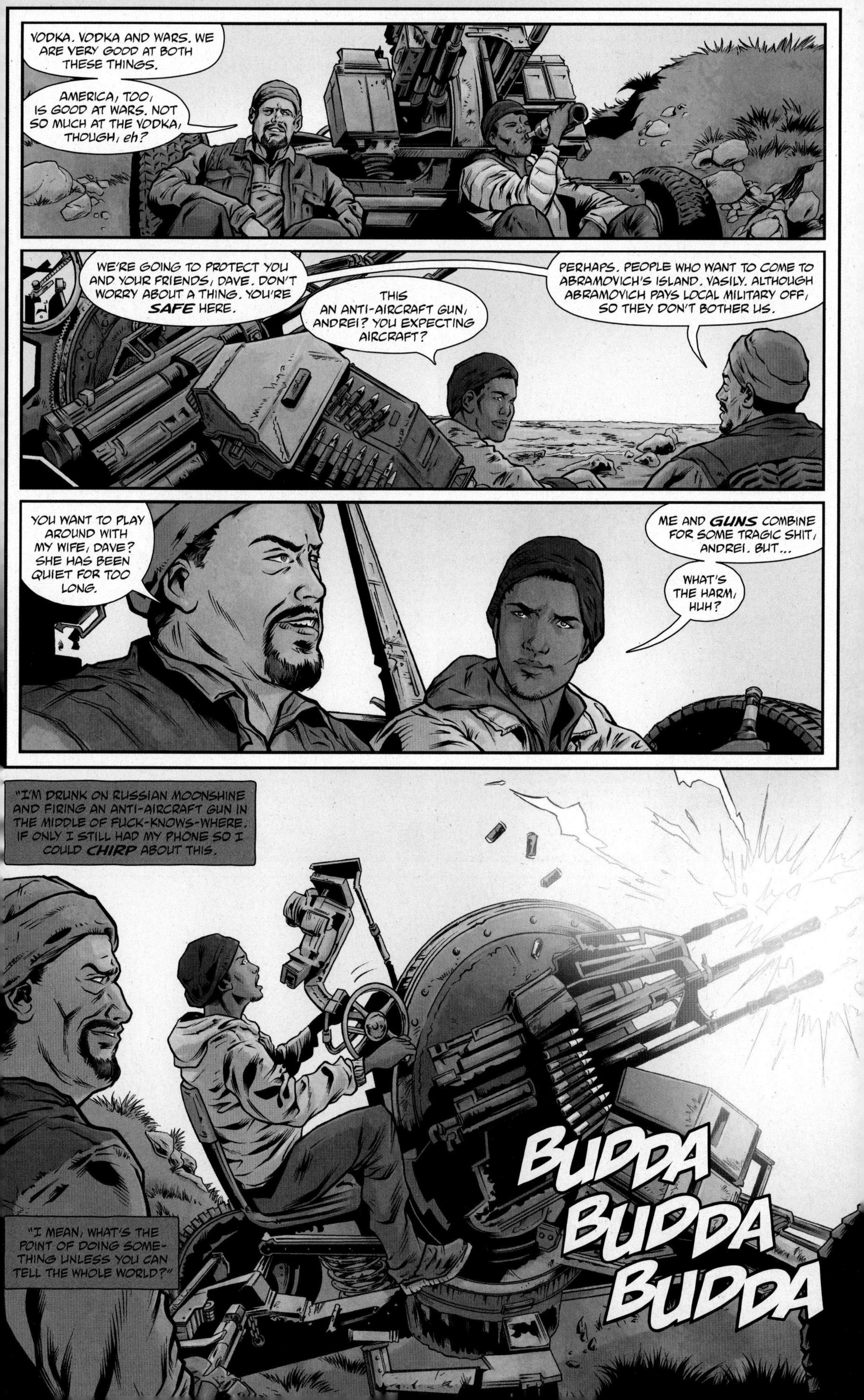
VODKA. VODKA AND WARS. WE ARE VERY GOOD AT BOTH THESE THINGS.
AMERICA, TOO, IS GOOD AT WARS. NOT SO MUCH AT THE VODKA, THOUGH, eh?
WE'RE GOING TO PROTECT YOU AND YOUR FRIENDS, DAVE. DON'T WORRY ABOUT A THING. YOU'RE SAFE HERE.
THIS AN ANTI-AIRCRAFT GUN, ANDREI? YOU EXPECTING AIRCRAFT?
PERHAPS. PEOPLE WHO WANT TO COME TO ABRAMOVICH'S ISLAND. VASILY. ALTHOUGH ABRAMOVICH PAYS LOCAL MILITARY OFF, SO THEY DON'T BOTHER US.
YOU WANT TO PLAY AROUND WITH MY WIFE, DAVE? SHE HAS BEEN QUIET FOR TOO LONG.
ME AND GUNS COMBINE FOR SOME TRAGIC SHIT, ANDREI. BUT...
WHAT'S THE HARM, HUH?
"I'M DRUNK ON RUSSIAN MOONSHINE AND FIRING AN ANTI-AIRCRAFT GUN IN THE MIDDLE OF FUCK-KNOWS-WHERE. IF ONLY I STILL HAD MY PHONE SO I COULD CHIRP ABOUT THIS.
"I MEAN, WHAT'S THE POINT OF DOING SOMETHING UNLESS YOU CAN TELL THE WHOLE WORLD?"
BUDDA
BUDDA
BUDDA

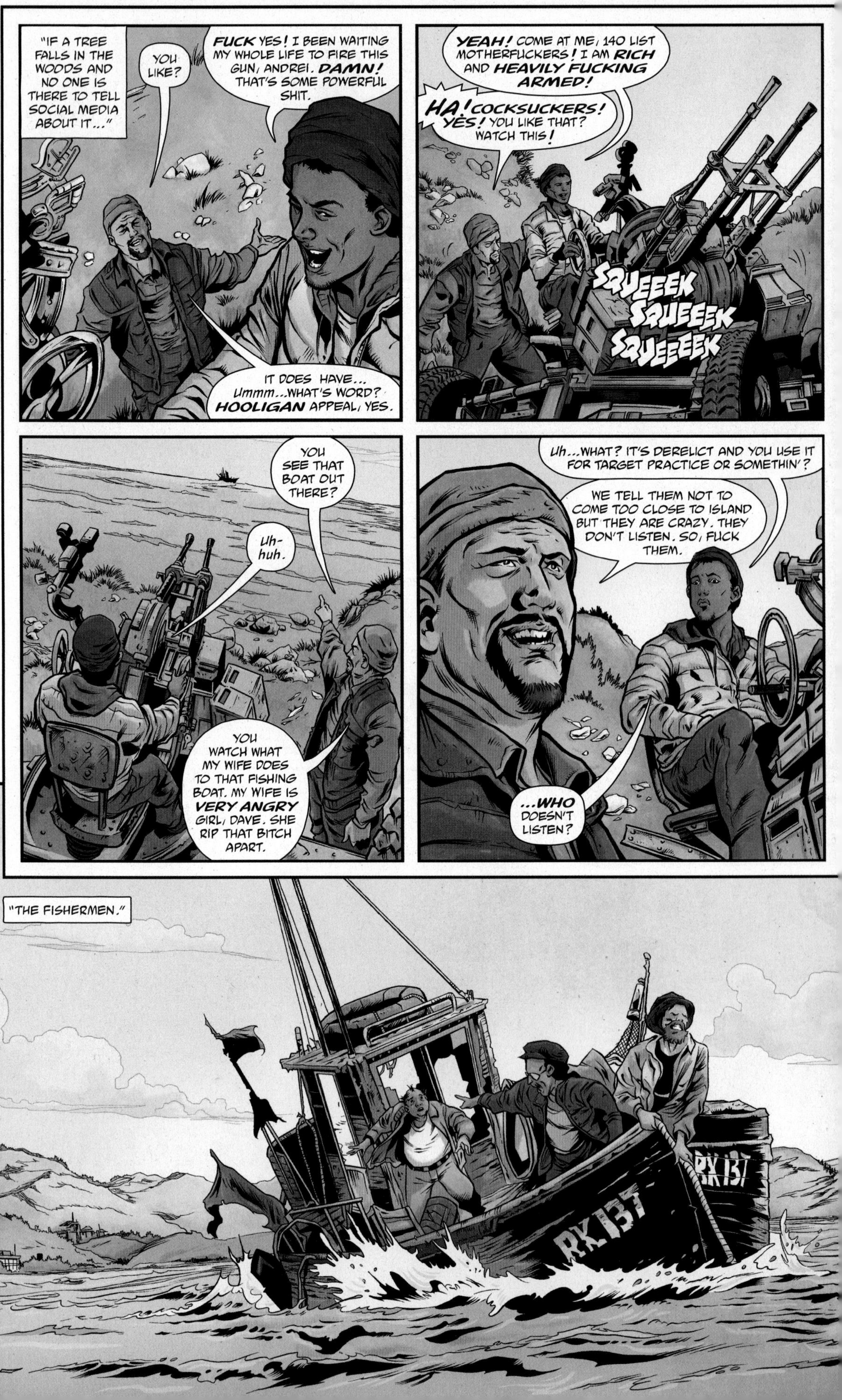
"IF A TREE FALLS IN THE WOODS AND NO ONE IS THERE TO TELL SOCIAL MEDIA ABOUT IT..."
YOU LIKE?
FUCK YES! I BEEN WAITING MY WHOLE LIFE TO FIRE THIS GUN, ANDREI. DAMN! THAT'S SOME POWERFUL SHIT.
IT DOES HAVE... UMMM...WHAT'S WORD? HOOLIGAN APPEAL, YES.
YEAH! COME AT ME, 140 LIST MOTHERFUCKERS! I AM RICH AND HEAVILY FUCKING ARMED!
HA! COCKSUCKERS! YES! YOU LIKE THAT? WATCH THIS!
SQUEEEK
SQUEEEK
SQUEEEEK
YOU SEE THAT BOAT OUT THERE?
UH-HUH.
YOU WATCH WHAT MY WIFE DOES TO THAT FISHING BOAT. MY WIFE IS VERY ANGRY GIRL, DAVE. SHE RIP THAT BITCH APART.
UH...WHAT? IT'S DERELICT AND YOU USE IT FOR TARGET PRACTICE OR SOMETHIN'?
WE TELL THEM NOT TO COME TOO CLOSE TO ISLAND BUT THEY ARE CRAZY. THEY DON'T LISTEN. SO, FUCK THEM.
...WHO DOESN'T LISTEN?
"THE FISHERMEN."
RK137
RK137

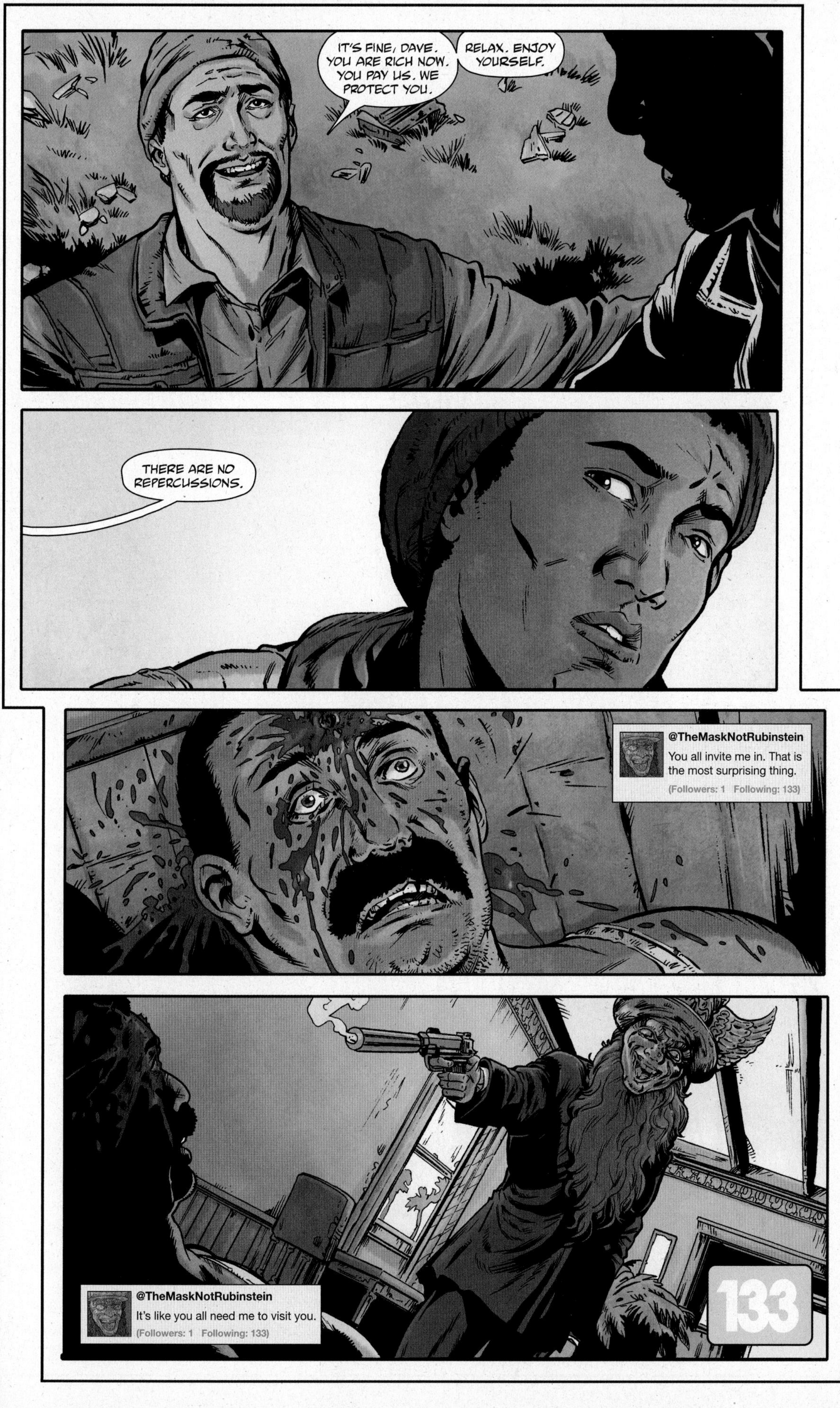

IT'S FINE, DAVE. YOU ARE RICH NOW. YOU PAY US. WE PROTECT YOU.
RELAX. ENJOY YOURSELF.
THERE ARE NO REPERCUSSIONS.
@TheMaskNotRubinstein
You all invite me in. That is the most surprising thing.
(Followers: 1 Following: 133)
@TheMaskNotRubinstein
It's like you all need me to visit you.
(Followers: 1 Following: 133)

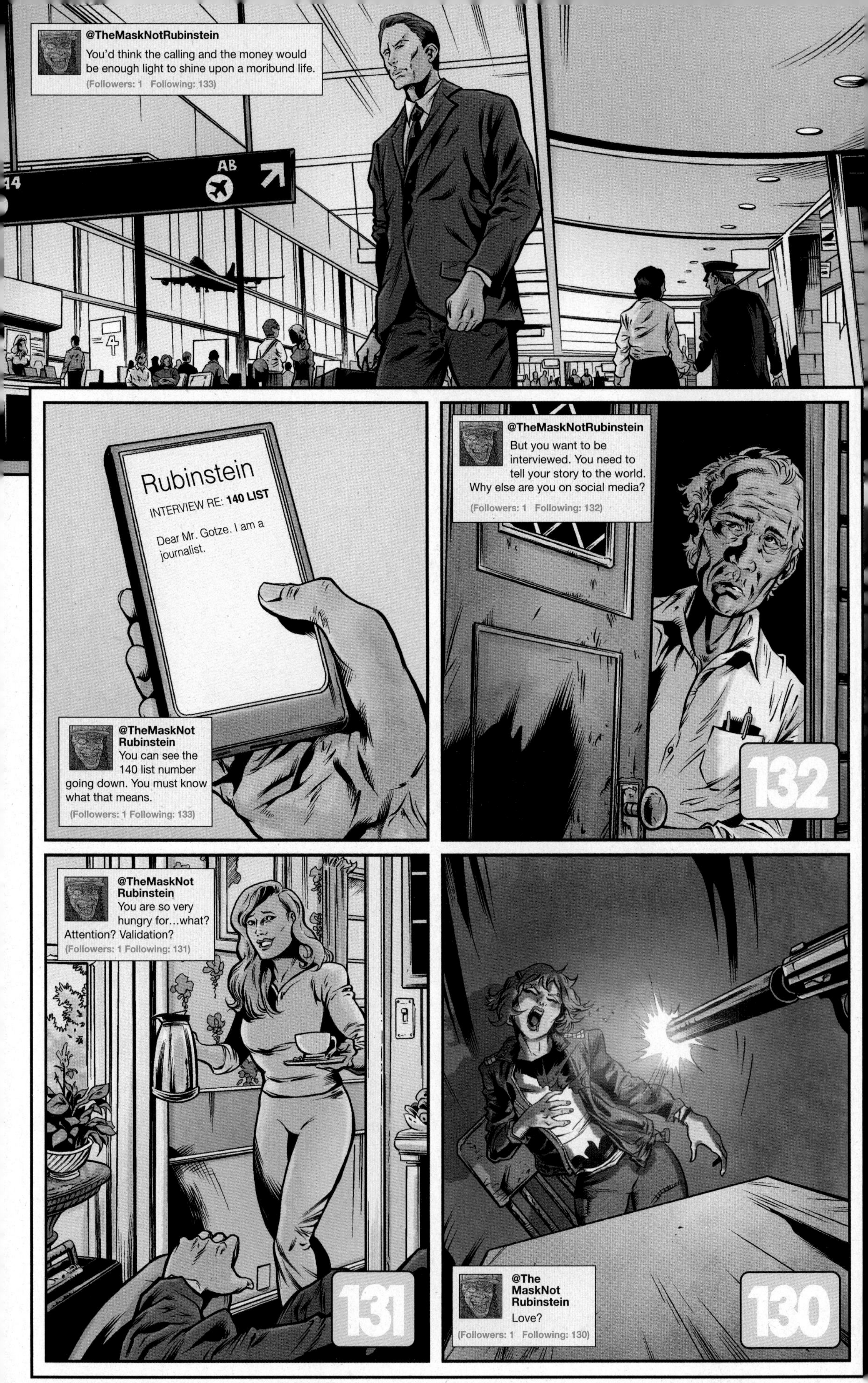

@TheMaskNotRubinstein
You'd think the calling and the money would be enough light to shine upon a moribund life.
(Followers: 1 Following: 133)
AB
Rubinstein
INTERVIEW RE: 140 LIST
Dear Mr. Gotze. I am a journalist.
@TheMaskNot Rubinstein
You can see the 140 list number going down. You must know what that means.
(Followers: 1 Following: 133)
@TheMaskNotRubinstein
But you want to be interviewed. You need to tell your story to the world. Why else are you on social media?
(Followers: 1 Following: 132)
132
@TheMaskNot Rubinstein
You are so very hungry for...what? Attention? Validation?
(Followers: 1 Following: 131)
131
@The MaskNot Rubinstein
Love?
(Followers: 1 Following: 130)
130

...KKKKKKK...

AHHHHH...

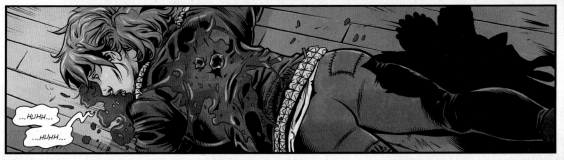

...HUHH...

...HUHH...

@TheMaskNotRubinstein
This was always about revealing THE TRUTH.
(Followers: 1   Following: 130)

@TheMask NotRubinstein
You were right about that, Larry. So...do you want to know the truth that I have discovered?
(Followers: 1   Following: 130)

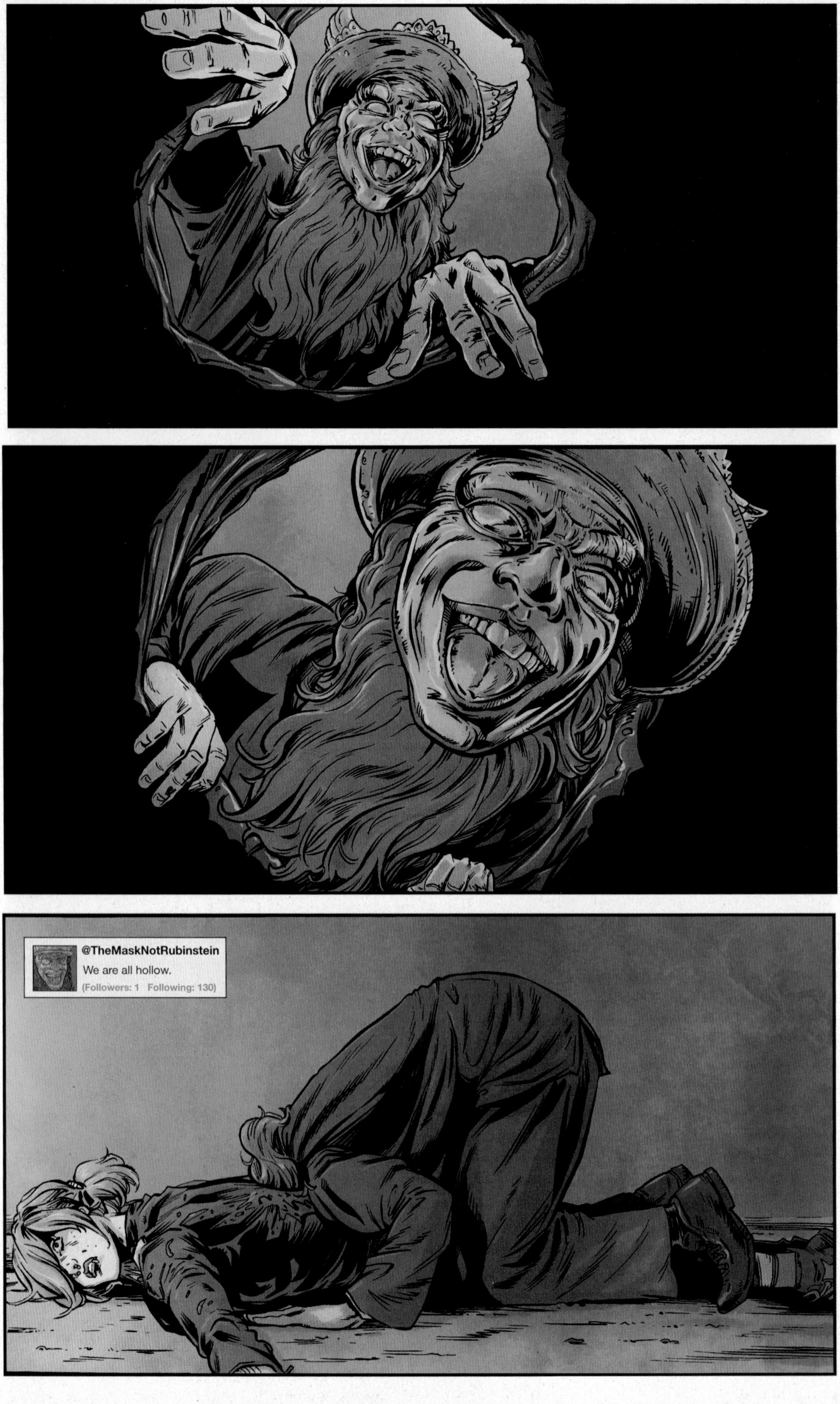
@TheMaskNotRubinstein
We are all hollow.
(Followers: 1 Following: 130)

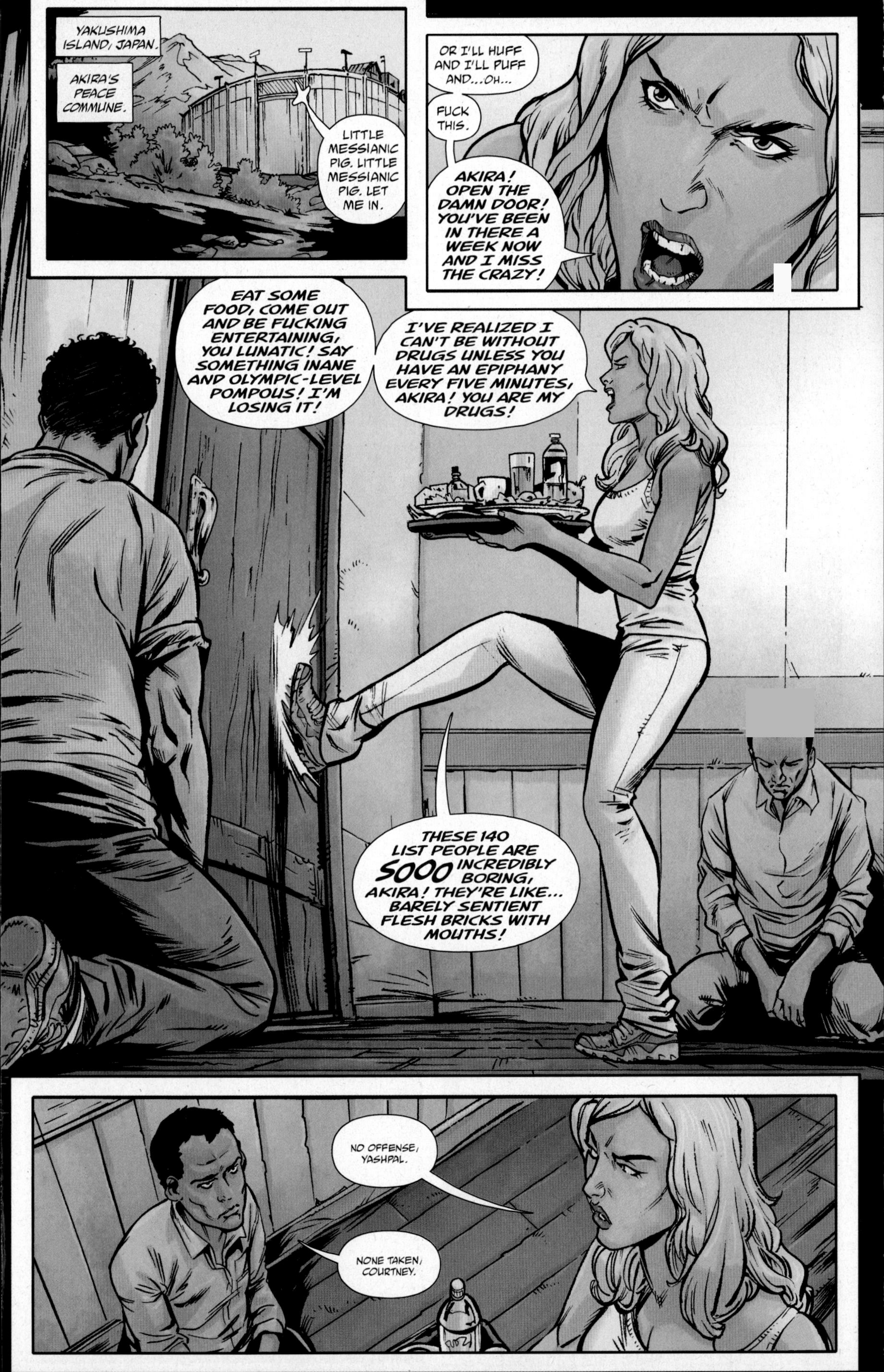
YAKUSHIMA ISLAND, JAPAN.
AKIRA'S PEACE COMMUNE.
LITTLE MESSIANIC PIG. LITTLE MESSIANIC PIG. LET ME IN.
OR I'LL HUFF AND I'LL PUFF AND...OH...
FUCK THIS.
AKIRA! OPEN THE DAMN DOOR! YOU'VE BEEN IN THERE A WEEK NOW AND I MISS THE CRAZY!
EAT SOME FOOD, COME OUT AND BE FUCKING ENTERTAINING, YOU LUNATIC! SAY SOMETHING INANE AND OLYMPIC-LEVEL POMPOUS! I'M LOSING IT!
I'VE REALIZED I CAN'T BE WITHOUT DRUGS UNLESS YOU HAVE AN EPIPHANY EVERY FIVE MINUTES, AKIRA! YOU ARE MY DRUGS!
THESE 140 LIST PEOPLE ARE SOOO INCREDIBLY BORING, AKIRA! THEY'RE LIKE... BARELY SENTIENT FLESH BRICKS WITH MOUTHS!
NO OFFENSE, YASHPAL.
NONE TAKEN, COURTNEY.

AKIRA HAS NOT LEFT HIS ROOM. HE HAS NOT EATEN OR BATHED.

HE CANNOT BE DISTURBED. HE IS *WRITING*, COURTNEY. HE IS CREATING HIS MASTERPIECE.

AND HE WILL SHOW THE WORLD *THE WAY* WITH IT.

DOES HE HAVE...A TOILET?

EXCUSE ME?

HE'S BECOMING A JESUS.

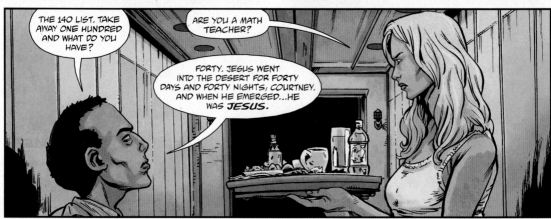

THE 140 LIST. TAKE AWAY ONE HUNDRED AND WHAT DO YOU HAVE?

ARE YOU A MATH TEACHER?

FORTY. JESUS WENT INTO THE DESERT FOR FORTY DAYS AND FORTY NIGHTS, COURTNEY. AND WHEN HE EMERGED...HE WAS *JESUS*.

HE WAS JESUS *BEFORE* HE WENT INTO THE DESERT, FUCKTARD.

AKIRA! YOU NEED TO EAT, MAN! C'MON. YOU'VE LEFT ME OUT HERE WITH MORONS.

BESIDES... YOU STILL HAVE TO DO THAT *PODCAST*. YOU KNOW...

...THE ONE THAT'S GONNA SAVE THE WORLD.

REMEMBER?

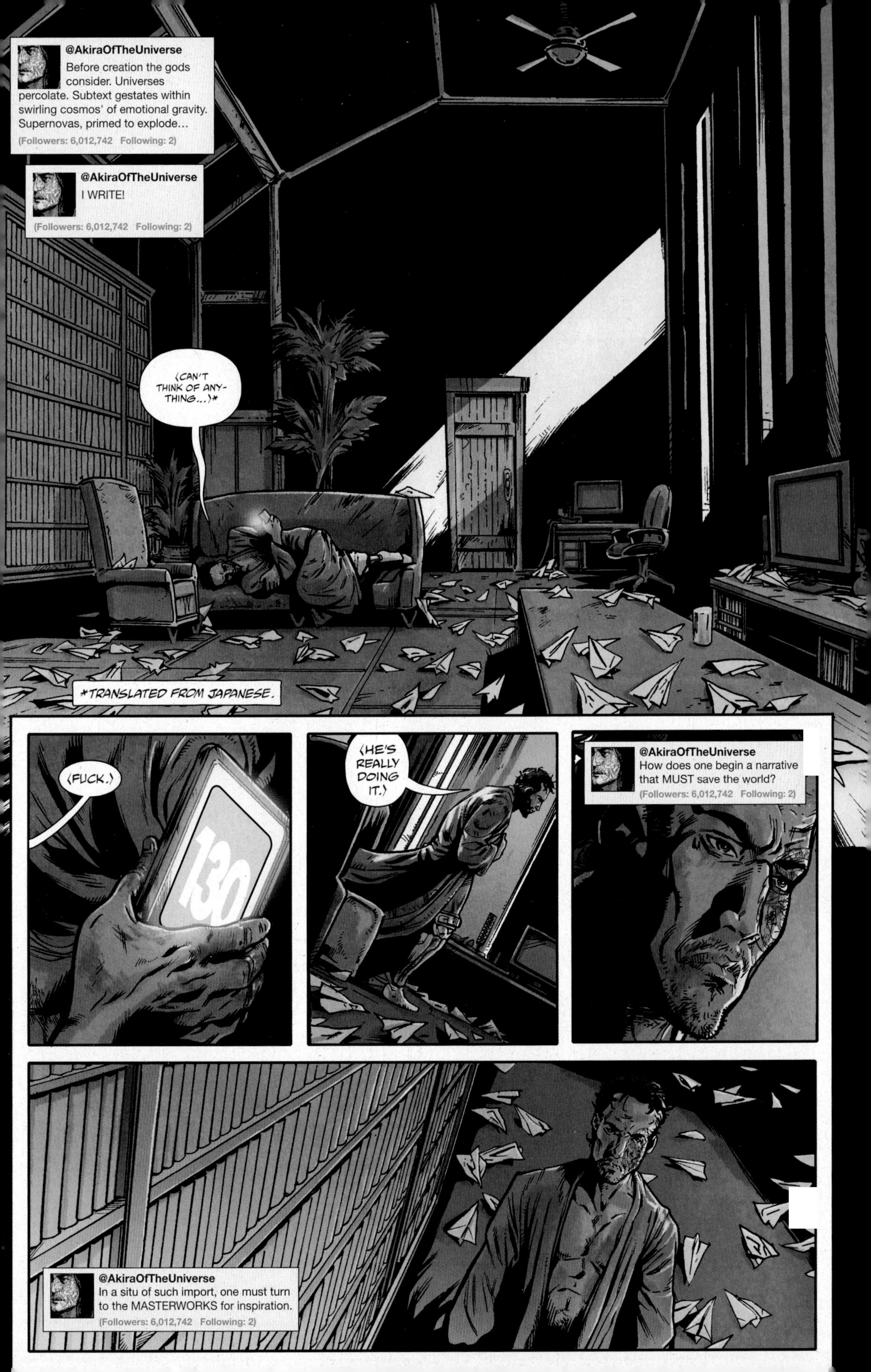
@AkiraOfTheUniverse
Before creation the gods consider. Universes percolate. Subtext gestates within swirling cosmos' of emotional gravity. Supernovas, primed to explode...
(Followers: 6,012,742 Following: 2)
@AkiraOfTheUniverse
I WRITE!
(Followers: 6,012,742 Following: 2)
(CAN'T THINK OF ANY-THING...)*
*TRANSLATED FROM JAPANESE.
(FUCK.)
130
(HE'S REALLY DOING IT.)
@AkiraOfTheUniverse
How does one begin a narrative that MUST save the world?
(Followers: 6,012,742 Following: 2)
@AkiraOfTheUniverse
In a situ of such import, one must turn to the MASTERWORKS for inspiration.
(Followers: 6,012,742 Following: 2)

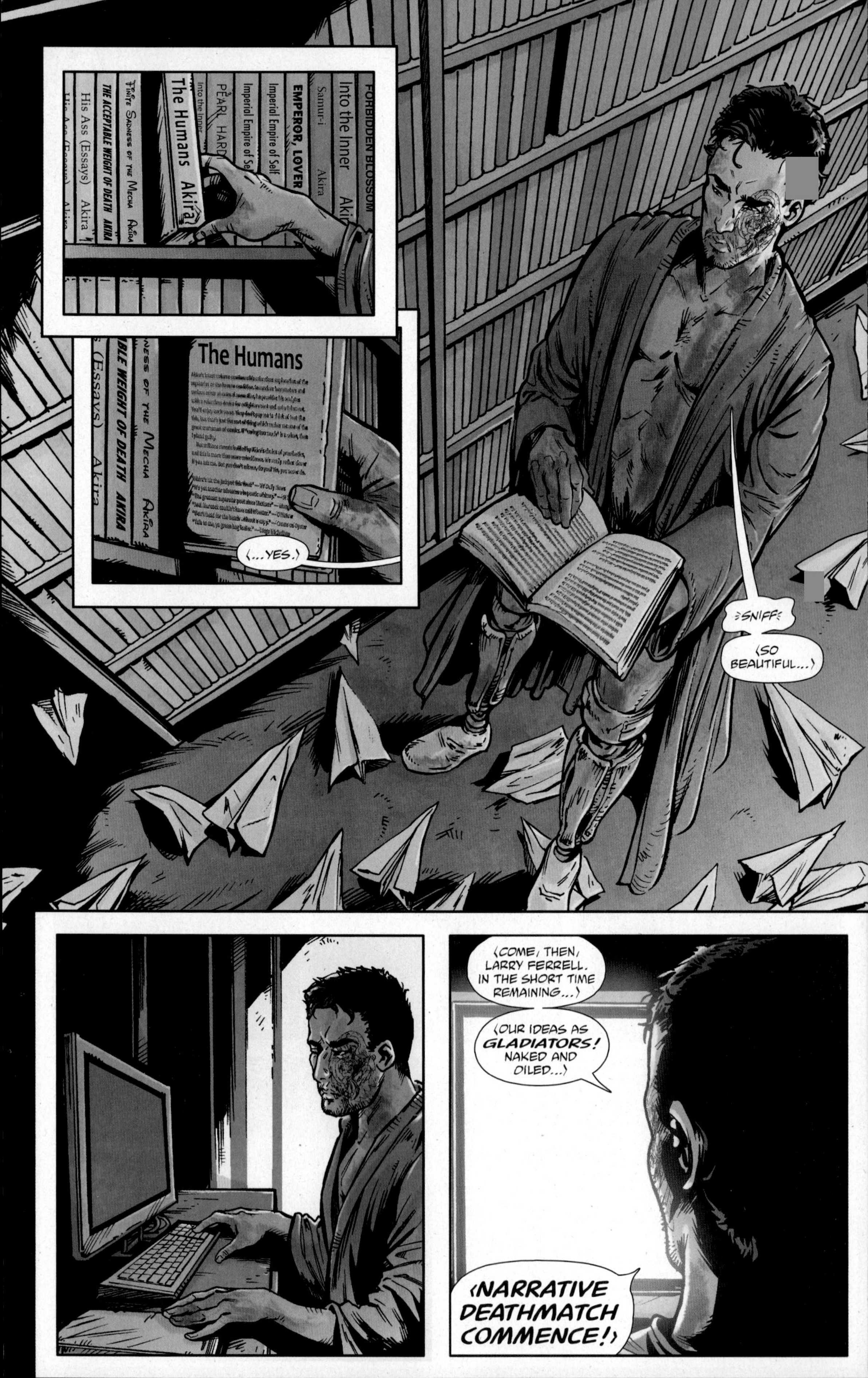

FORBIDDEN BLOSSOM
Into the Inner Akira
Samur-i Akira
EMPEROR, LOVER
Imperial Empire of Self
The Humans Akira
The Finite Sadness of the Mecha Akira
THE ACCEPTABLE WEIGHT OF DEATH AKIRA
His Ass (Essays) Akira
The Humans
‹...YES.›
SNIFF
‹SO BEAUTIFUL...›
‹COME, THEN, LARRY FERRELL. IN THE SHORT TIME REMAINING...›
‹OUR IDEAS AS GLADIATORS! NAKED AND OILED...›
‹NARRATIVE DEATHMATCH COMMENCE!›

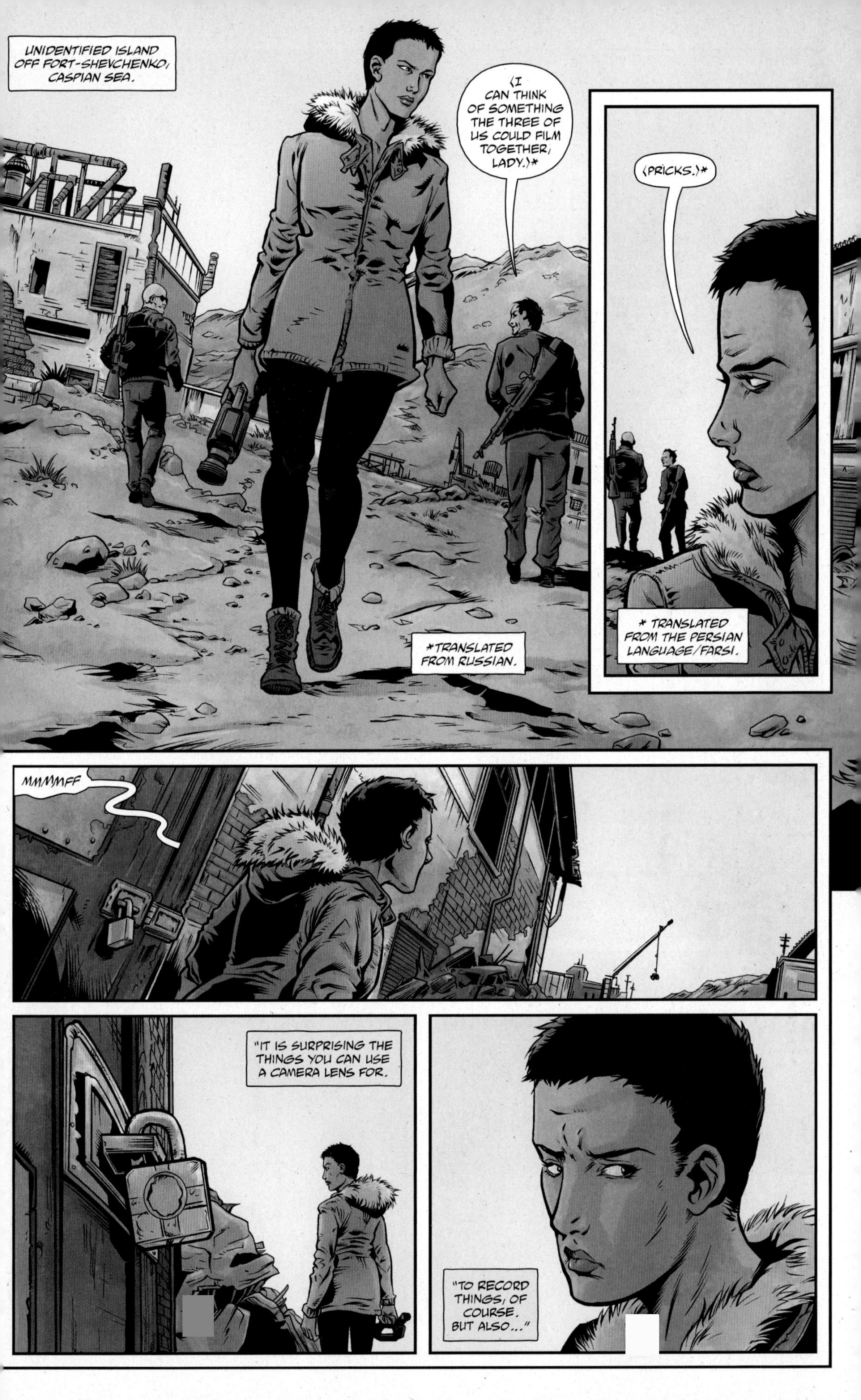
UNIDENTIFIED ISLAND OFF FORT-SHEVCHENKO, CASPIAN SEA.
⟨I CAN THINK OF SOMETHING THE THREE OF US COULD FILM TOGETHER, LADY.⟩*
*TRANSLATED FROM RUSSIAN.
⟨PRICKS.⟩*
* TRANSLATED FROM THE PERSIAN LANGUAGE/FARSI.
MMMMFF
"IT IS SURPRISING THE THINGS YOU CAN USE A CAMERA LENS FOR.
"TO RECORD THINGS, OF COURSE. BUT ALSO..."

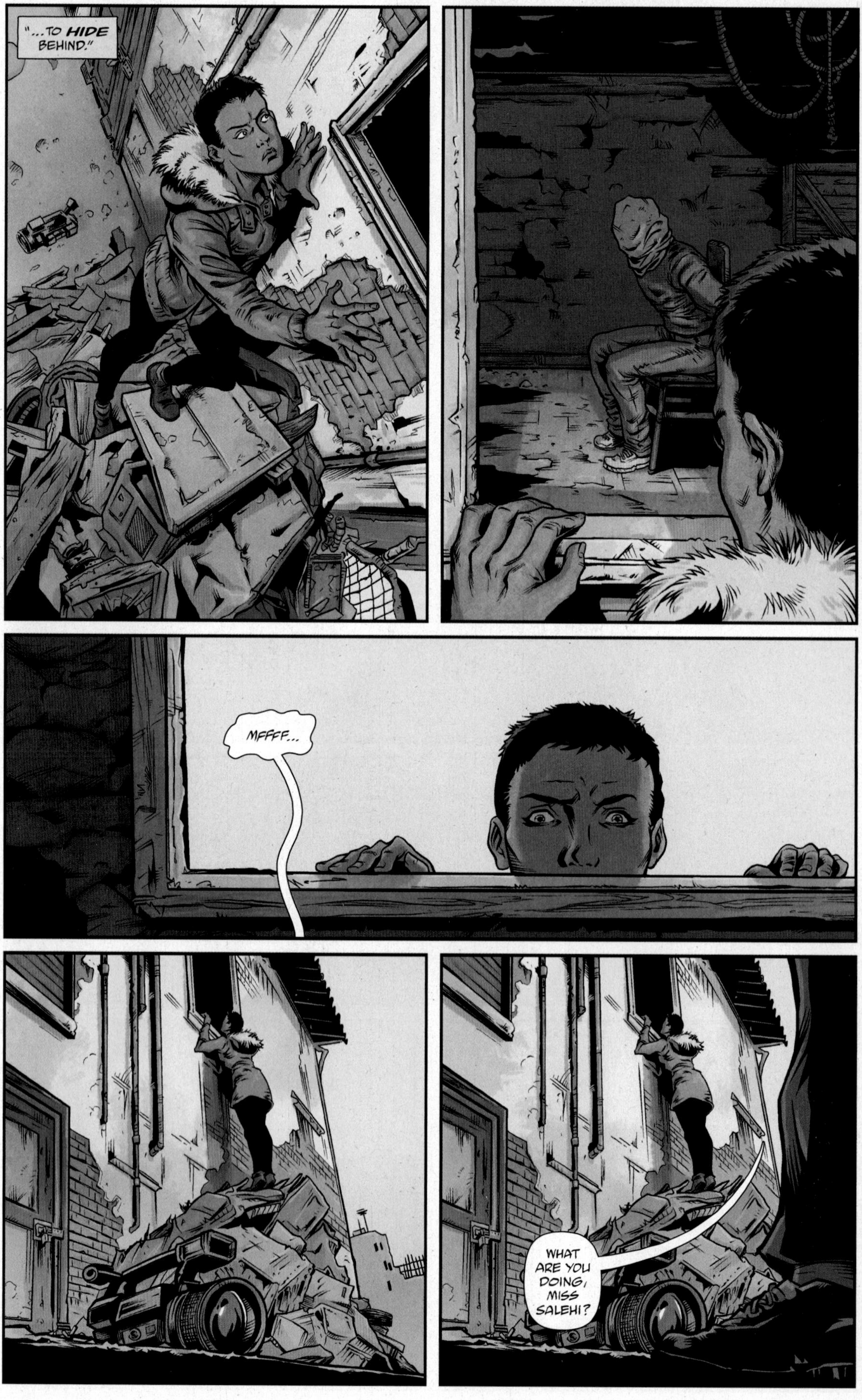
"...TO HIDE BEHIND."
MFFFF...
WHAT ARE YOU DOING, MISS SALEHI?

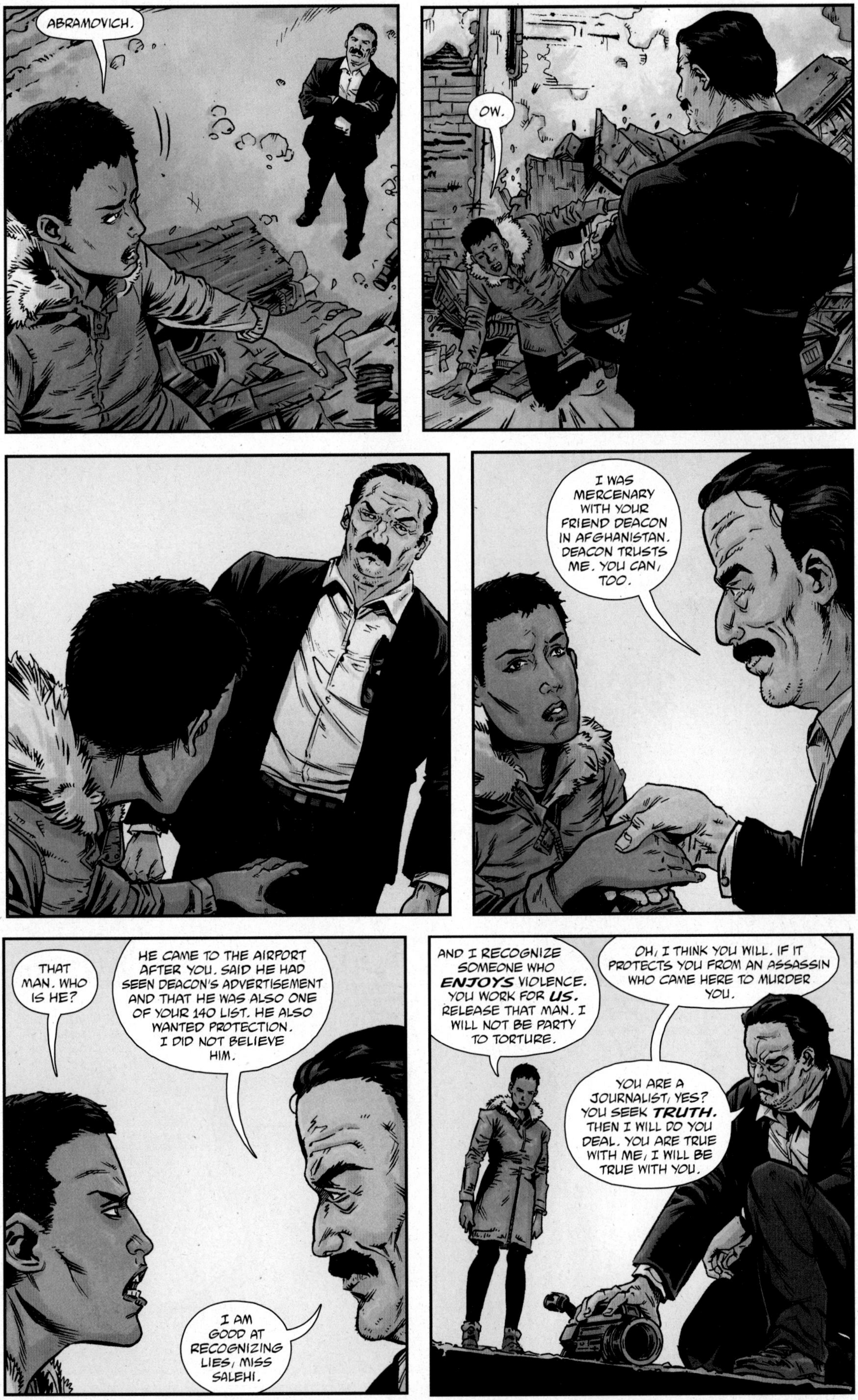
ABRAMOVICH.
OW.
I WAS MERCENARY WITH YOUR FRIEND DEACON IN AFGHANISTAN. DEACON TRUSTS ME. YOU CAN, TOO.
THAT MAN. WHO IS HE?
HE CAME TO THE AIRPORT AFTER YOU. SAID HE HAD SEEN DEACON'S ADVERTISEMENT AND THAT HE WAS ALSO ONE OF YOUR 140 LIST. HE ALSO WANTED PROTECTION. I DID NOT BELIEVE HIM.
I AM GOOD AT RECOGNIZING LIES, MISS SALEHI.
AND I RECOGNIZE SOMEONE WHO ENJOYS VIOLENCE. YOU WORK FOR US. RELEASE THAT MAN. I WILL NOT BE PARTY TO TORTURE.
OH, I THINK YOU WILL. IF IT PROTECTS YOU FROM AN ASSASSIN WHO CAME HERE TO MURDER YOU.
YOU ARE A JOURNALIST, YES? YOU SEEK TRUTH. THEN I WILL DO YOU DEAL. YOU ARE TRUE WITH ME, I WILL BE TRUE WITH YOU.

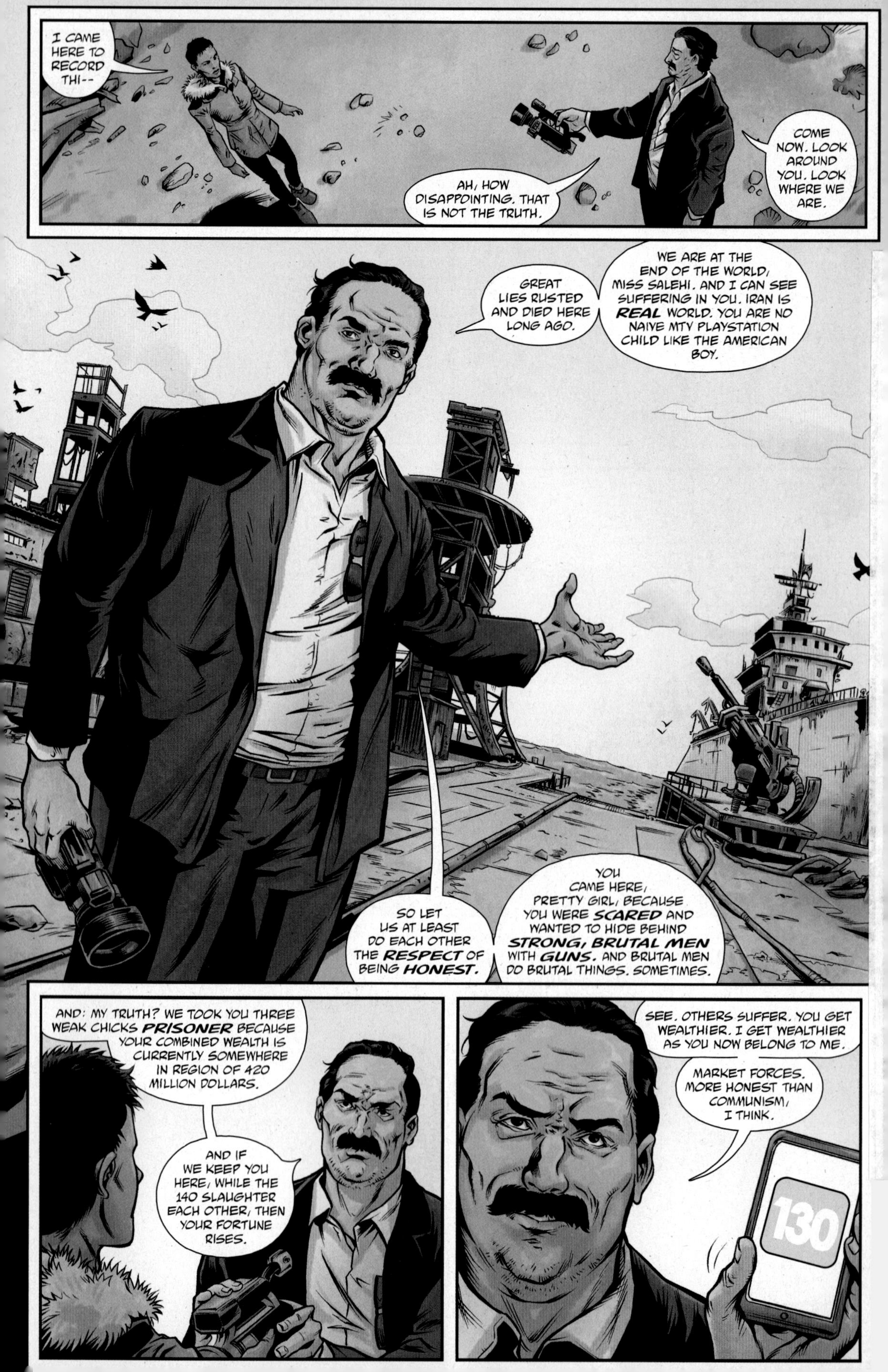
I CAME HERE TO RECORD THI--
AH, HOW DISAPPOINTING. THAT IS NOT THE TRUTH.
COME NOW. LOOK AROUND YOU. LOOK WHERE WE ARE.
GREAT LIES RUSTED AND DIED HERE LONG AGO.
WE ARE AT THE END OF THE WORLD, MISS SALEHI. AND I CAN SEE SUFFERING IN YOU. IRAN IS REAL WORLD. YOU ARE NO NAIVE MTV PLAYSTATION CHILD LIKE THE AMERICAN BOY.
SO LET US AT LEAST DO EACH OTHER THE RESPECT OF BEING HONEST.
YOU CAME HERE, PRETTY GIRL, BECAUSE YOU WERE SCARED AND WANTED TO HIDE BEHIND STRONG, BRUTAL MEN WITH GUNS. AND BRUTAL MEN DO BRUTAL THINGS. SOMETIMES.
AND: MY TRUTH? WE TOOK YOU THREE WEAK CHICKS PRISONER BECAUSE YOUR COMBINED WEALTH IS CURRENTLY SOMEWHERE IN REGION OF 420 MILLION DOLLARS.
AND IF WE KEEP YOU HERE, WHILE THE 140 SLAUGHTER EACH OTHER, THEN YOUR FORTUNE RISES.
SEE. OTHERS SUFFER. YOU GET WEALTHIER. I GET WEALTHIER AS YOU NOW BELONG TO ME.
MARKET FORCES. MORE HONEST THAN COMMUNISM, I THINK.
130

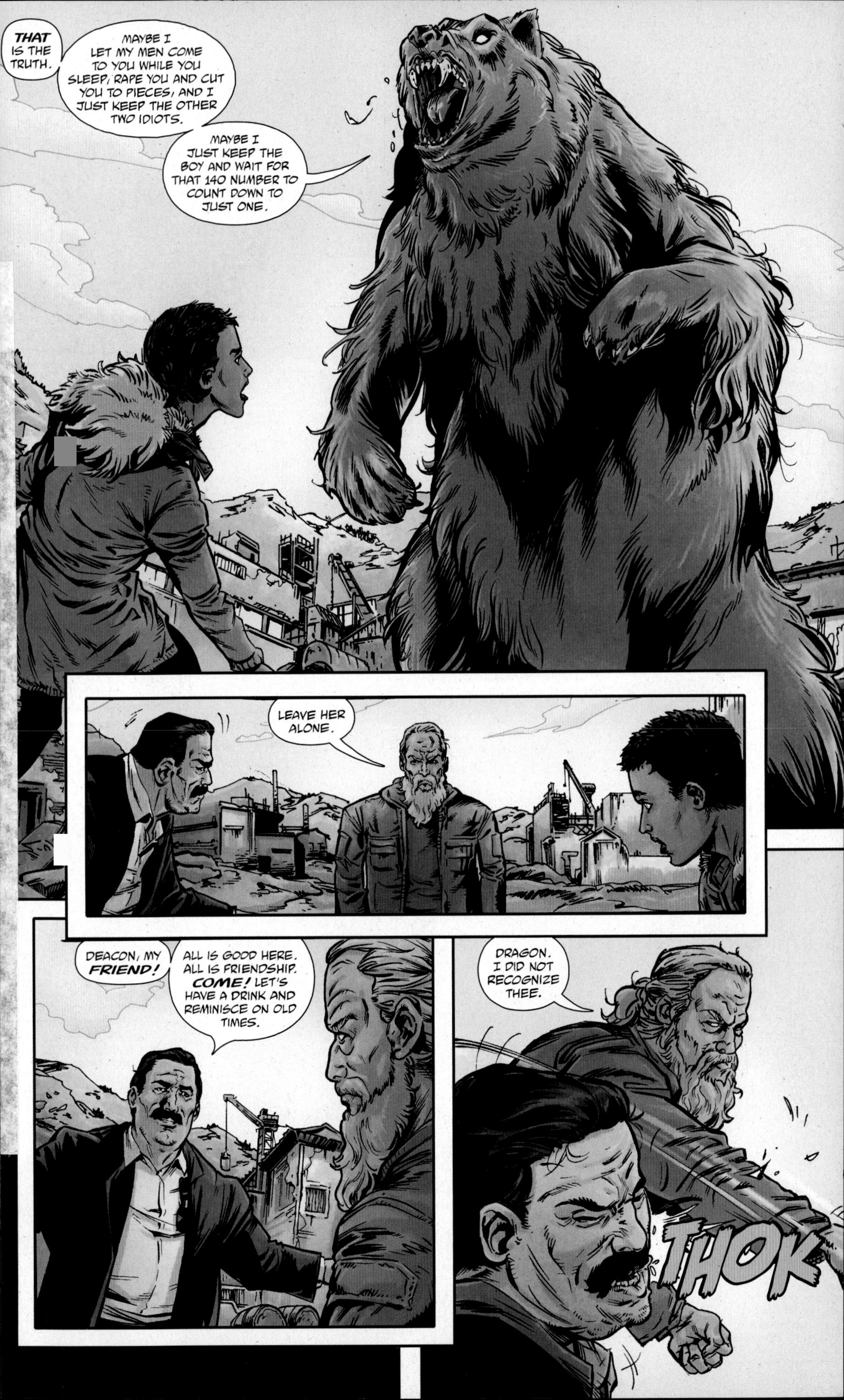

THAT IS THE TRUTH.
MAYBE I LET MY MEN COME TO YOU WHILE YOU SLEEP, RAPE YOU AND CUT YOU TO PIECES, AND I JUST KEEP THE OTHER TWO IDIOTS.
MAYBE I JUST KEEP THE BOY AND WAIT FOR THAT 140 NUMBER TO COUNT DOWN TO JUST ONE.
LEAVE HER ALONE.
DEACON, MY FRIEND!
ALL IS GOOD HERE. ALL IS FRIENDSHIP. COME! LET'S HAVE A DRINK AND REMINISCE ON OLD TIMES.
DRAGON. I DID NOT RECOGNIZE THEE.
THOK

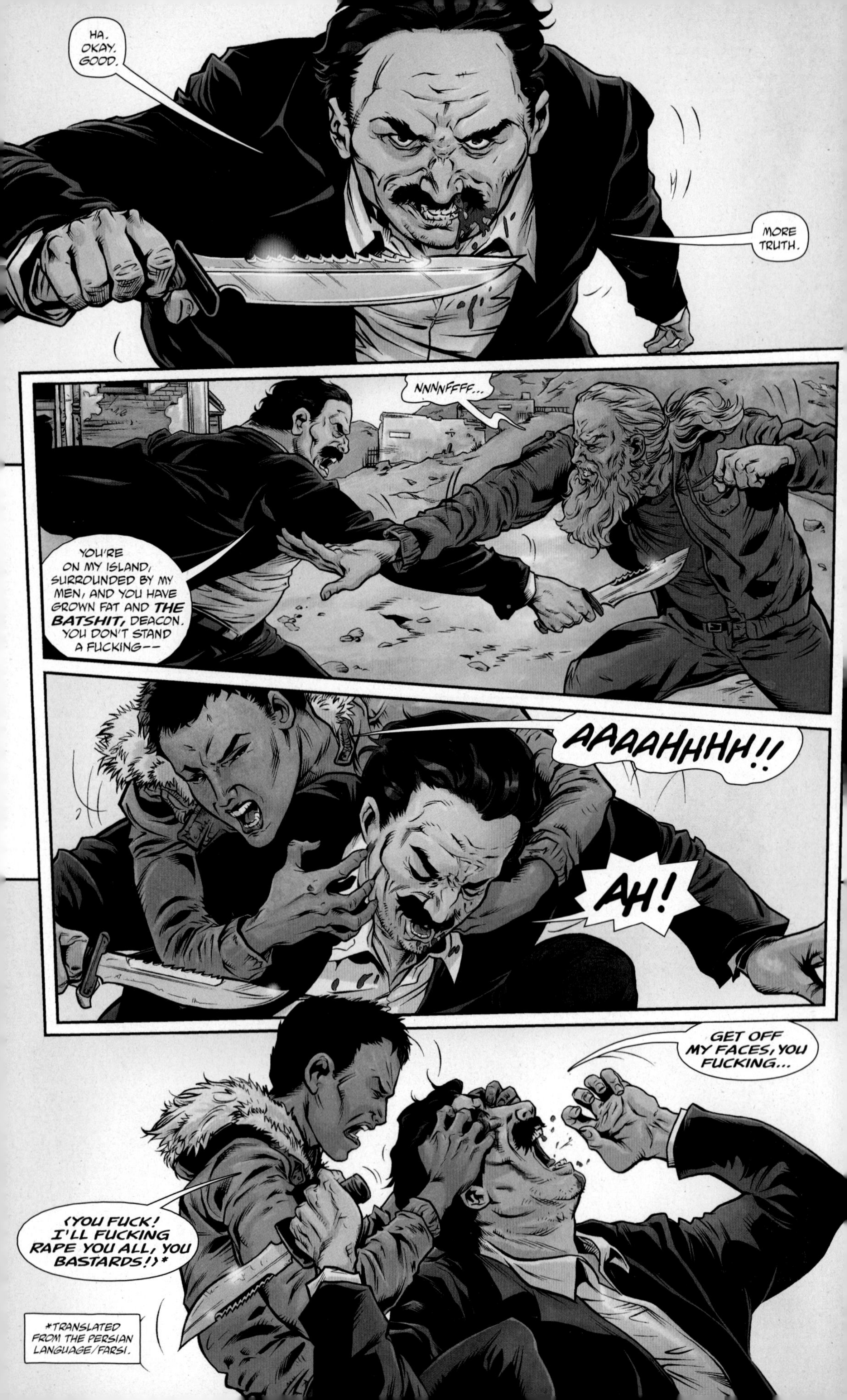
HA. OKAY. GOOD.
MORE TRUTH.
NNNNFFFF...
YOU'RE ON MY ISLAND, SURROUNDED BY MY MEN, AND YOU HAVE GROWN FAT AND THE BATSHIT, DEACON. YOU DON'T STAND A FUCKING--
AAAAHHHH!!
AH!
GET OFF MY FACES, YOU FUCKING...
‹YOU FUCK! I'LL FUCKING RAPE YOU ALL, YOU BASTARDS!›*
*TRANSLATED FROM THE PERSIAN LANGUAGE/FARSI.

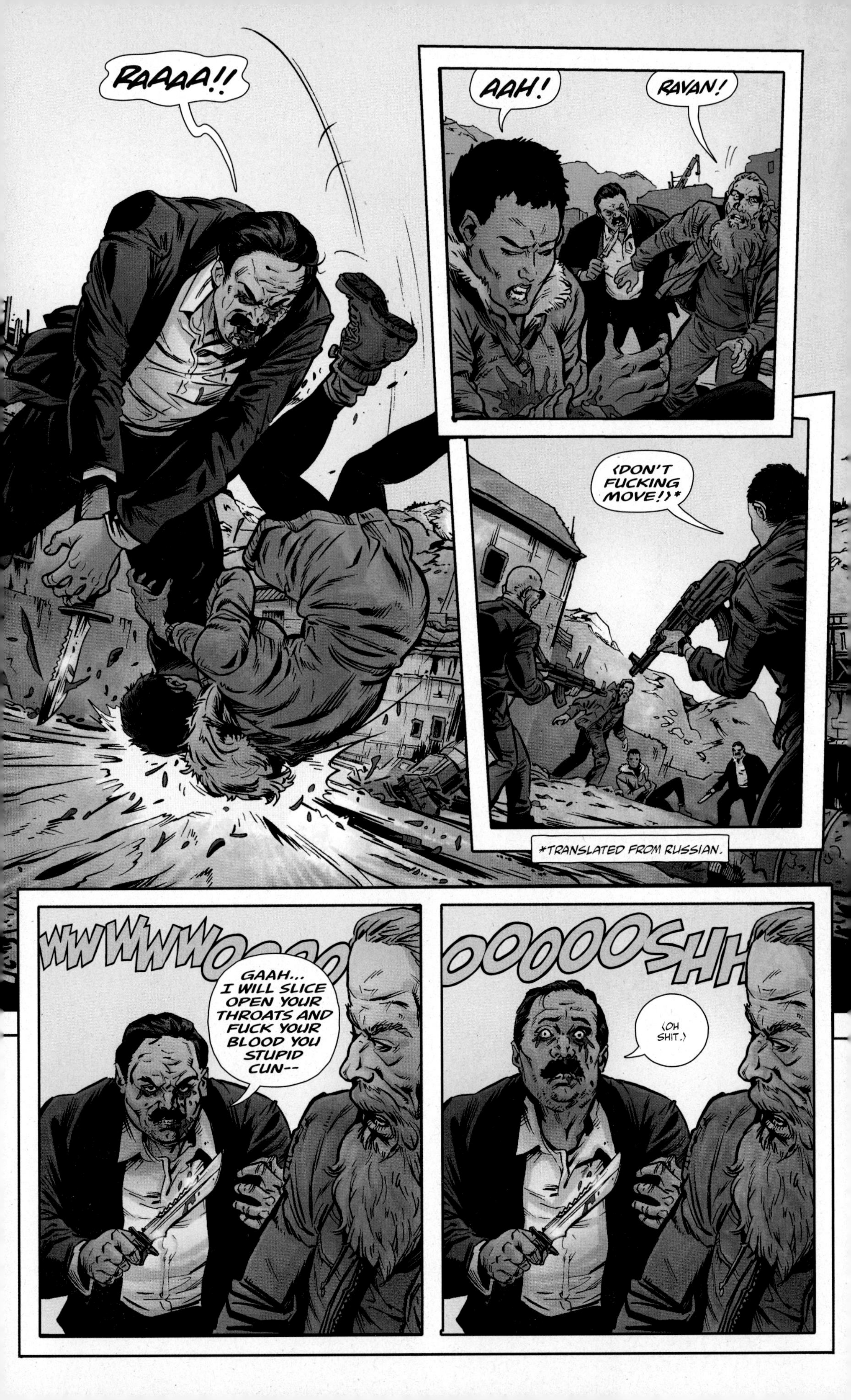
RAAAA!!
AAH!
RAVAN!
⟨DON'T FUCKING MOVE!⟩*
*TRANSLATED FROM RUSSIAN.
WWWWOOOOOOOOOOOSHH
GAAH... I WILL SLICE OPEN YOUR THROATS AND FUCK YOUR BLOOD YOU STUPID CUN--
⟨OH SHIT.⟩

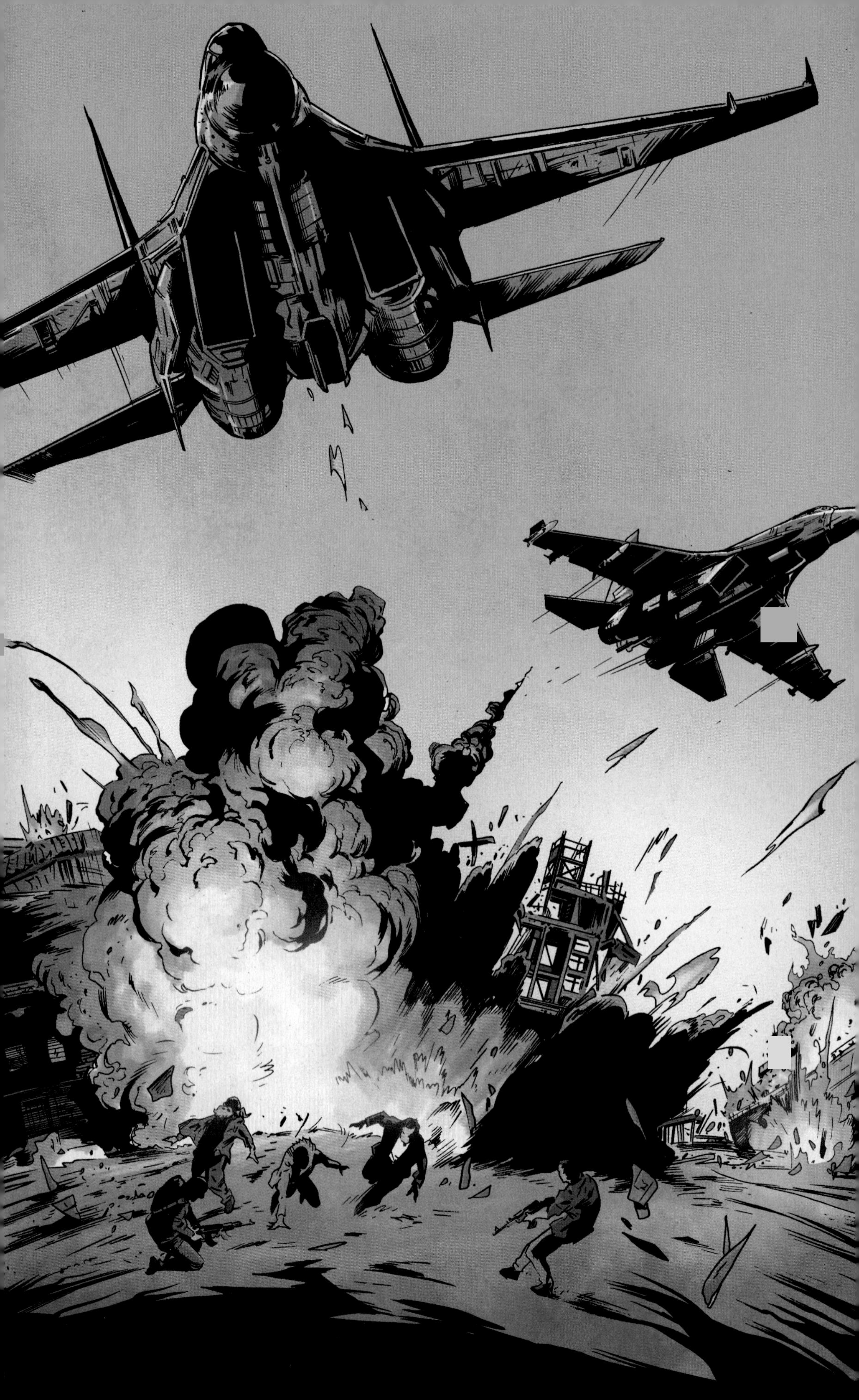

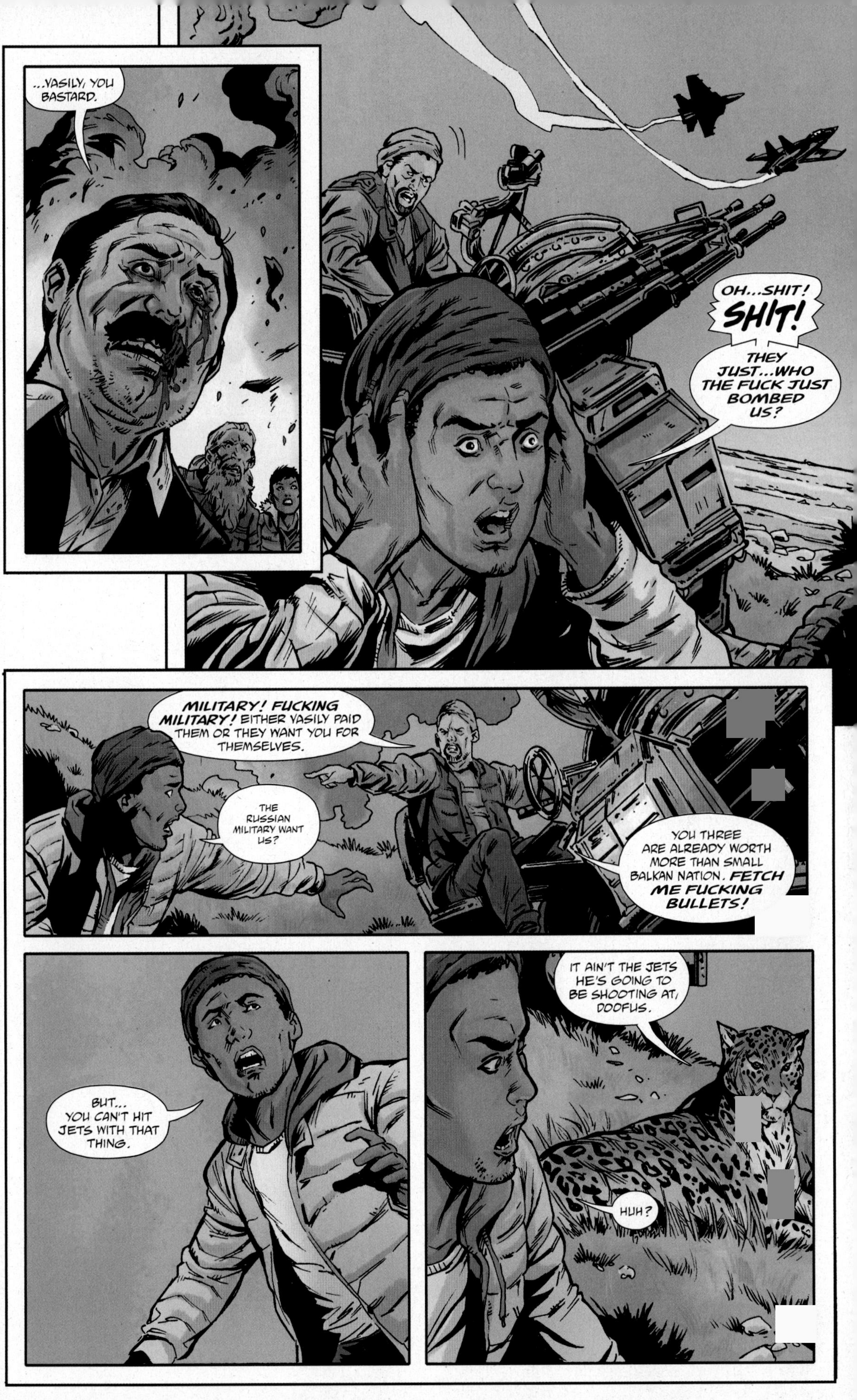
...VASILY, YOU BASTARD.
OH...SHIT! SHIT!
THEY JUST...WHO THE FUCK JUST BOMBED US?
MILITARY! FUCKING MILITARY! EITHER VASILY PAID THEM OR THEY WANT YOU FOR THEMSELVES.
THE RUSSIAN MILITARY WANT US?
YOU THREE ARE ALREADY WORTH MORE THAN SMALL BALKAN NATION. FETCH ME FUCKING BULLETS!
BUT... YOU CAN'T HIT JETS WITH THAT THING.
IT AIN'T THE JETS HE'S GOING TO BE SHOOTING AT, DOOFUS.
HUH?

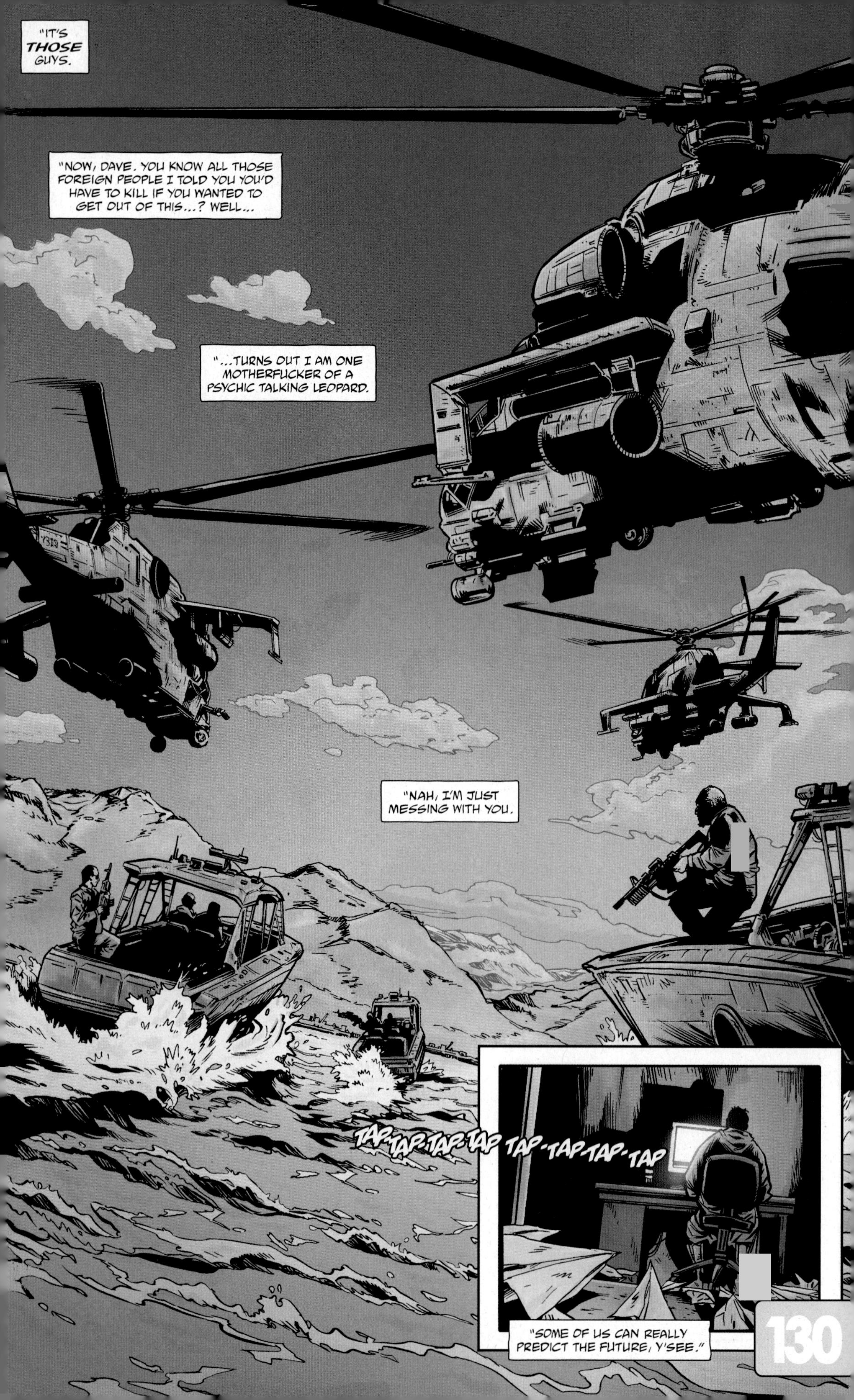
"IT'S THOSE GUYS.
"NOW, DAVE. YOU KNOW ALL THOSE FOREIGN PEOPLE I TOLD YOU YOU'D HAVE TO KILL IF YOU WANTED TO GET OUT OF THIS...? WELL...
"...TURNS OUT I AM ONE MOTHERFUCKER OF A PSYCHIC TALKING LEOPARD.
"NAH, I'M JUST MESSING WITH YOU.
TAP-TAP-TAP-TAP TAP-TAP-TAP-TAP
"SOME OF US CAN REALLY PREDICT THE FUTURE, Y'SEE."

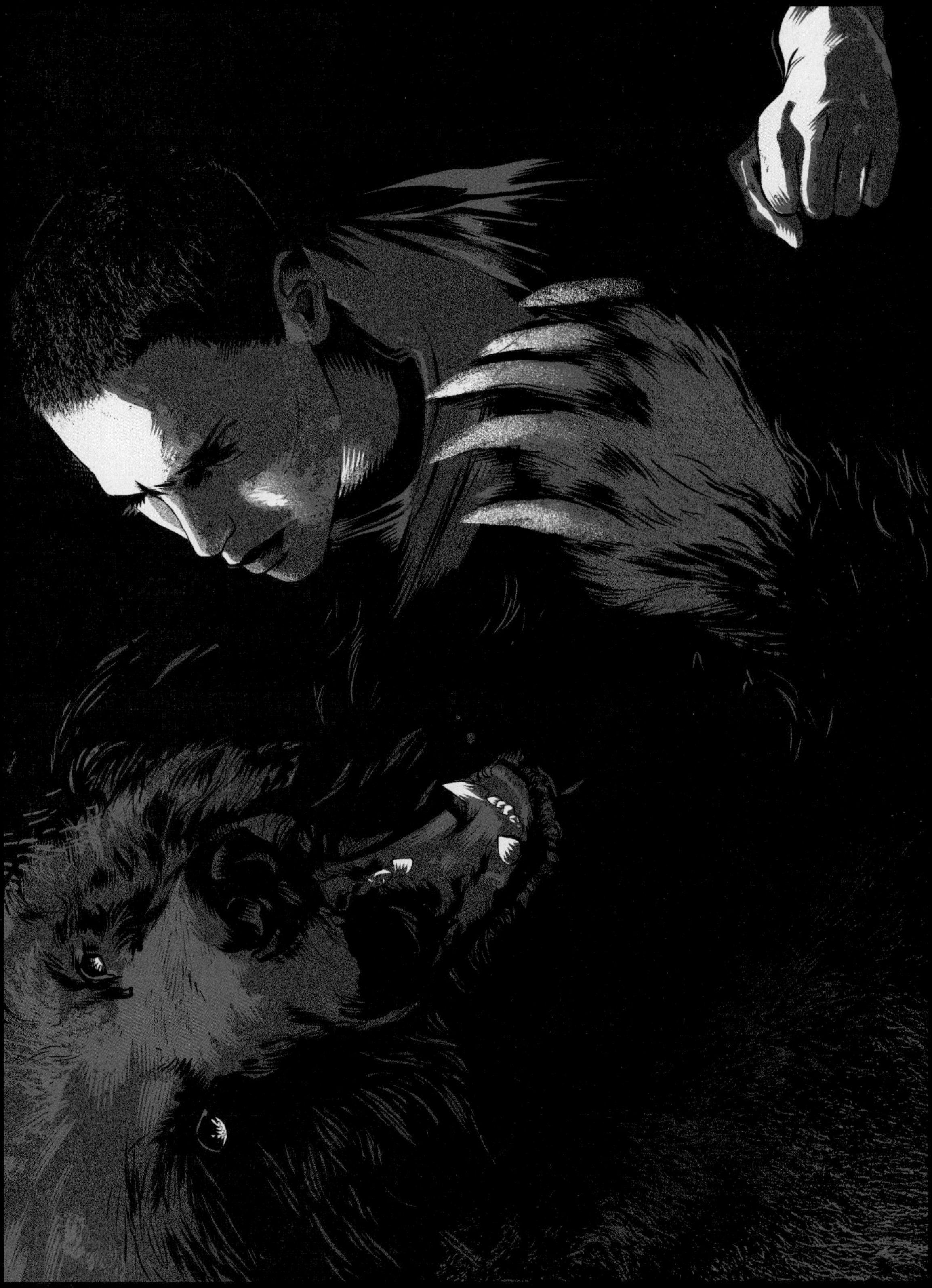

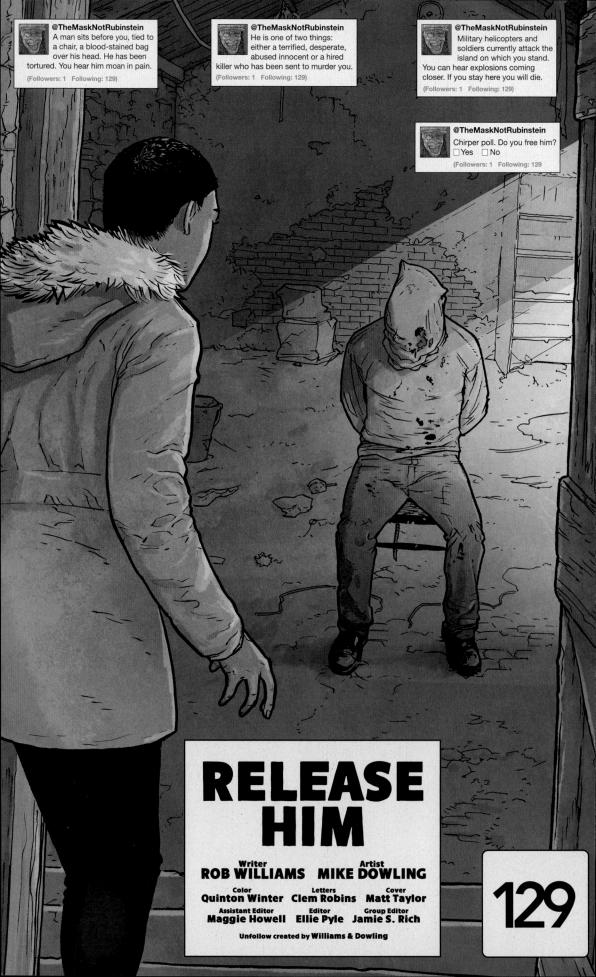

@TheMaskNotRubinstein
A man sits before you, tied to a chair, a blood-stained bag over his head. He has been tortured. You hear him moan in pain.
(Followers: 1   Following: 129)

@TheMaskNotRubinstein
He is one of two things: either a terrified, desperate, abused innocent or a hired killer who has been sent to murder you.
(Followers: 1   Following: 129)

@TheMaskNotRubinstein
Military helicopters and soldiers currently attack the island on which you stand. You can hear explosions coming closer. If you stay here you will die.
(Followers: 1   Following: 129)

@TheMaskNotRubinstein
Chirper poll. Do you free him?
☐ Yes   ☐ No
(Followers: 1   Following: 129)

RELEASE HIM

Writer
ROB WILLIAMS

Artist
MIKE DOWLING

Color
Quinton Winter

Letters
Clem Robins

Cover
Matt Taylor

Assistant Editor
Maggie Howell

Editor
Ellie Pyle

Group Editor
Jamie S. Rich

Unfollow created by Williams & Dowling

129

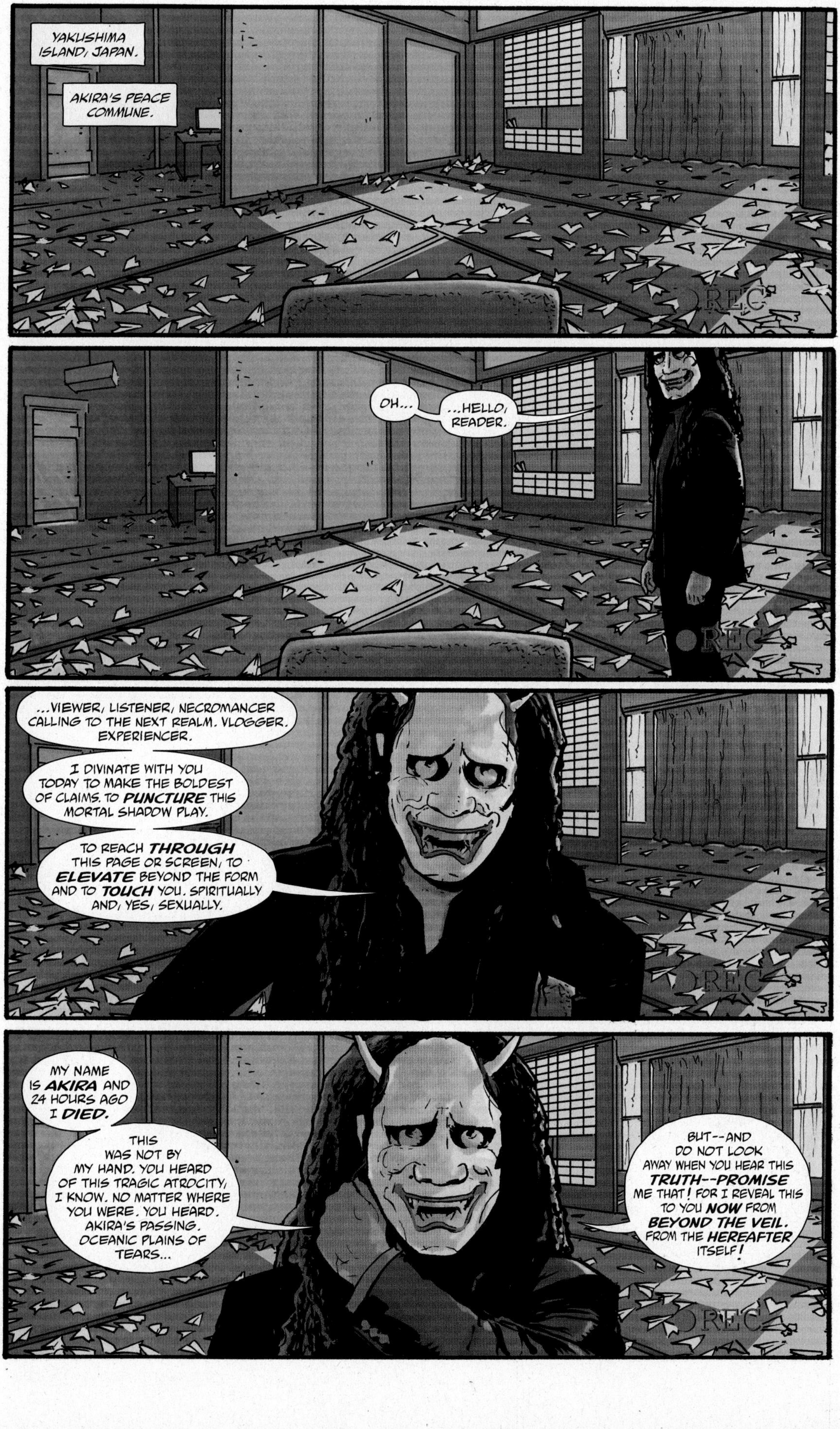

YAKUSHIMA ISLAND, JAPAN.
AKIRA'S PEACE COMMUNE.
REC
OH...
...HELLO, READER.
REC
...VIEWER, LISTENER, NECROMANCER CALLING TO THE NEXT REALM. VLOGGER. EXPERIENCER.
I DIVINATE WITH YOU TODAY TO MAKE THE BOLDEST OF CLAIMS. TO **PUNCTURE** THIS MORTAL SHADOW PLAY.
TO REACH **THROUGH** THIS PAGE OR SCREEN, TO **ELEVATE** BEYOND THE FORM AND TO **TOUCH** YOU. SPIRITUALLY AND, YES, SEXUALLY.
REC
MY NAME IS **AKIRA** AND 24 HOURS AGO I **DIED.**
THIS WAS NOT BY MY HAND. YOU HEARD OF THIS TRAGIC ATROCITY, I KNOW. NO MATTER WHERE YOU WERE, YOU HEARD. AKIRA'S PASSING. OCEANIC PLAINS OF TEARS...
BUT--AND DO NOT LOOK AWAY WHEN YOU HEAR THIS **TRUTH--PROMISE** ME THAT! FOR I REVEAL THIS TO YOU **NOW** FROM **BEYOND THE VEIL.** FROM THE **HEREAFTER** ITSELF!
REC

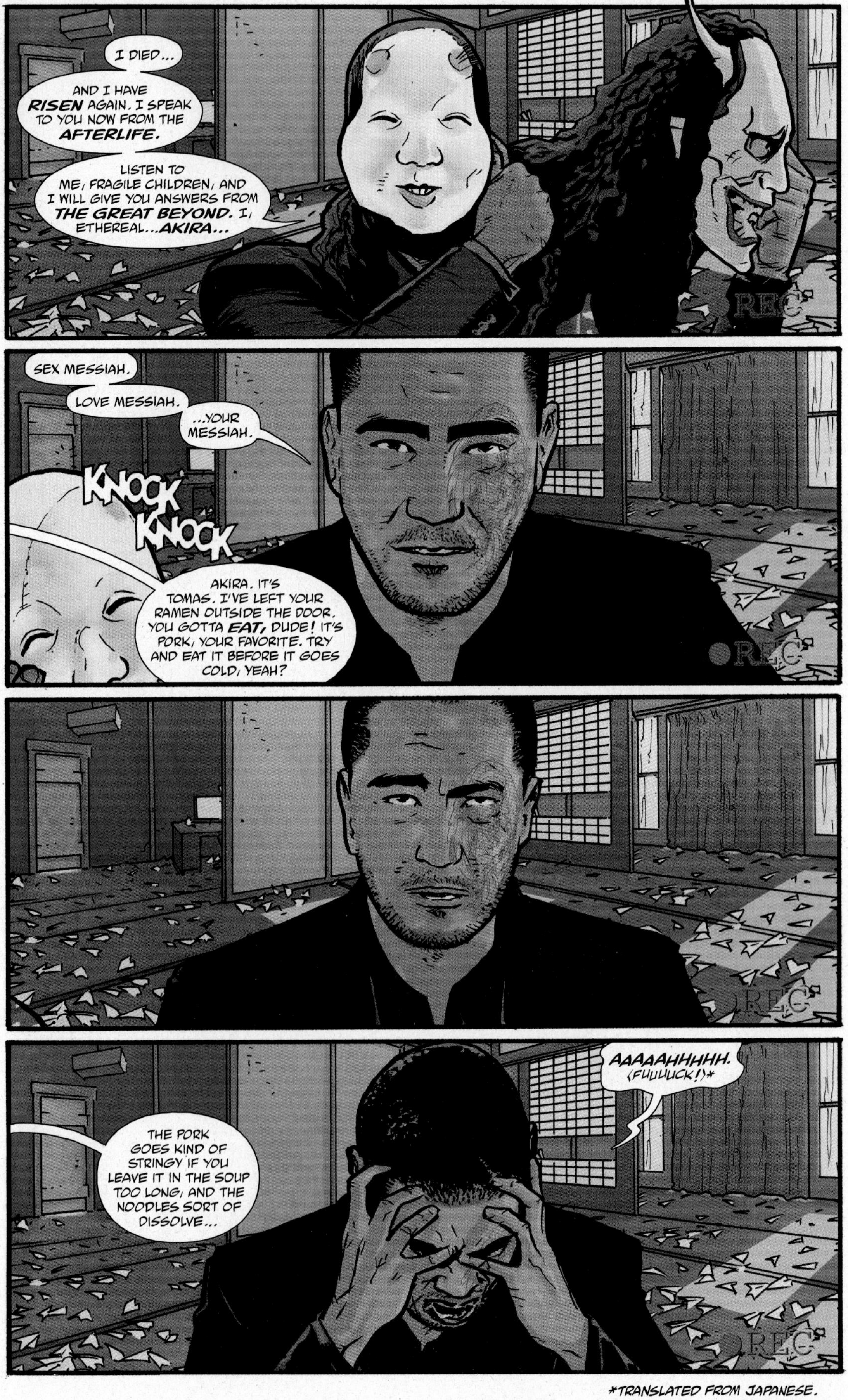
I DIED...
AND I HAVE RISEN AGAIN. I SPEAK TO YOU NOW FROM THE AFTERLIFE.
LISTEN TO ME, FRAGILE CHILDREN, AND I WILL GIVE YOU ANSWERS FROM THE GREAT BEYOND. I, ETHEREAL...AKIRA...
REC
SEX MESSIAH.
LOVE MESSIAH.
...YOUR MESSIAH.
KNOCK KNOCK
AKIRA. IT'S TOMAS. I'VE LEFT YOUR RAMEN OUTSIDE THE DOOR. YOU GOTTA EAT, DUDE! IT'S PORK, YOUR FAVORITE. TRY AND EAT IT BEFORE IT GOES COLD, YEAH?
REC
REC
AAAAAHHHHH. (FUUUUCK!)*
THE PORK GOES KIND OF STRINGY IF YOU LEAVE IT IN THE SOUP TOO LONG, AND THE NOODLES SORT OF DISSOLVE...
REC

*TRANSLATED FROM JAPANESE.

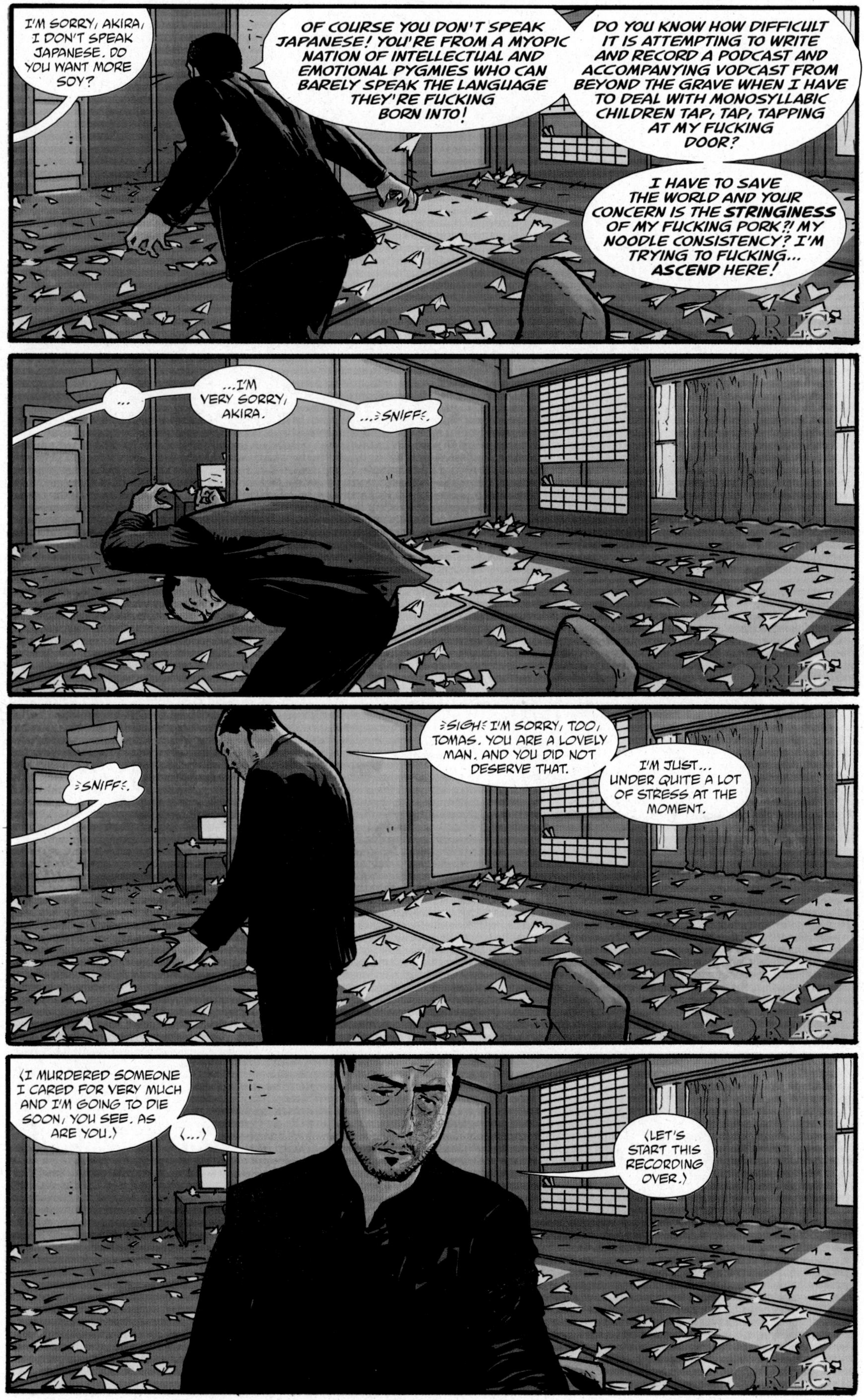
I'M SORRY, AKIRA, I DON'T SPEAK JAPANESE. DO YOU WANT MORE SOY?
OF COURSE YOU DON'T SPEAK JAPANESE! YOU'RE FROM A MYOPIC NATION OF INTELLECTUAL AND EMOTIONAL PYGMIES WHO CAN BARELY SPEAK THE LANGUAGE THEY'RE FUCKING BORN INTO!
DO YOU KNOW HOW DIFFICULT IT IS ATTEMPTING TO WRITE AND RECORD A PODCAST AND ACCOMPANYING VODCAST FROM BEYOND THE GRAVE WHEN I HAVE TO DEAL WITH MONOSYLLABIC CHILDREN TAP, TAP, TAPPING AT MY FUCKING DOOR?
I HAVE TO SAVE THE WORLD AND YOUR CONCERN IS THE STRINGINESS OF MY FUCKING PORK?! MY NOODLE CONSISTENCY? I'M TRYING TO FUCKING... ASCEND HERE!
REC
...
...I'M VERY SORRY, AKIRA.
...⸗SNIFF⸗.
REC
⸗SNIFF⸗.
⸗SIGH⸗ I'M SORRY, TOO, TOMAS. YOU ARE A LOVELY MAN. AND YOU DID NOT DESERVE THAT.
I'M JUST... UNDER QUITE A LOT OF STRESS AT THE MOMENT.
REC
⟨I MURDERED SOMEONE I CARED FOR VERY MUCH AND I'M GOING TO DIE SOON, YOU SEE. AS ARE YOU.⟩
⟨...⟩
⟨LET'S START THIS RECORDING OVER.⟩
REC

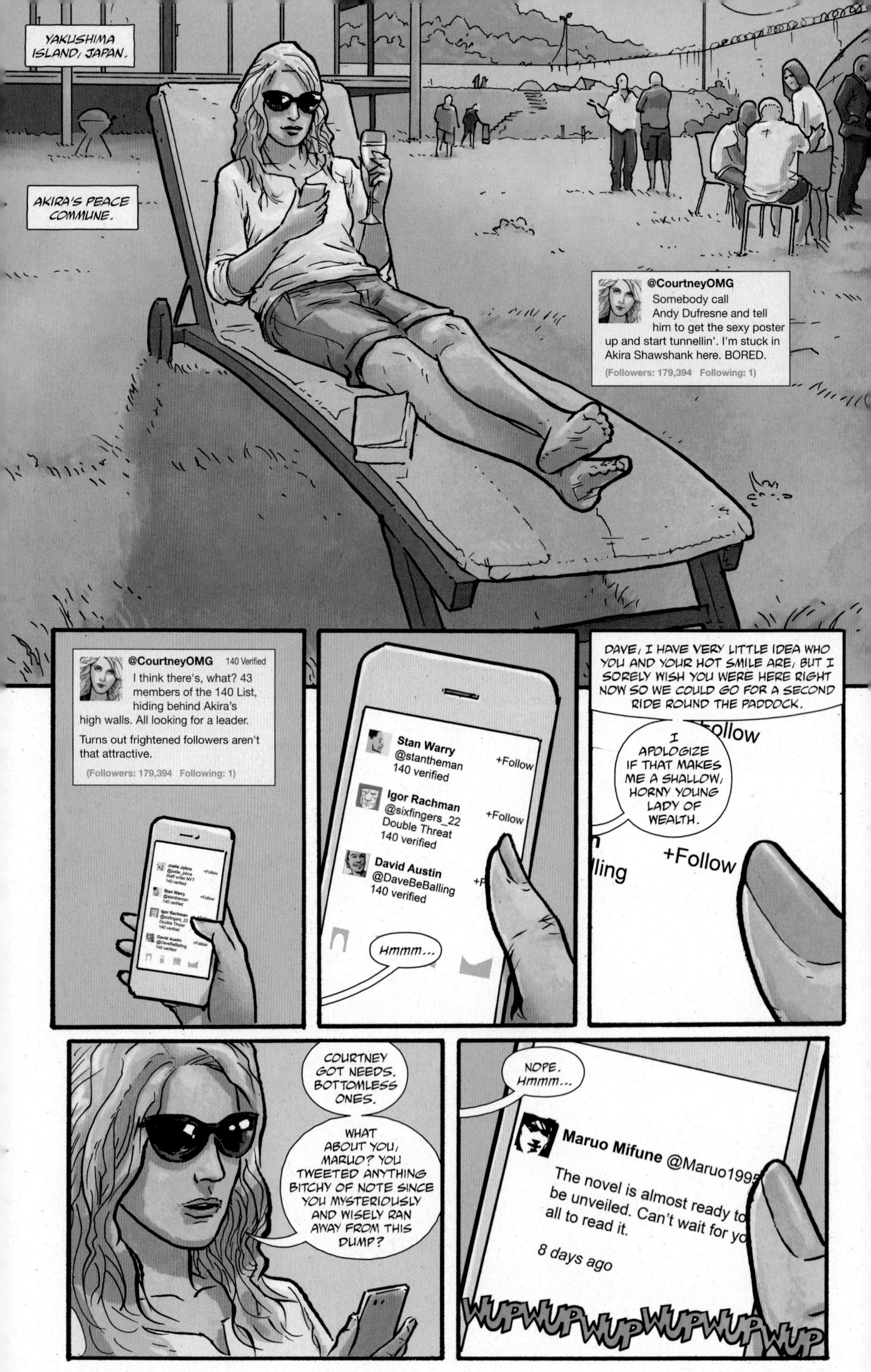

YAKUSHIMA ISLAND, JAPAN.
AKIRA'S PEACE COMMUNE.
@CourtneyOMG
Somebody call Andy Dufresne and tell him to get the sexy poster up and start tunnellin'. I'm stuck in Akira Shawshank here. BORED.
(Followers: 179,394 Following: 1)
@CourtneyOMG 140 Verified
I think there's, what? 43 members of the 140 List, hiding behind Akira's high walls. All looking for a leader.
Turns out frightened followers aren't that attractive.
(Followers: 179,394 Following: 1)
Stan Warry @stantheman 140 verified +Follow
Igor Rachman @sixfingers_22 Double Threat 140 verified +Follow
David Austin @DaveBeBalling 140 verified
Hmmm...
DAVE, I HAVE VERY LITTLE IDEA WHO YOU AND YOUR HOT SMILE ARE, BUT I SORELY WISH YOU WERE HERE RIGHT NOW SO WE COULD GO FOR A SECOND RIDE ROUND THE PADDOCK.
I APOLOGIZE IF THAT MAKES ME A SHALLOW, HORNY YOUNG LADY OF WEALTH.
+Follow
COURTNEY GOT NEEDS. BOTTOMLESS ONES.
WHAT ABOUT YOU, MARUO? YOU TWEETED ANYTHING BITCHY OF NOTE SINCE YOU MYSTERIOUSLY AND WISELY RAN AWAY FROM THIS DUMP?
NOPE. Hmmm...
Maruo Mifune @Maruo1995
The novel is almost ready to be unveiled. Can't wait for yo all to read it.
8 days ago
WUPWUPWUPWUPWUPWUP

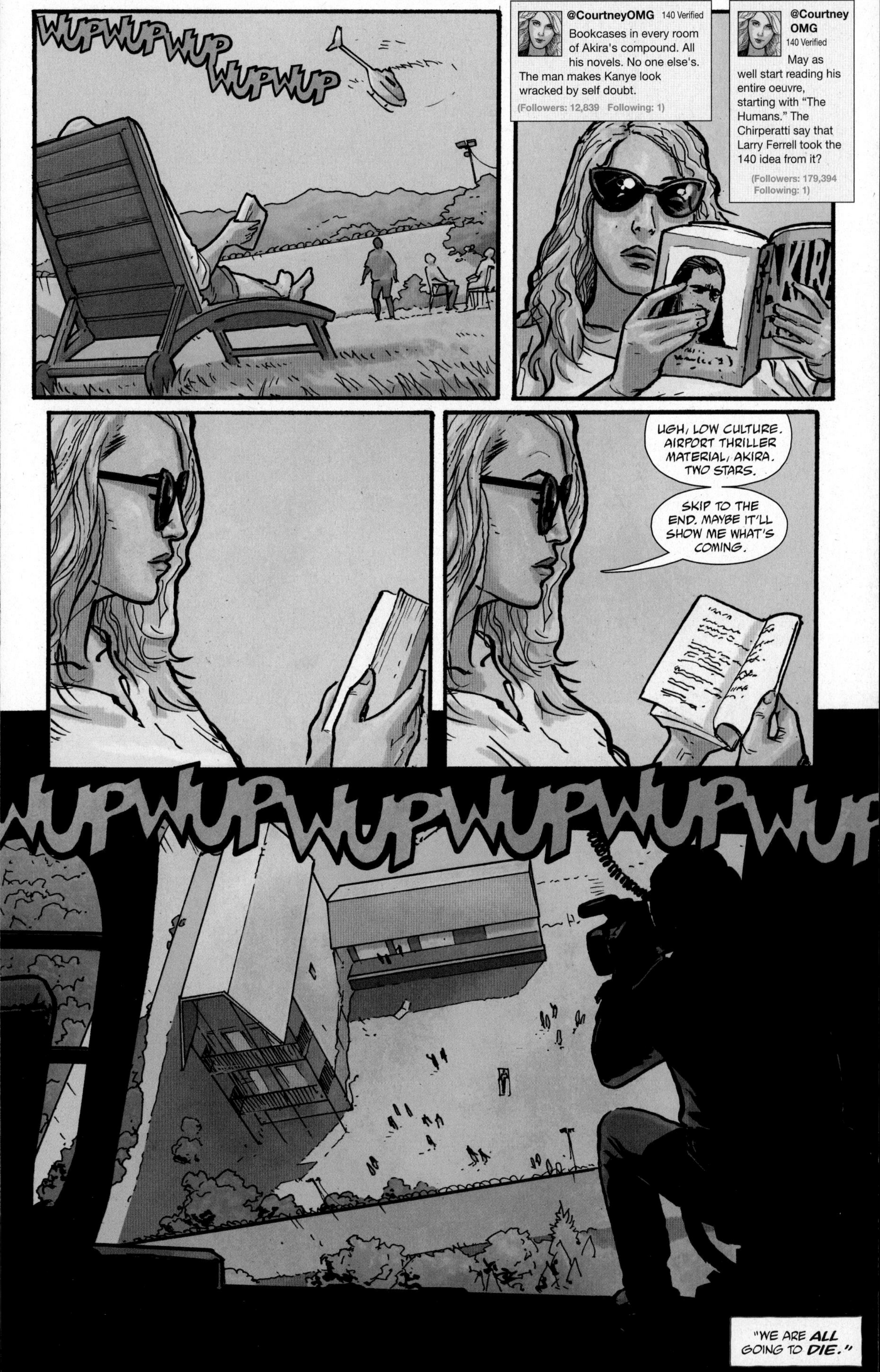
WUPWUPWUP
WUPWUP
@CourtneyOMG 140 Verified
Bookcases in every room of Akira's compound. All his novels. No one else's. The man makes Kanye look wracked by self doubt.
(Followers: 12,839 Following: 1)
@CourtneyOMG 140 Verified
May as well start reading his entire oeuvre, starting with "The Humans." The Chirperatti say that Larry Ferrell took the 140 idea from it?
(Followers: 179,394 Following: 1)
UGH, LOW CULTURE. AIRPORT THRILLER MATERIAL, AKIRA. TWO STARS.
SKIP TO THE END. MAYBE IT'LL SHOW ME WHAT'S COMING.
WUPWUPWUPWUPWUP
"WE ARE ALL GOING TO DIE."

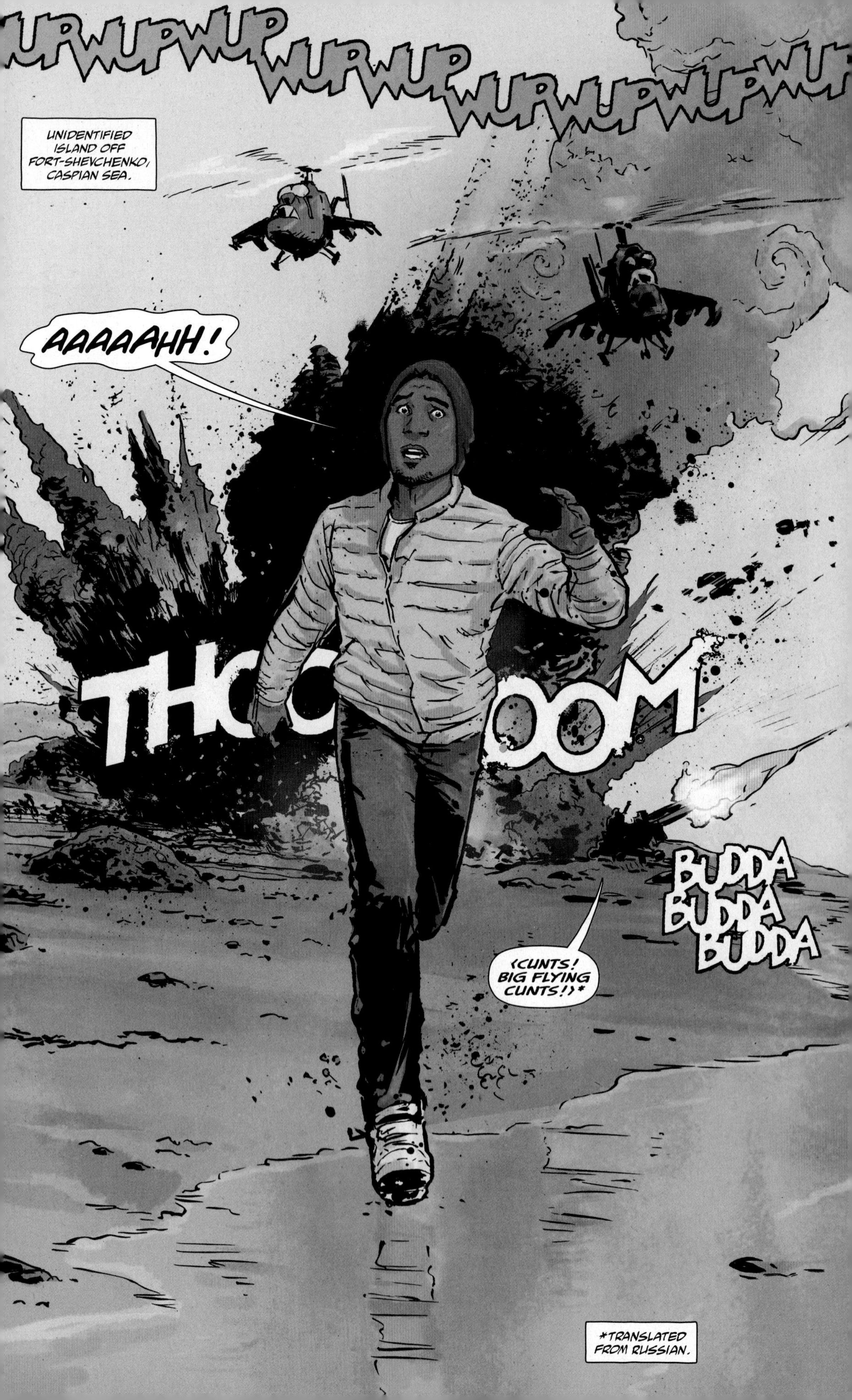
WUPWUPWUP WUPWUP WUPWUPWUPWUPWU
UNIDENTIFIED ISLAND OFF FORT-SHEVCHENKO, CASPIAN SEA.
AAAAAHH!
THOOOOM
BUDDA BUDDA BUDDA
‹CUNTS! BIG FLYING CUNTS!›*
*TRANSLATED FROM RUSSIAN.

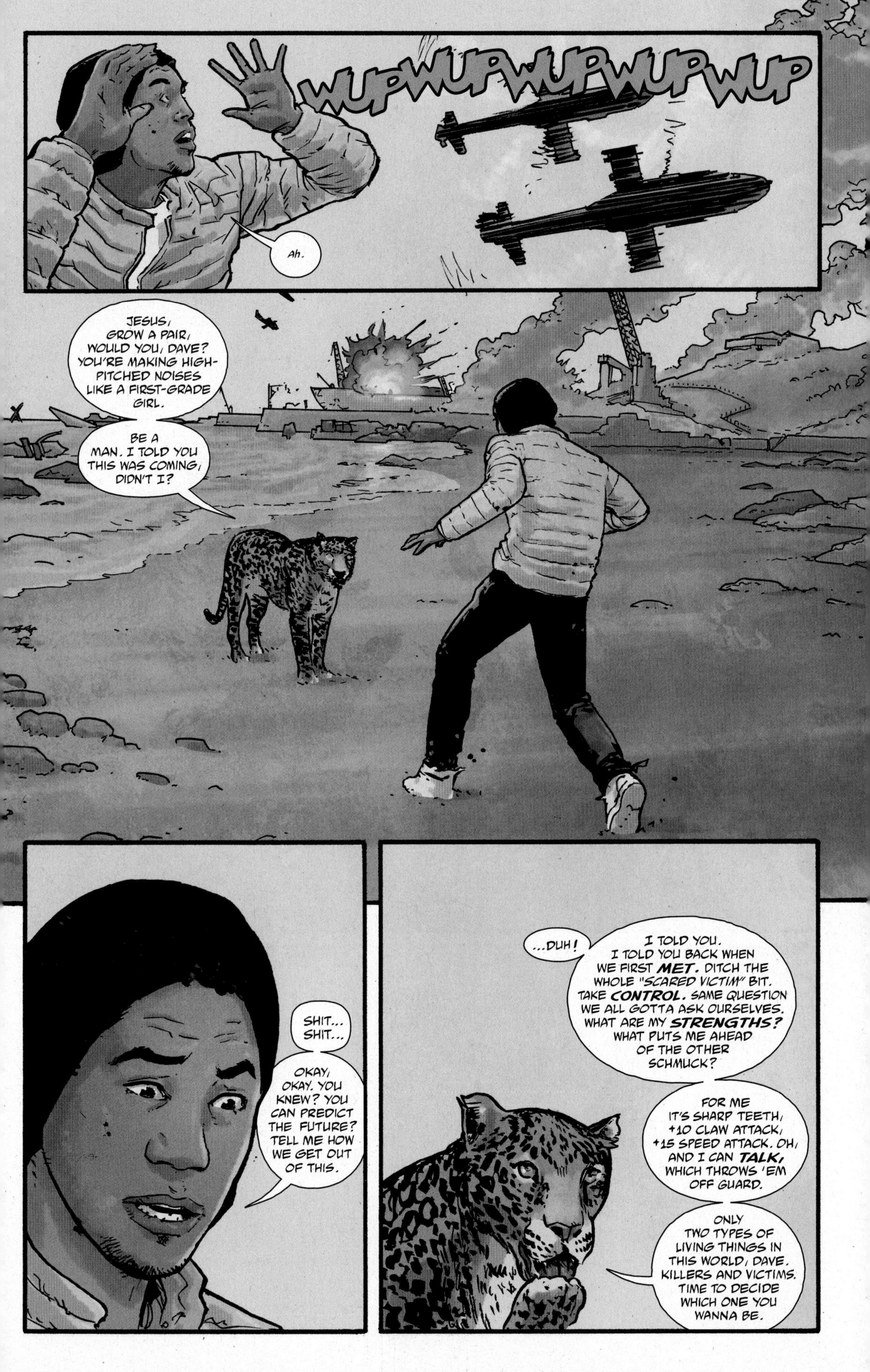
WUPWUPWUPWUPWUP
Ah.
JESUS, GROW A PAIR, WOULD YOU, DAVE? YOU'RE MAKING HIGH-PITCHED NOISES LIKE A FIRST-GRADE GIRL.
BE A MAN. I TOLD YOU THIS WAS COMING, DIDN'T I?
SHIT... SHIT...
OKAY, OKAY. YOU KNEW? YOU CAN PREDICT THE FUTURE? TELL ME HOW WE GET OUT OF THIS.
...DUH!
I TOLD YOU. I TOLD YOU BACK WHEN WE FIRST MET. DITCH THE WHOLE "SCARED VICTIM" BIT. TAKE CONTROL. SAME QUESTION WE ALL GOTTA ASK OURSELVES. WHAT ARE MY STRENGTHS? WHAT PUTS ME AHEAD OF THE OTHER SCHMUCK?
FOR ME IT'S SHARP TEETH, +10 CLAW ATTACK, +15 SPEED ATTACK. OH, AND I CAN TALK, WHICH THROWS 'EM OFF GUARD.
ONLY TWO TYPES OF LIVING THINGS IN THIS WORLD, DAVE. KILLERS AND VICTIMS. TIME TO DECIDE WHICH ONE YOU WANNA BE.

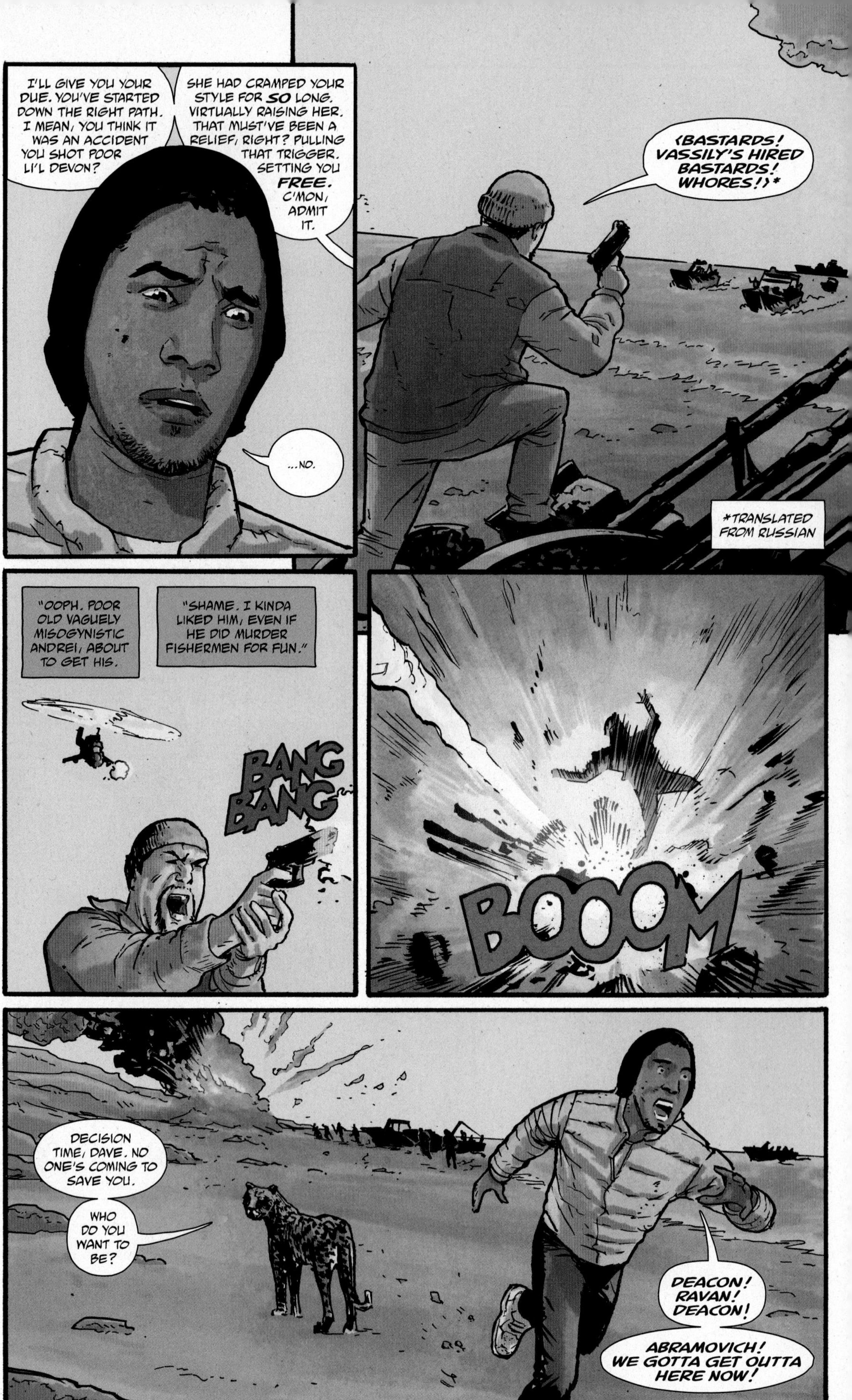
I'LL GIVE YOU YOUR DUE. YOU'VE STARTED DOWN THE RIGHT PATH. I MEAN, YOU THINK IT WAS AN ACCIDENT YOU SHOT POOR LI'L DEVON?
SHE HAD CRAMPED YOUR STYLE FOR SO LONG. VIRTUALLY RAISING HER. THAT MUST'VE BEEN A RELIEF, RIGHT? PULLING THAT TRIGGER. SETTING YOU FREE.
C'MON, ADMIT IT.
...NO.
‹BASTARDS! VASSILY'S HIRED BASTARDS! WHORES!›*
*TRANSLATED FROM RUSSIAN
"OOPH. POOR OLD VAGUELY MISOGYNISTIC ANDREI, ABOUT TO GET HIS.
"SHAME. I KINDA LIKED HIM, EVEN IF HE DID MURDER FISHERMEN FOR FUN."
BANG BANG
BOOOM
DECISION TIME, DAVE. NO ONE'S COMING TO SAVE YOU.
WHO DO YOU WANT TO BE?
DEACON! RAVAN! DEACON!
ABRAMOVICH! WE GOTTA GET OUTTA HERE NOW!

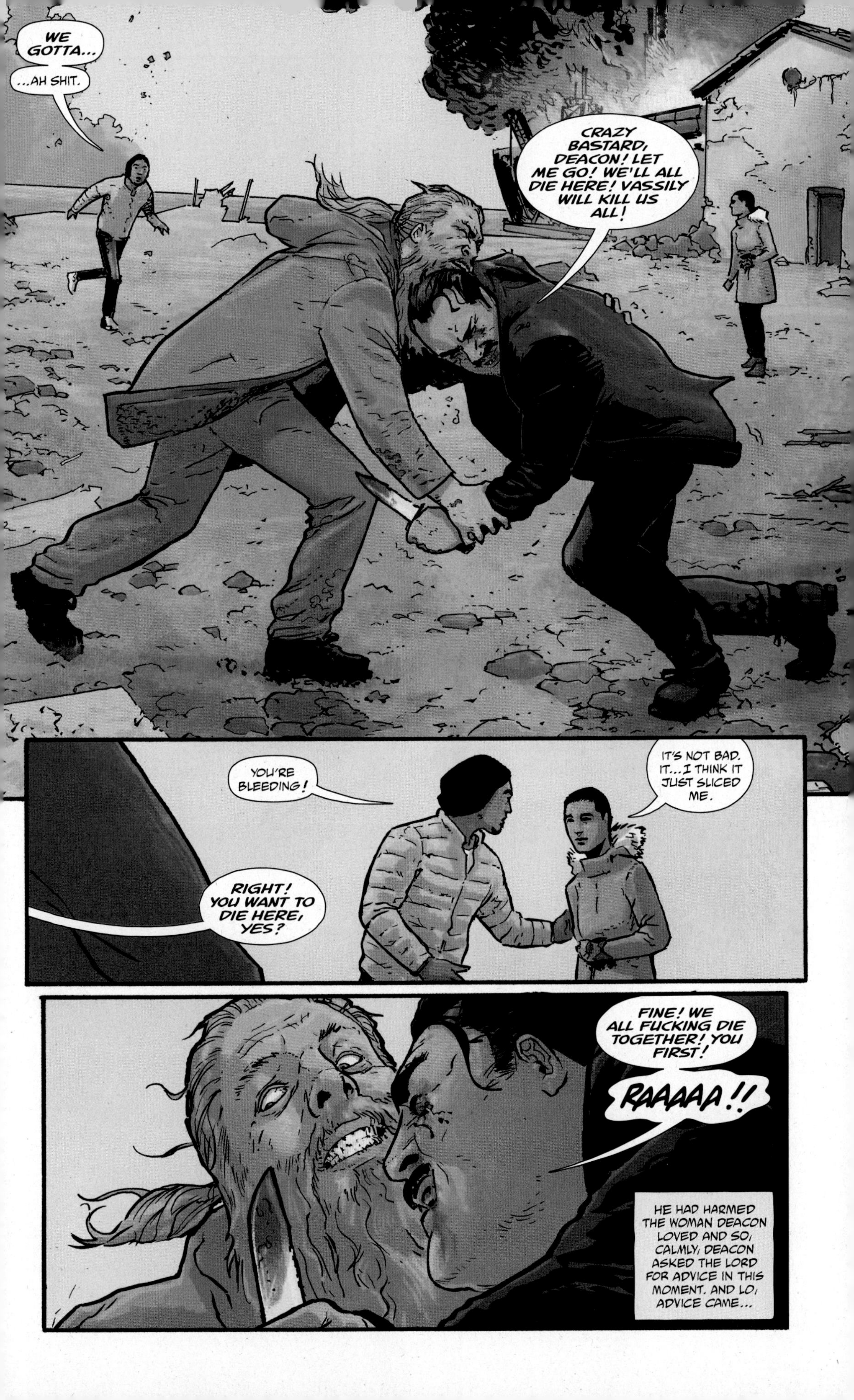
WE GOTTA...
...AH SHIT.
CRAZY BASTARD, DEACON! LET ME GO! WE'LL ALL DIE HERE! VASSILY WILL KILL US ALL!
YOU'RE BLEEDING!
IT'S NOT BAD. IT... I THINK IT JUST SLICED ME.
RIGHT! YOU WANT TO DIE HERE, YES?
FINE! WE ALL FUCKING DIE TOGETHER! YOU FIRST!
RAAAAA!!
HE HAD HARMED THE WOMAN DEACON LOVED AND SO, CALMLY, DEACON ASKED THE LORD FOR ADVICE IN THIS MOMENT. AND LO, ADVICE CAME...

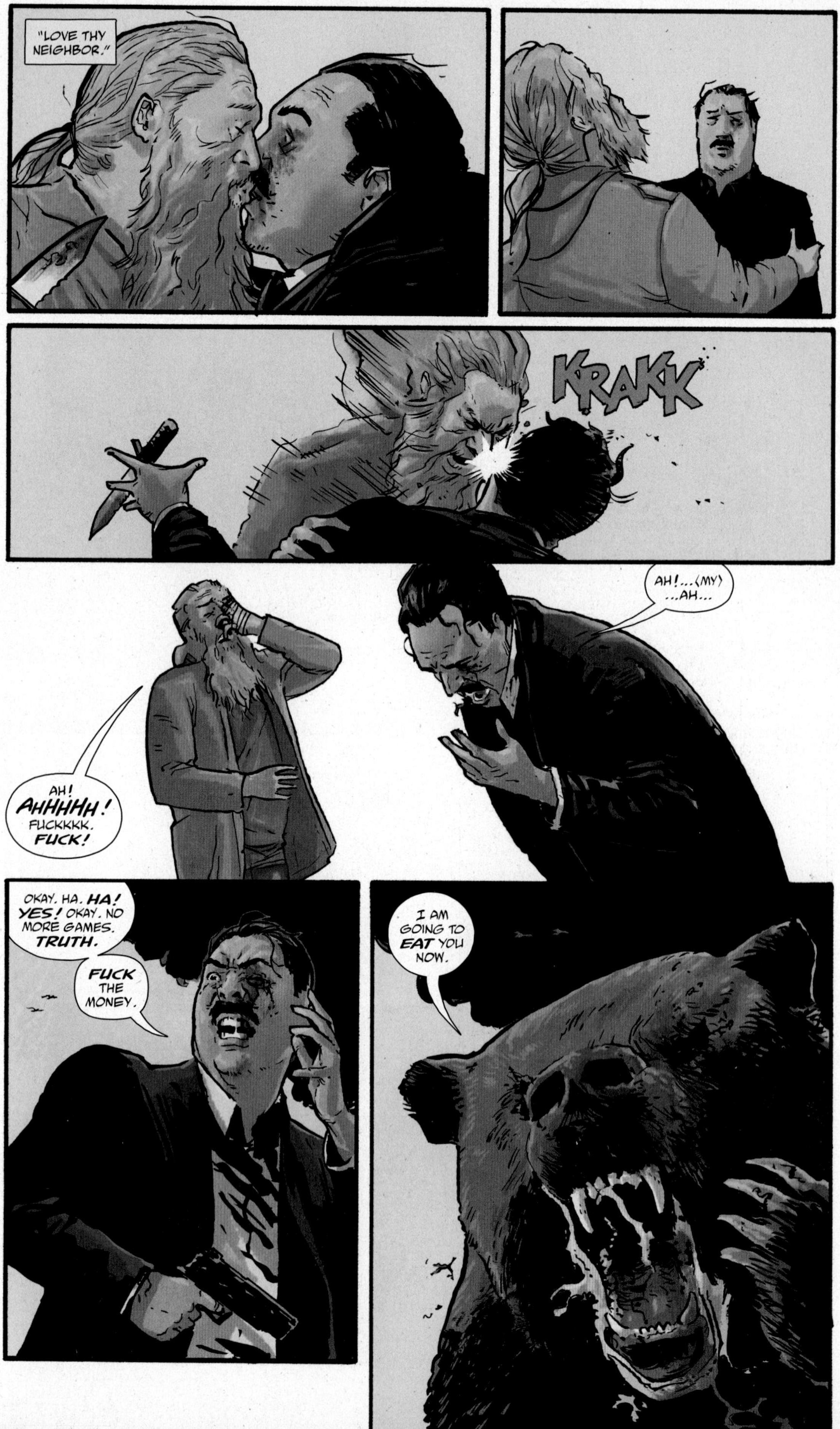

"LOVE THY NEIGHBOR."
KRAKK
AH!...(MY) ...AH...
AH! AHHHHH! FUCKKKK. FUCK!
OKAY. HA. HA! YES! OKAY. NO MORE GAMES. TRUTH.
FUCK THE MONEY.
I AM GOING TO EAT YOU NOW.

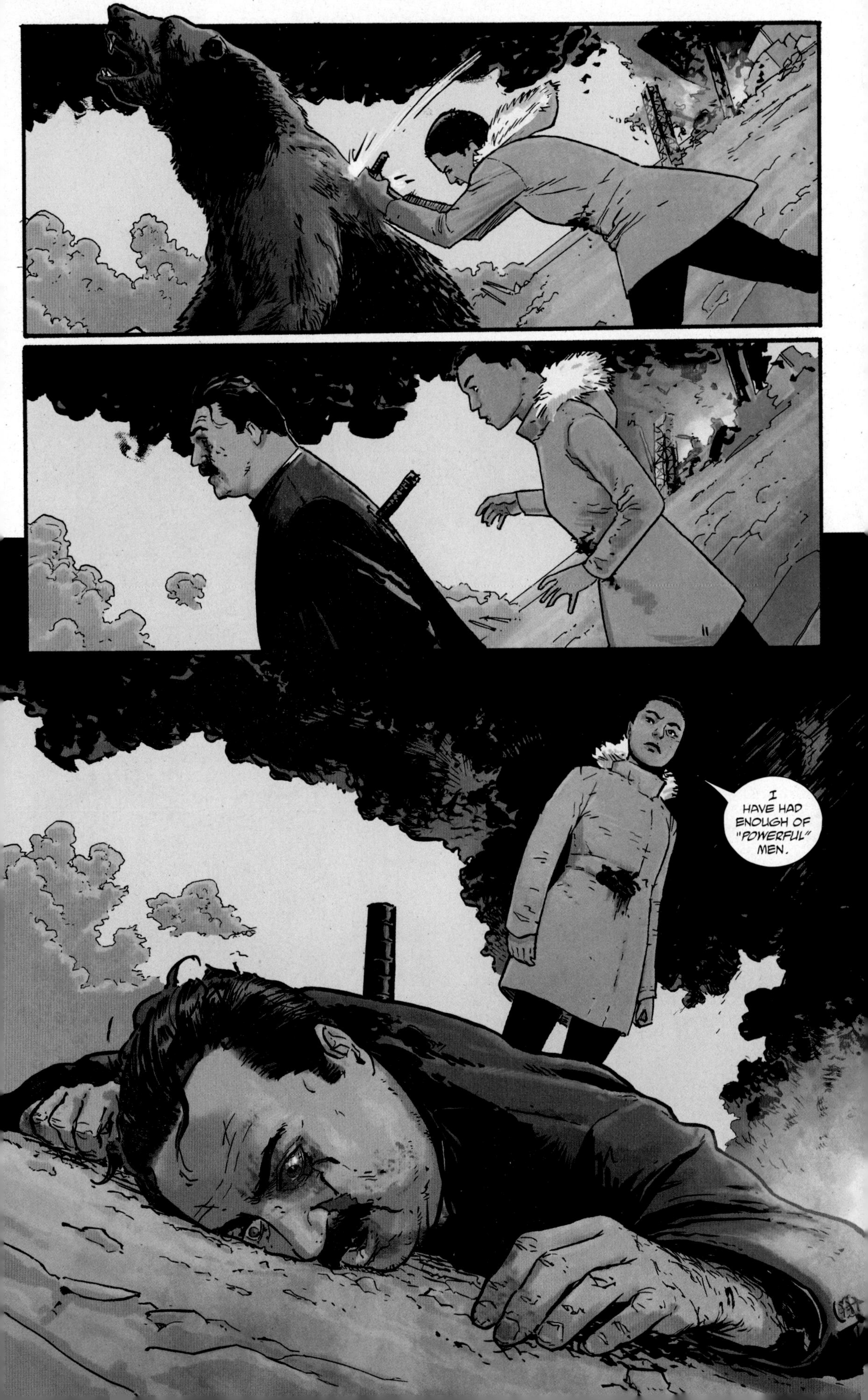
I HAVE HAD ENOUGH OF "POWERFUL" MEN.

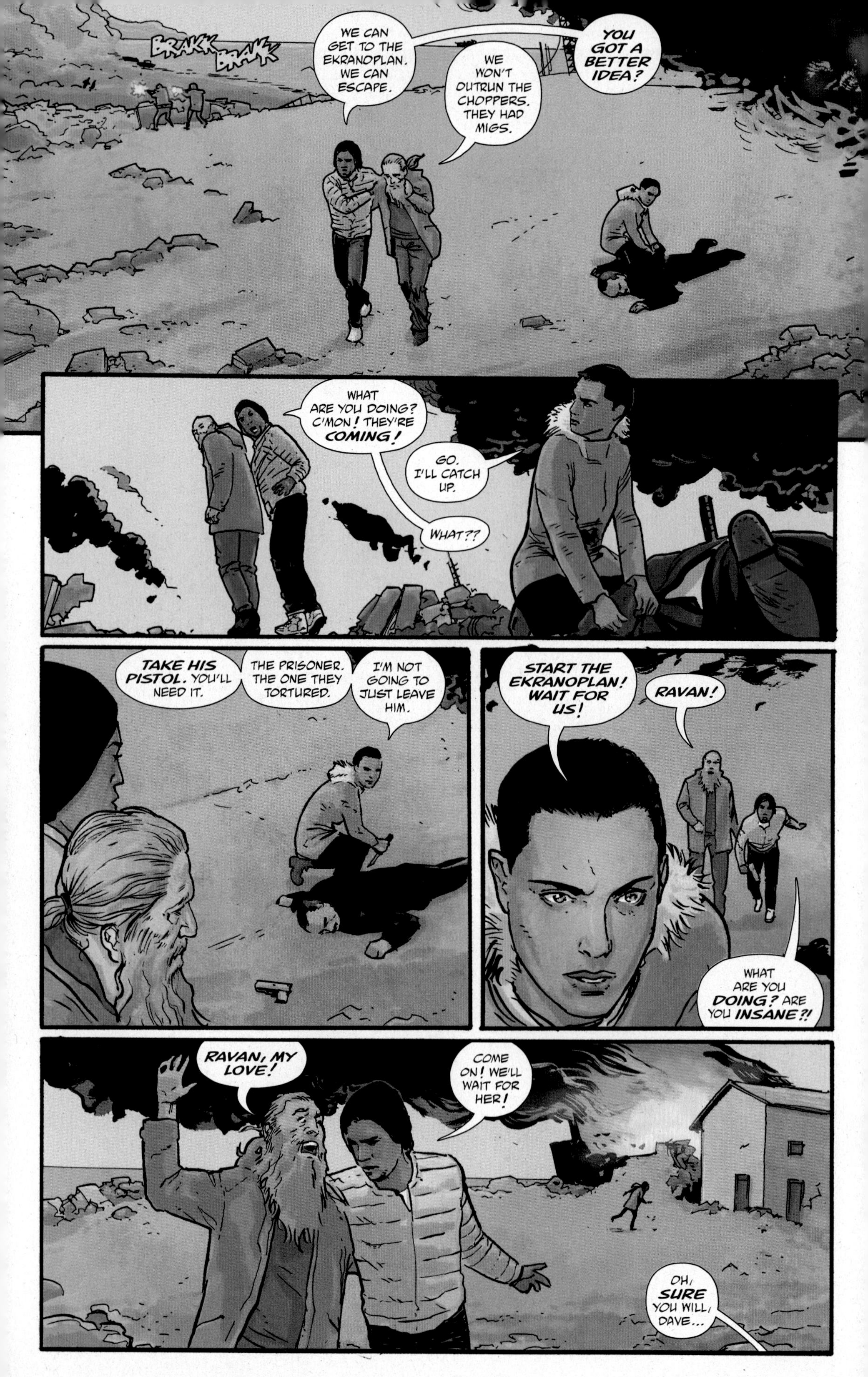
BRAKK BRAKK
WE CAN GET TO THE EKRANOPLAN. WE CAN ESCAPE.
WE WON'T OUTRUN THE CHOPPERS. THEY HAD MIGS.
YOU GOT A BETTER IDEA?
WHAT ARE YOU DOING? C'MON! THEY'RE COMING!
GO. I'LL CATCH UP.
WHAT??
TAKE HIS PISTOL. YOU'LL NEED IT.
THE PRISONER. THE ONE THEY TORTURED.
I'M NOT GOING TO JUST LEAVE HIM.
START THE EKRANOPLAN! WAIT FOR US!
RAVAN!
WHAT ARE YOU DOING? ARE YOU INSANE?!
RAVAN, MY LOVE!
COME ON! WE'LL WAIT FOR HER!
OH, SURE YOU WILL, DAVE...

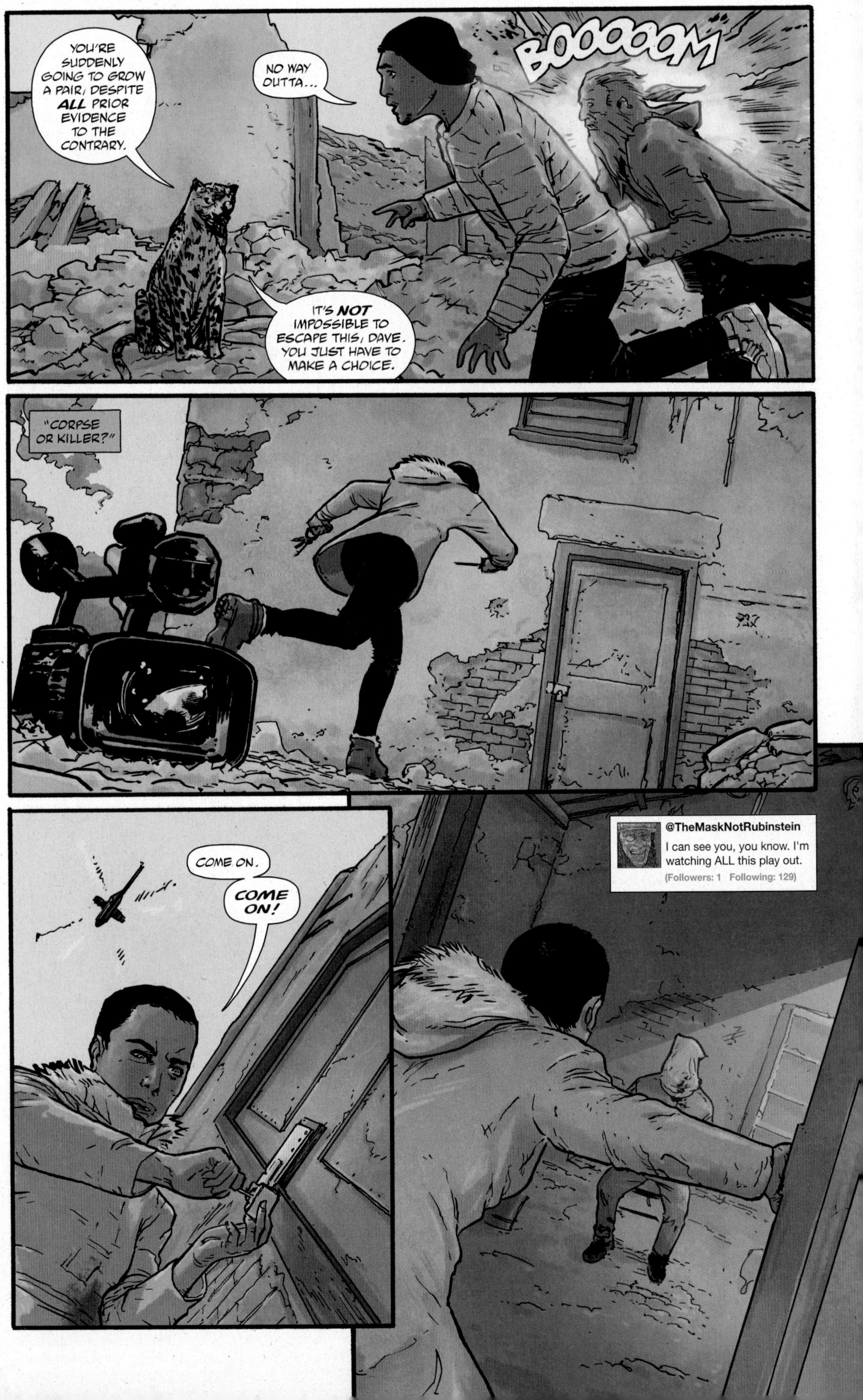
YOU'RE SUDDENLY GOING TO GROW A PAIR, DESPITE ALL PRIOR EVIDENCE TO THE CONTRARY.
NO WAY OUTTA...
BOOOOOOM
IT'S NOT IMPOSSIBLE TO ESCAPE THIS, DAVE. YOU JUST HAVE TO MAKE A CHOICE.
"CORPSE OR KILLER?"
COME ON.
COME ON!
@TheMaskNotRubinstein
I can see you, you know. I'm watching ALL this play out.
(Followers: 1 Following: 129)

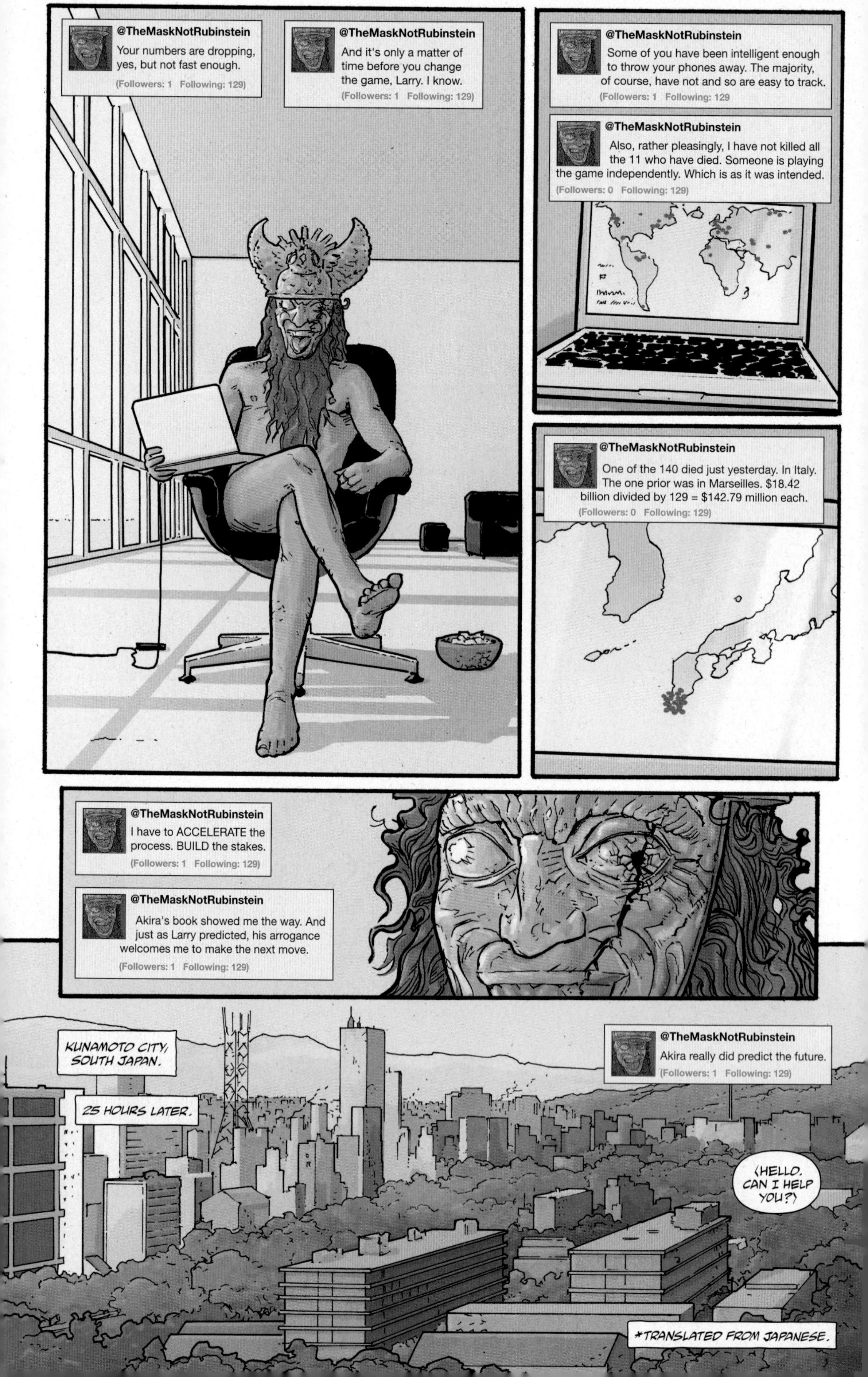
@TheMaskNotRubinstein
Your numbers are dropping, yes, but not fast enough.
(Followers: 1 Following: 129)
@TheMaskNotRubinstein
And it's only a matter of time before you change the game, Larry. I know.
(Followers: 1 Following: 129)
@TheMaskNotRubinstein
Some of you have been intelligent enough to throw your phones away. The majority, of course, have not and so are easy to track.
(Followers: 1 Following: 129
@TheMaskNotRubinstein
Also, rather pleasingly, I have not killed all the 11 who have died. Someone is playing the game independently. Which is as it was intended.
(Followers: 0 Following: 129)
@TheMaskNotRubinstein
One of the 140 died just yesterday. In Italy. The one prior was in Marseilles. $18.42 billion divided by 129 = $142.79 million each.
(Followers: 0 Following: 129)
@TheMaskNotRubinstein
I have to ACCELERATE the process. BUILD the stakes.
(Followers: 1 Following: 129)
@TheMaskNotRubinstein
Akira's book showed me the way. And just as Larry predicted, his arrogance welcomes me to make the next move.
(Followers: 1 Following: 129)
KUNAMOTO CITY, SOUTH JAPAN.
25 HOURS LATER.
@TheMaskNotRubinstein
Akira really did predict the future.
(Followers: 1 Following: 129)
⟨HELLO. CAN I HELP YOU?⟩
*TRANSLATED FROM JAPANESE.

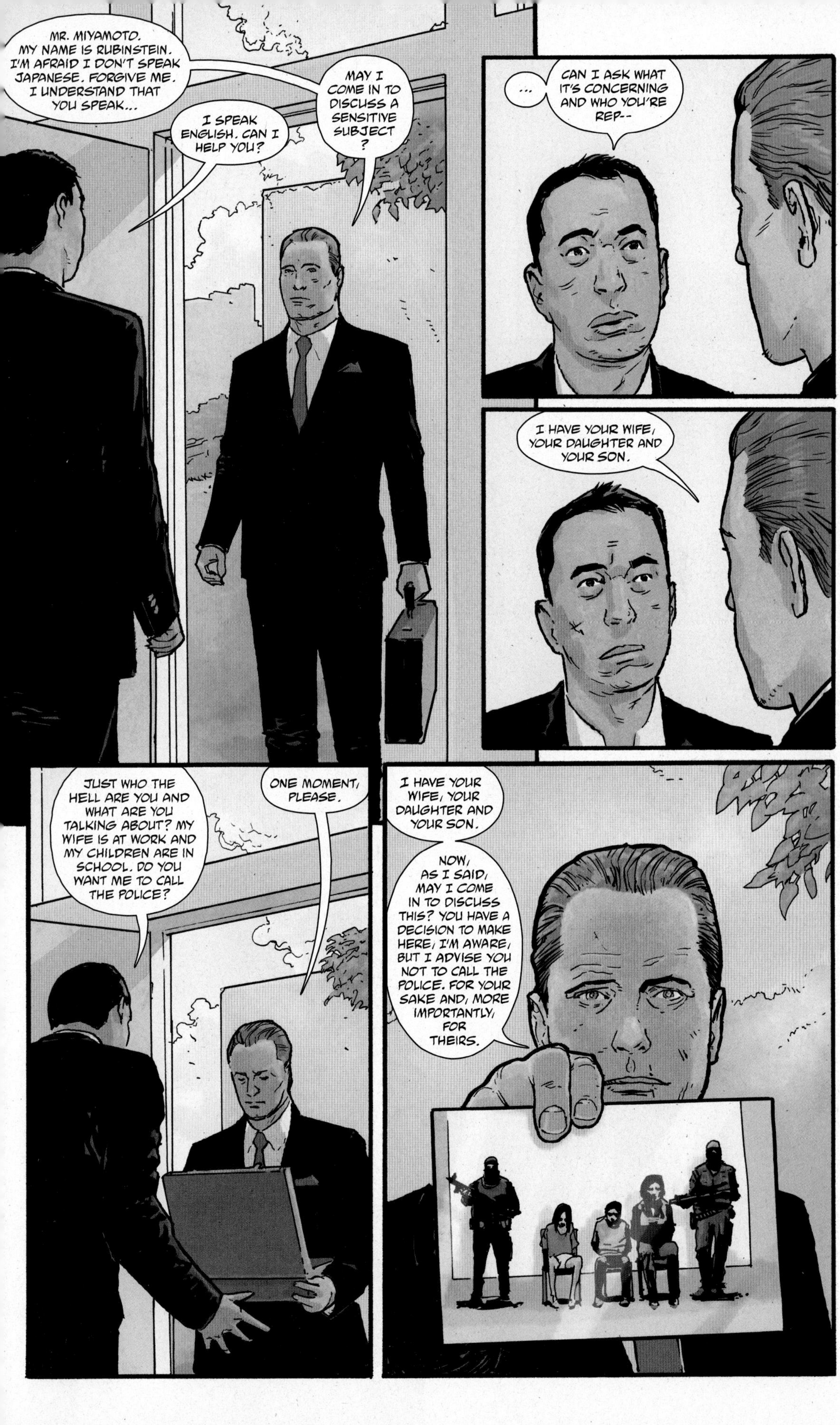
MR. MIYAMOTO. MY NAME IS RUBINSTEIN. I'M AFRAID I DON'T SPEAK JAPANESE. FORGIVE ME. I UNDERSTAND THAT YOU SPEAK...
I SPEAK ENGLISH. CAN I HELP YOU?
MAY I COME IN TO DISCUSS A SENSITIVE SUBJECT?
...
CAN I ASK WHAT IT'S CONCERNING AND WHO YOU'RE REP--
I HAVE YOUR WIFE, YOUR DAUGHTER AND YOUR SON.
JUST WHO THE HELL ARE YOU AND WHAT ARE YOU TALKING ABOUT? MY WIFE IS AT WORK AND MY CHILDREN ARE IN SCHOOL. DO YOU WANT ME TO CALL THE POLICE?
ONE MOMENT, PLEASE.
I HAVE YOUR WIFE, YOUR DAUGHTER AND YOUR SON.
NOW, AS I SAID, MAY I COME IN TO DISCUSS THIS? YOU HAVE A DECISION TO MAKE HERE, I'M AWARE, BUT I ADVISE YOU NOT TO CALL THE POLICE. FOR YOUR SAKE AND, MORE IMPORTANTLY, FOR THEIRS.

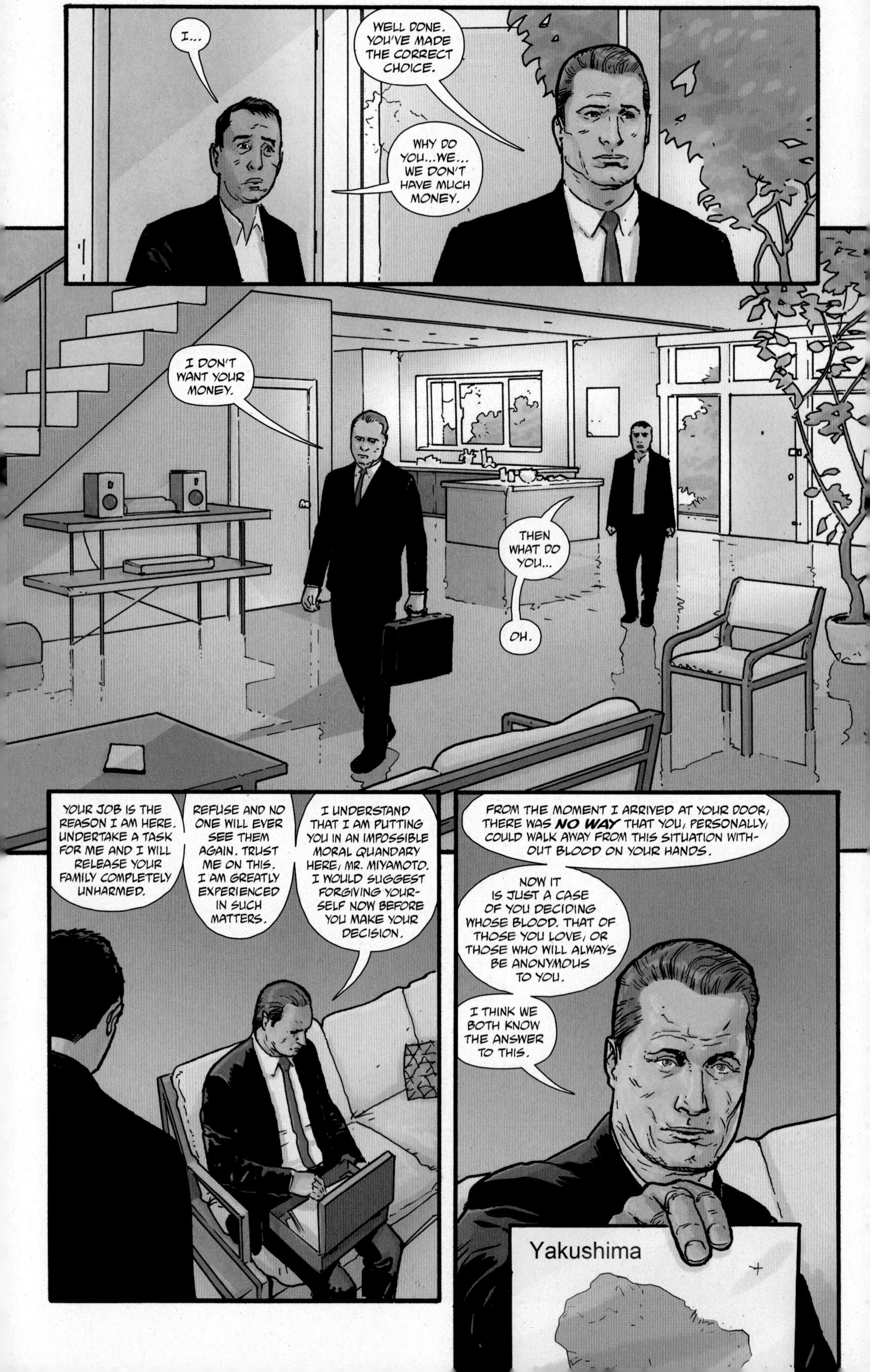
I...
WELL DONE. YOU'VE MADE THE CORRECT CHOICE.
WHY DO YOU...WE... WE DON'T HAVE MUCH MONEY.
I DON'T WANT YOUR MONEY.
THEN WHAT DO YOU...
OH.
YOUR JOB IS THE REASON I AM HERE. UNDERTAKE A TASK FOR ME AND I WILL RELEASE YOUR FAMILY COMPLETELY UNHARMED.
REFUSE AND NO ONE WILL EVER SEE THEM AGAIN. TRUST ME ON THIS. I AM GREATLY EXPERIENCED IN SUCH MATTERS.
I UNDERSTAND THAT I AM PUTTING YOU IN AN IMPOSSIBLE MORAL QUANDARY HERE, MR. MIYAMOTO. I WOULD SUGGEST FORGIVING YOUR-SELF NOW BEFORE YOU MAKE YOUR DECISION.
FROM THE MOMENT I ARRIVED AT YOUR DOOR, THERE WAS NO WAY THAT YOU, PERSONALLY, COULD WALK AWAY FROM THIS SITUATION WITH-OUT BLOOD ON YOUR HANDS.
NOW IT IS JUST A CASE OF YOU DECIDING WHOSE BLOOD. THAT OF THOSE YOU LOVE, OR THOSE WHO WILL ALWAYS BE ANONYMOUS TO YOU.
I THINK WE BOTH KNOW THE ANSWER TO THIS.
Yakushima

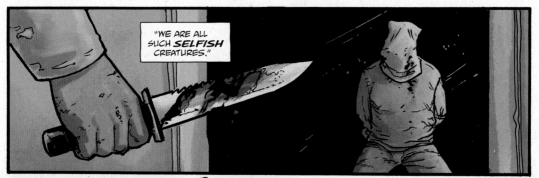

"WE ARE ALL SUCH *SELFISH* CREATURES."

I THINK ABRAMOVICH WAS RIGHT ABOUT US ALL HIDING BEHIND BRUTAL MEN.

EVERY CIVILIZED PERSON DOES THIS.

BUT I KNOW WHAT IT IS TO SIT IN THAT CHAIR.

AND I WOULD RATHER *DIE* THAN STAND BY WHILE THE INNOCENT SUFFER.

YOU... YOU'RE ONE OF THE 140, TOO?

...YES.

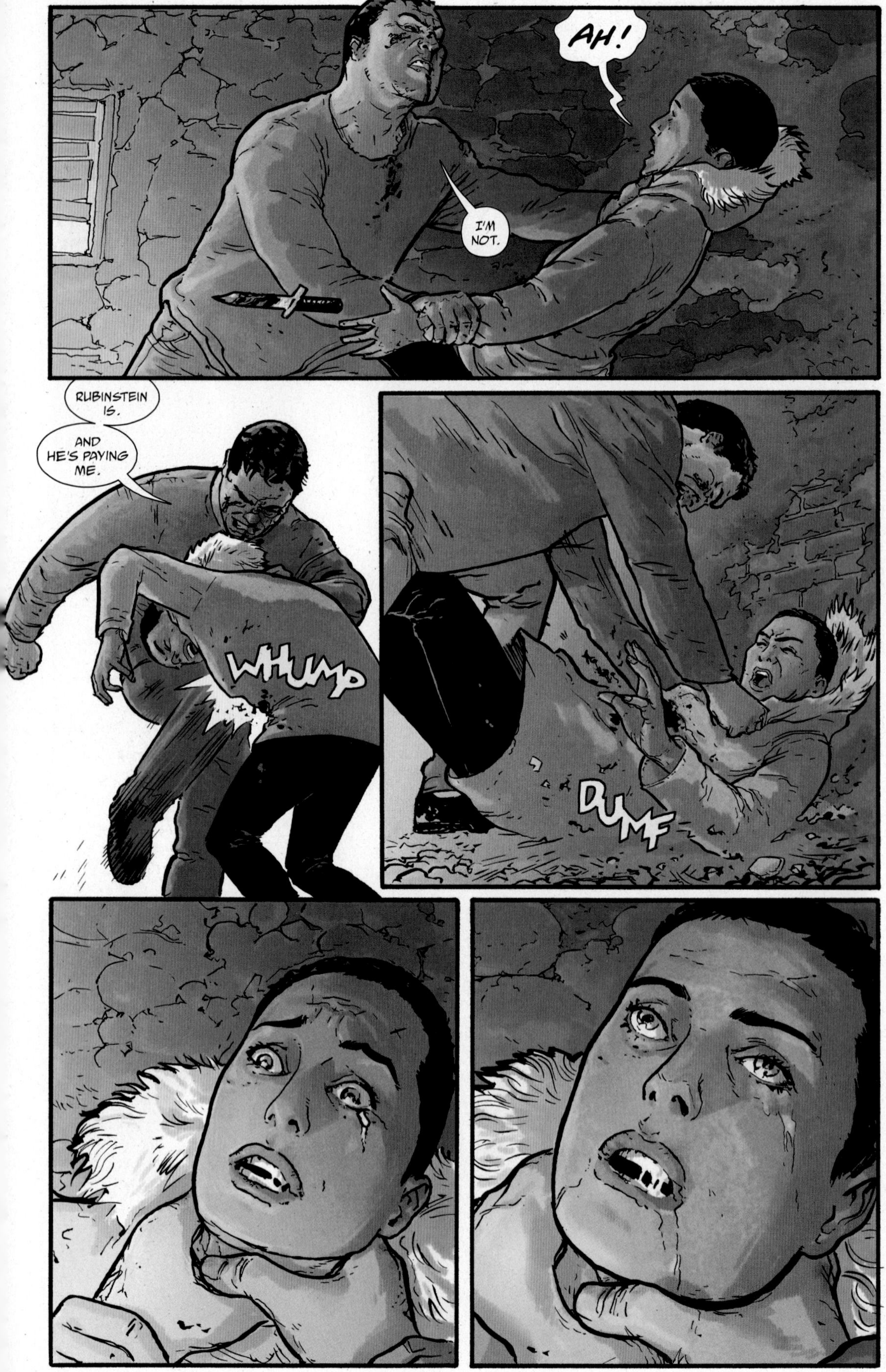
AH!
I'M NOT.
RUBINSTEIN IS.
AND HE'S PAYING ME.
WHUMP
DUMF

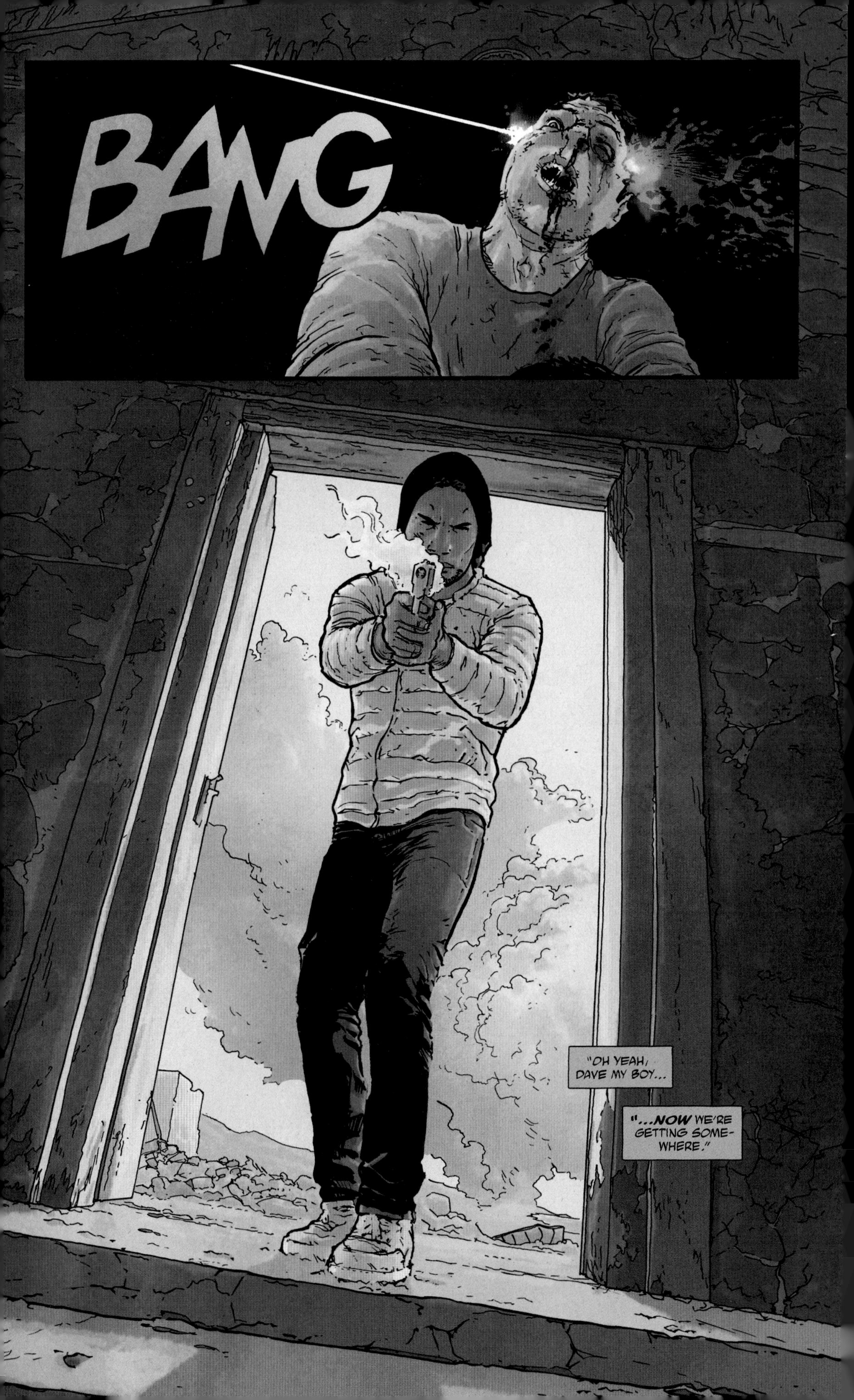
BANG
"OH YEAH, DAVE MY BOY...
"...NOW WE'RE GETTING SOME-WHERE."

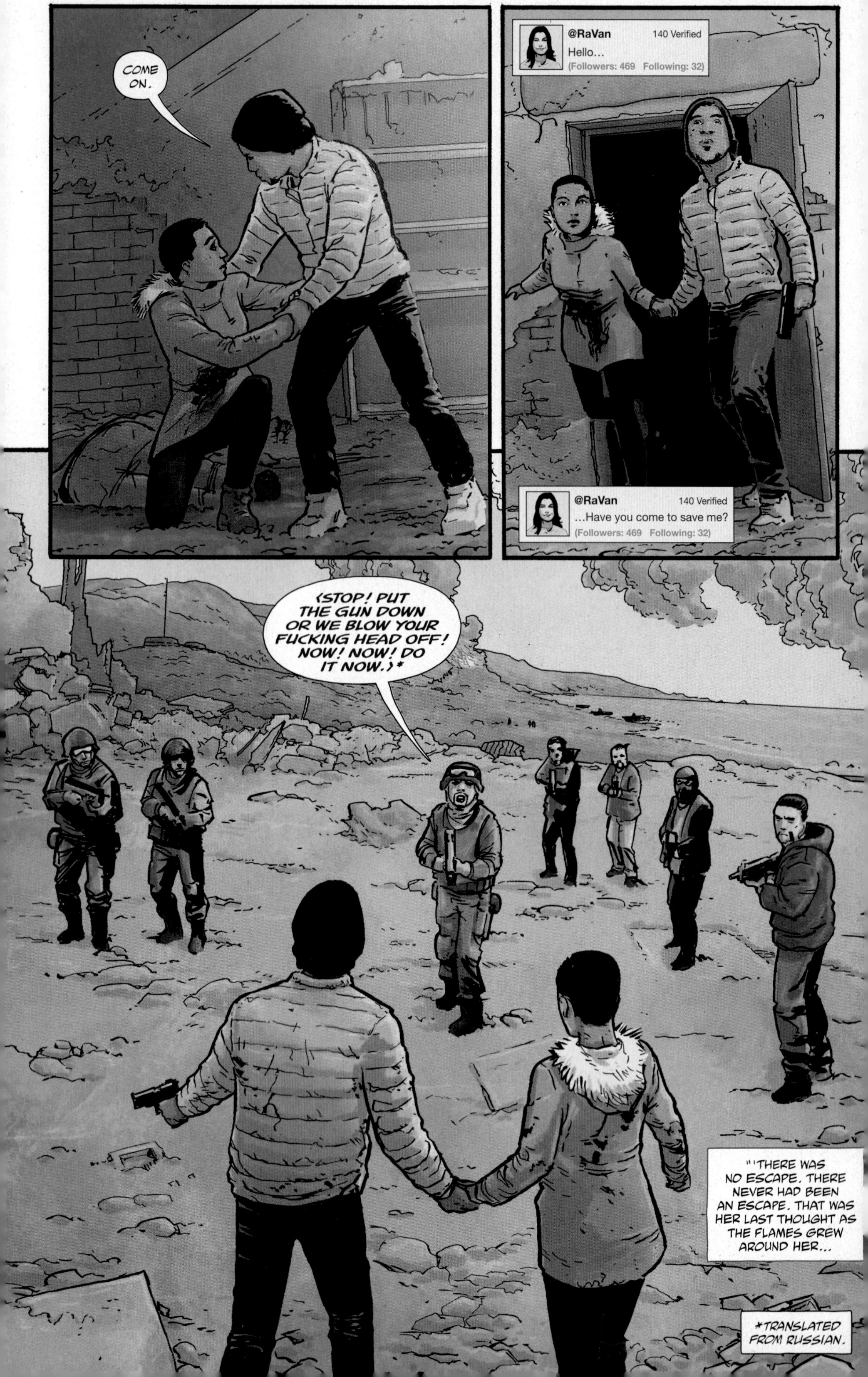
COME ON.
@RaVan 140 Verified
Hello...
(Followers: 469 Following: 32)
@RaVan 140 Verified
...Have you come to save me?
(Followers: 469 Following: 32)
‹STOP! PUT THE GUN DOWN OR WE BLOW YOUR FUCKING HEAD OFF! NOW! NOW! DO IT NOW.›*
"'THERE WAS NO ESCAPE. THERE NEVER HAD BEEN AN ESCAPE. THAT WAS HER LAST THOUGHT AS THE FLAMES GREW AROUND HER...
*TRANSLATED FROM RUSSIAN.

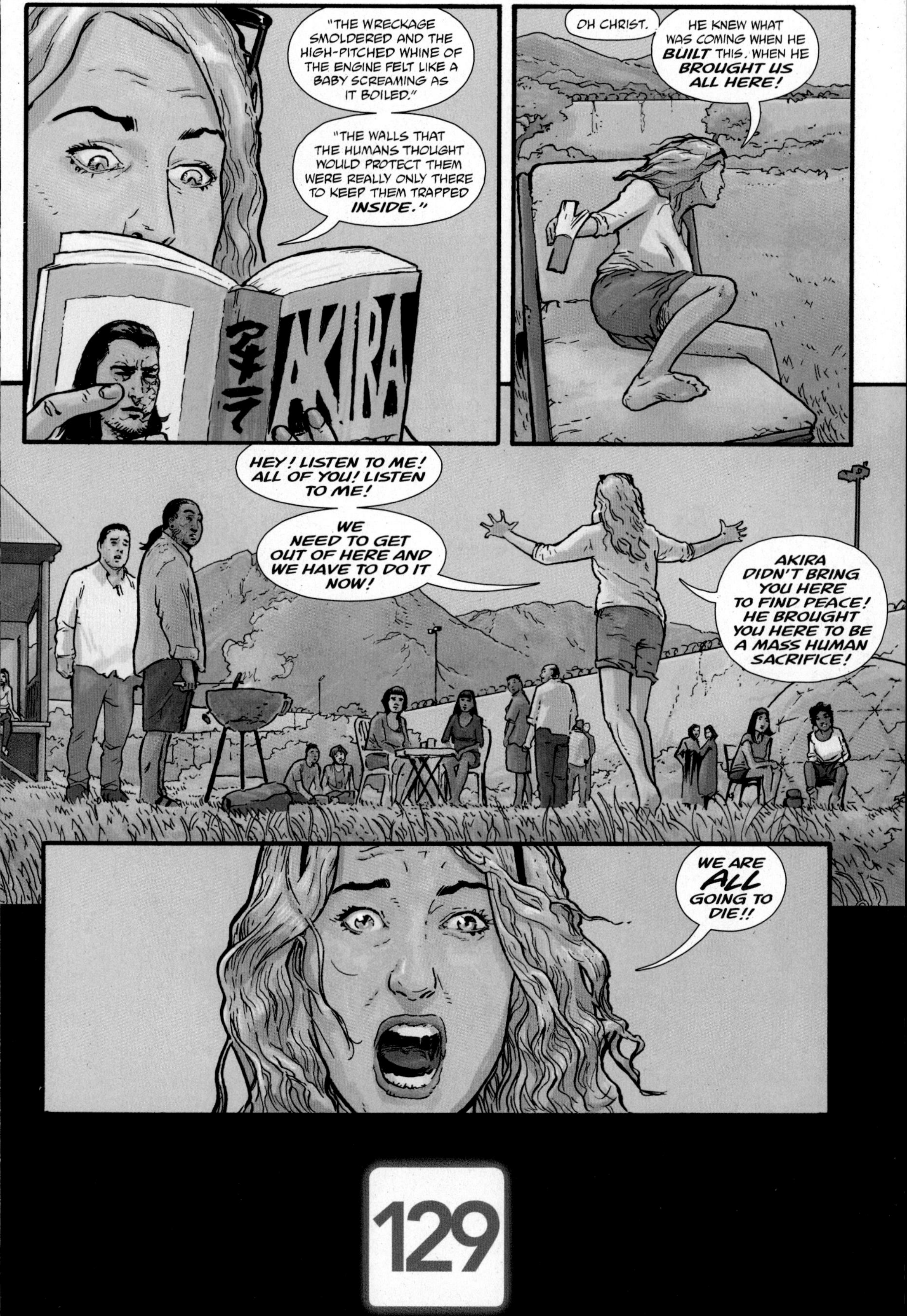
"THE WRECKAGE SMOLDERED AND THE HIGH-PITCHED WHINE OF THE ENGINE FELT LIKE A BABY SCREAMING AS IT BOILED."
"THE WALLS THAT THE HUMANS THOUGHT WOULD PROTECT THEM WERE REALLY ONLY THERE TO KEEP THEM TRAPPED INSIDE."
AKIRA
OH CHRIST.
HE KNEW WHAT WAS COMING WHEN HE BUILT THIS. WHEN HE BROUGHT US ALL HERE!
HEY! LISTEN TO ME! ALL OF YOU! LISTEN TO ME!
WE NEED TO GET OUT OF HERE AND WE HAVE TO DO IT NOW!
AKIRA DIDN'T BRING YOU HERE TO FIND PEACE! HE BROUGHT YOU HERE TO BE A MASS HUMAN SACRIFICE!
WE ARE ALL GOING TO DIE!!

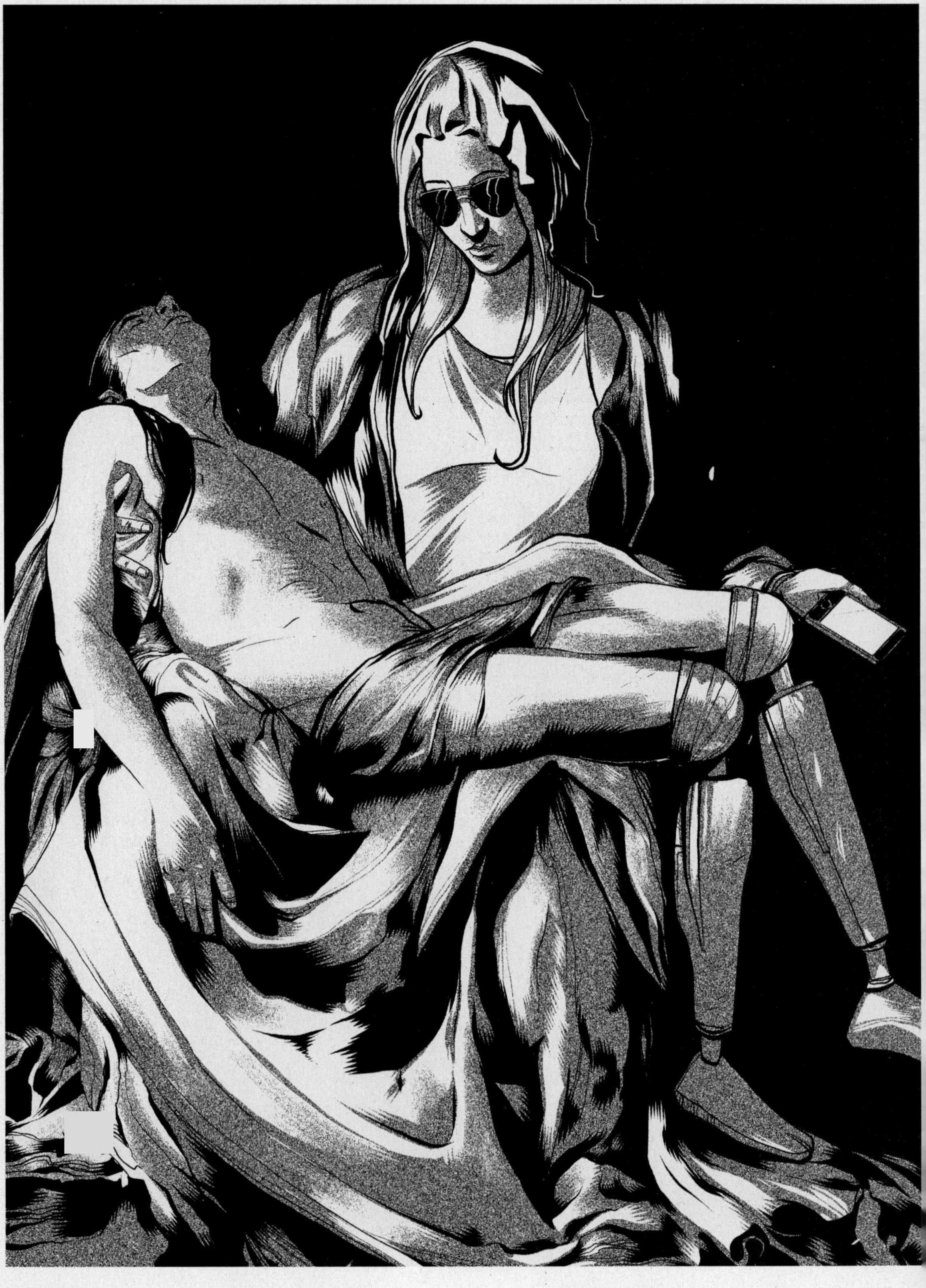

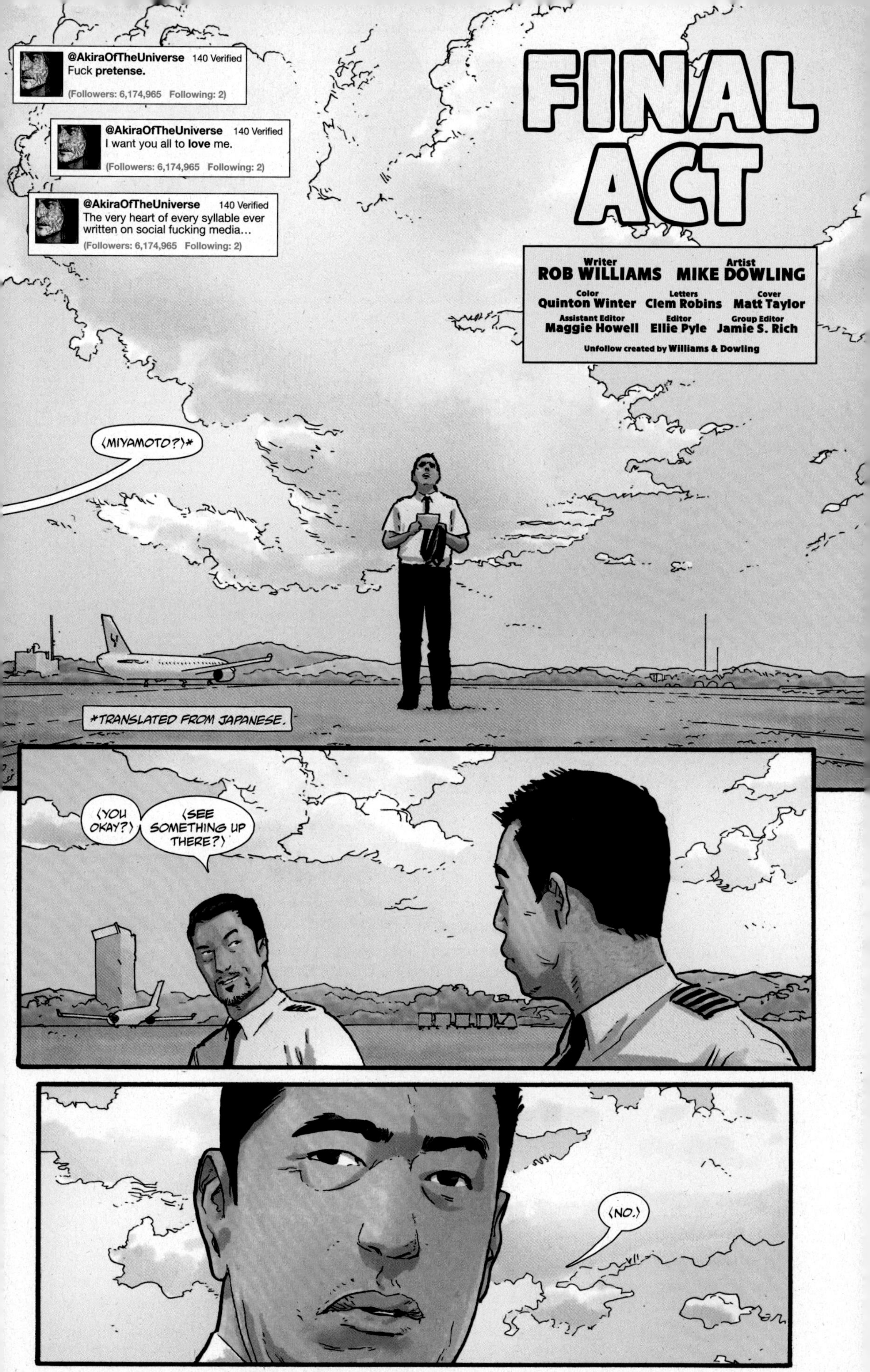

@AkiraOfTheUniverse 140 Verified
Fuck pretense.
(Followers: 6,174,965 Following: 2)
@AkiraOfTheUniverse 140 Verified
I want you all to love me.
(Followers: 6,174,965 Following: 2)
@AkiraOfTheUniverse 140 Verified
The very heart of every syllable ever written on social fucking media…
(Followers: 6,174,965 Following: 2)
FINAL ACT
Writer ROB WILLIAMS
Artist MIKE DOWLING
Color Quinton Winter
Letters Clem Robins
Cover Matt Taylor
Assistant Editor Maggie Howell
Editor Ellie Pyle
Group Editor Jamie S. Rich
Unfollow created by Williams & Dowling
⟨MIYAMOTO?⟩*
*TRANSLATED FROM JAPANESE.
⟨YOU OKAY?⟩
⟨SEE SOMETHING UP THERE?⟩
⟨NO.⟩

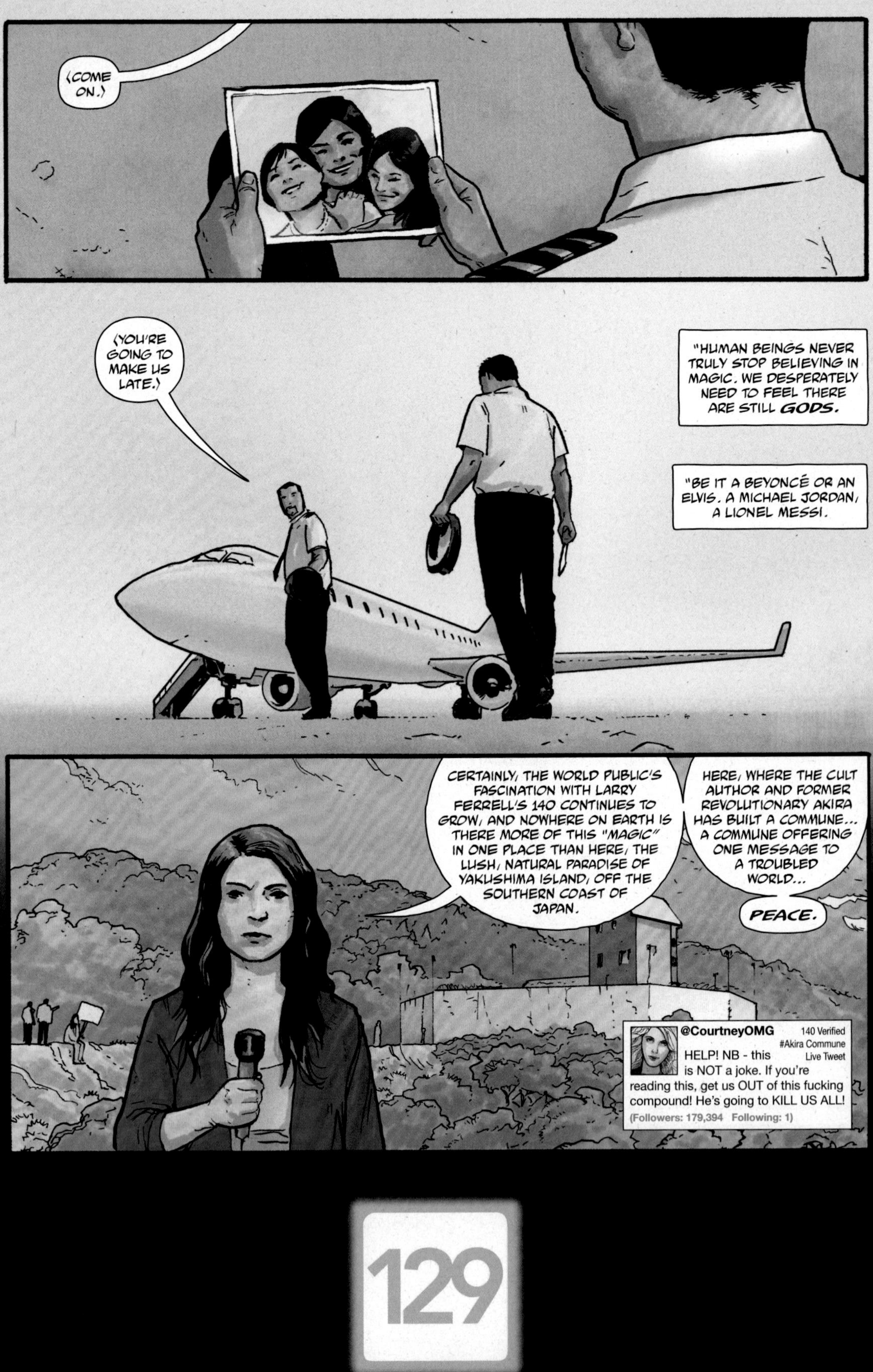
(COME ON.)
(YOU'RE GOING TO MAKE US LATE.)
"HUMAN BEINGS NEVER TRULY STOP BELIEVING IN MAGIC. WE DESPERATELY NEED TO FEEL THERE ARE STILL GODS.
"BE IT A BEYONCÉ OR AN ELVIS. A MICHAEL JORDAN, A LIONEL MESSI.
CERTAINLY, THE WORLD PUBLIC'S FASCINATION WITH LARRY FERRELL'S 140 CONTINUES TO GROW, AND NOWHERE ON EARTH IS THERE MORE OF THIS "MAGIC" IN ONE PLACE THAN HERE, THE LUSH, NATURAL PARADISE OF YAKUSHIMA ISLAND, OFF THE SOUTHERN COAST OF JAPAN.
HERE, WHERE THE CULT AUTHOR AND FORMER REVOLUTIONARY AKIRA HAS BUILT A COMMUNE... A COMMUNE OFFERING ONE MESSAGE TO A TROUBLED WORLD...
PEACE.
@CourtneyOMG
140 Verified
#Akira Commune
Live Tweet
HELP! NB - this is NOT a joke. If you're reading this, get us OUT of this fucking compound! He's going to KILL US ALL!
(Followers: 179,394 Following: 1)
129

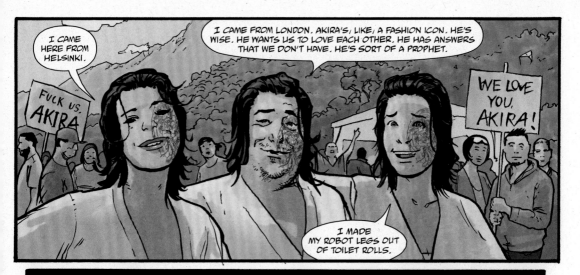

I CAME HERE FROM HELSINKI.

I CAME FROM LONDON. AKIRA'S, LIKE, A FASHION ICON. HE'S WISE. HE WANTS US TO LOVE EACH OTHER. HE HAS ANSWERS THAT WE DON'T HAVE. HE'S SORT OF A PROPHET.

FUCK US, AKIRA

WE LOVE YOU, AKIRA!

I MADE MY ROBOT LEGS OUT OF TOILET ROLLS.

"MEANWHILE, LARRY FERRELL'S APP CONTINUES TO COUNT DOWN.

"ELEVEN MEMBERS OF THE '140' HAVE BEEN KILLED SINCE FERRELL BEQUEATHED HIS FORTUNE. SOME IN BRUTAL, PUBLIC MURDERS. A TWISTED SOCIAL EXPERIMENT INTO THE NATURE OF SOCIAL MEDIA.

"YET AKIRA AND 43 OF HIS FOLLOWERS ARE STAGING THEIR OWN GANDHI-ESQUE NON-VIOLENT PROTEST HERE. TRYING, THEY CLAIM, TO SHOW THAT WE ARE NOT ALL *ANIMALS*.

129

"AND NOW A NEW APP HAS BEEN LAUNCHED BY AKIRA HIMSELF TO ACT AS DIRECT COUNTERPOINT TO FERRELL.

"NOT YET ACTIVE BUT DOWNLOADABLE AND FREE, HIS *PR* CLAIMS THAT, VERY SOON, IT WILL OFFER, WITHOUT HYPERBOLE, 'SECRETS FROM BEYOND ALL PRESENTLY KNOWN HUMAN EXPERIENCE.'

"DISPATCHES FROM *HEAVEN* ITSELF.

"THE DIARY OF A NEW *GOD.*"

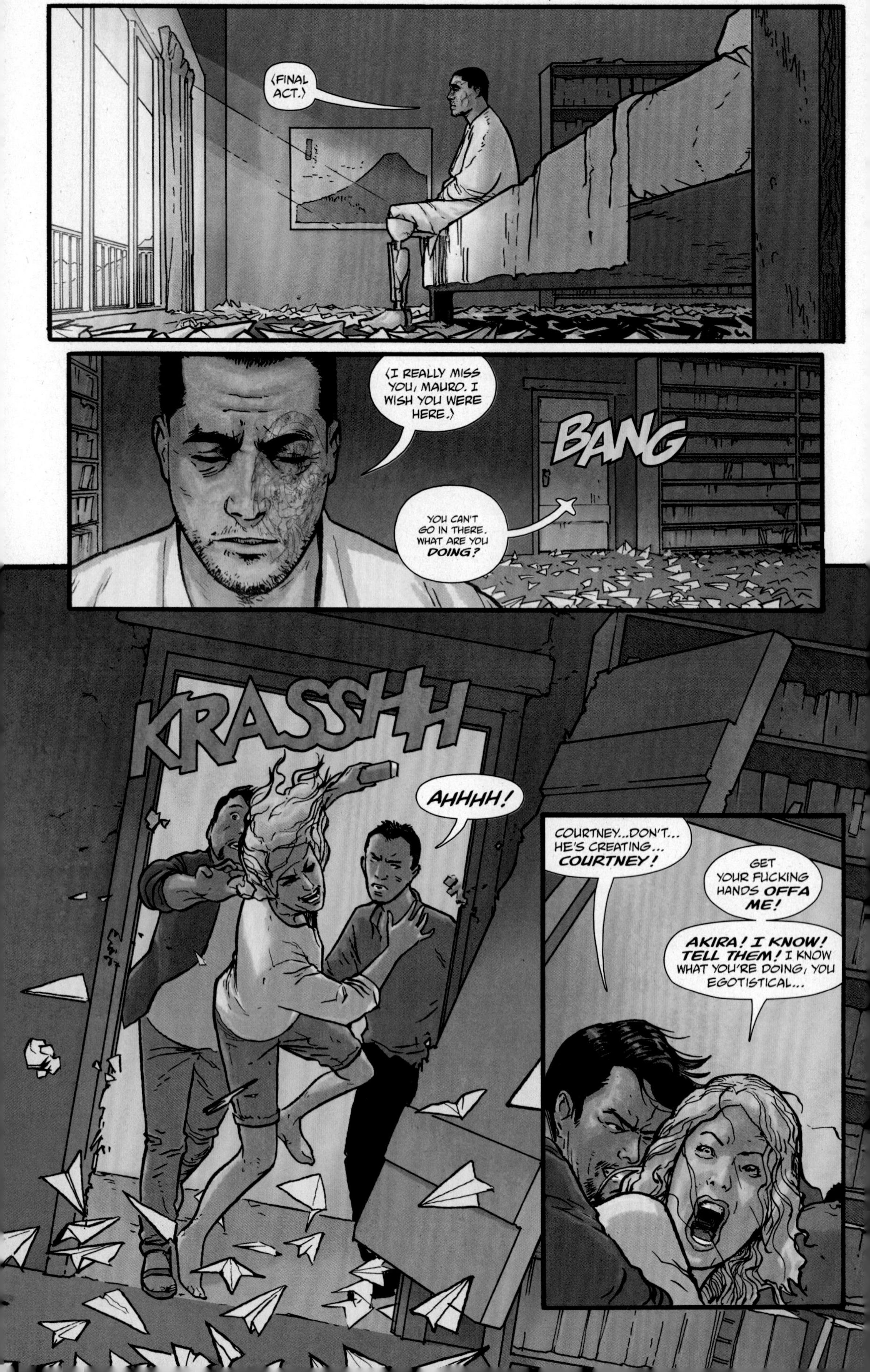
⟨FINAL ACT.⟩
⟨I REALLY MISS YOU, MAURO. I WISH YOU WERE HERE.⟩
BANG
YOU CAN'T GO IN THERE. WHAT ARE YOU DOING?
KRASSHH
AHHHH!
COURTNEY...DON'T... HE'S CREATING... COURTNEY!
GET YOUR FUCKING HANDS OFFA ME!
AKIRA! I KNOW! TELL THEM! I KNOW WHAT YOU'RE DOING, YOU EGOTISTICAL...

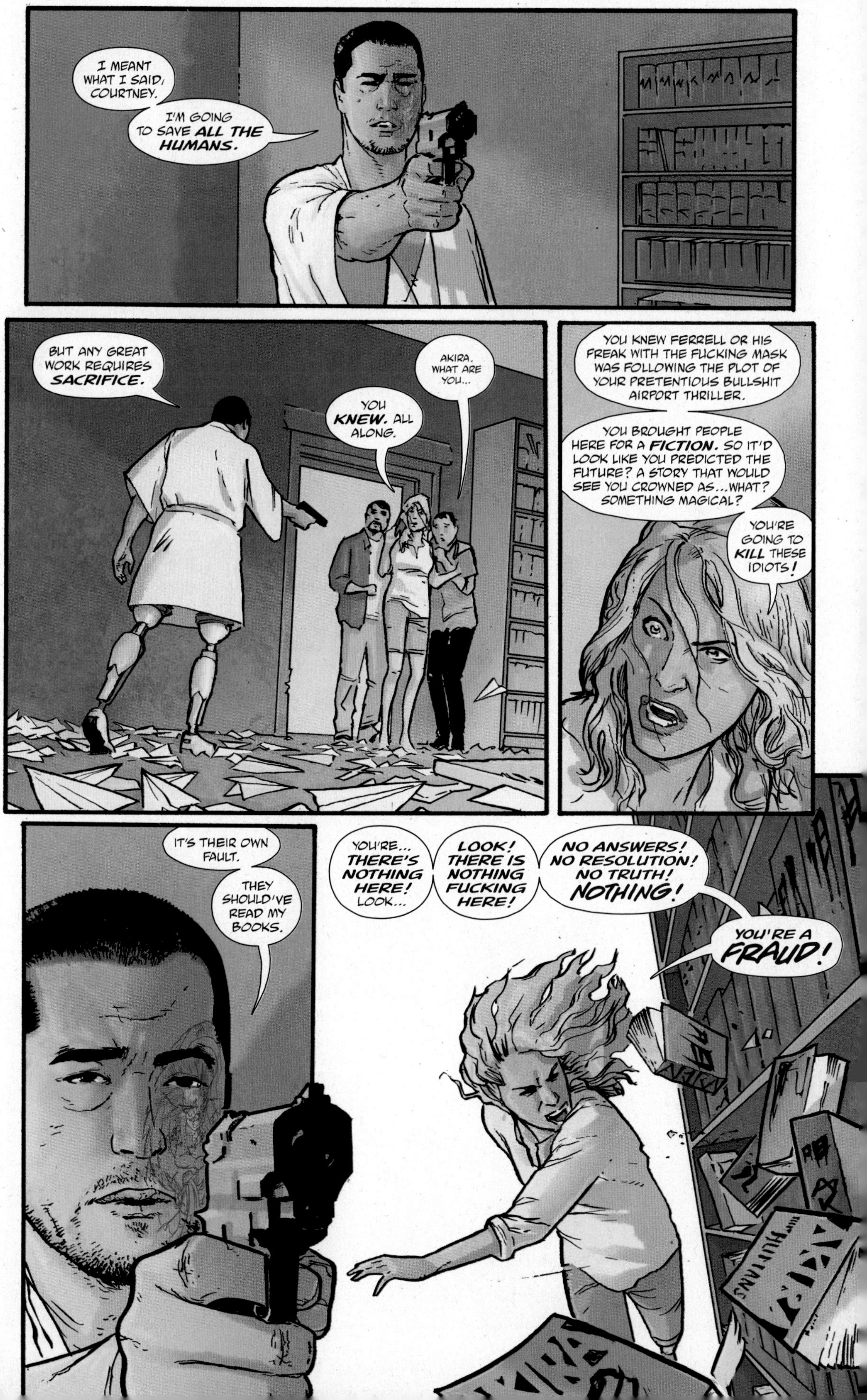
I MEANT WHAT I SAID, COURTNEY.
I'M GOING TO SAVE **ALL THE HUMANS.**
BUT ANY GREAT WORK REQUIRES **SACRIFICE.**
AKIRA. WHAT ARE YOU...
YOU **KNEW.** ALL ALONG.
YOU KNEW FERRELL OR HIS FREAK WITH THE FUCKING MASK WAS FOLLOWING THE PLOT OF YOUR PRETENTIOUS BULLSHIT AIRPORT THRILLER.
YOU BROUGHT PEOPLE HERE FOR A **FICTION.** SO IT'D LOOK LIKE YOU PREDICTED THE FUTURE? A STORY THAT WOULD SEE YOU CROWNED AS...WHAT? SOMETHING MAGICAL?
YOU'RE GOING TO **KILL** THESE IDIOTS!
IT'S THEIR OWN FAULT.
THEY SHOULD'VE READ MY BOOKS.
YOU'RE... **THERE'S NOTHING HERE!** LOOK...
LOOK! THERE IS NOTHING FUCKING HERE!
NO ANSWERS! NO RESOLUTION! NO TRUTH! NOTHING!
YOU'RE A FRAUD!

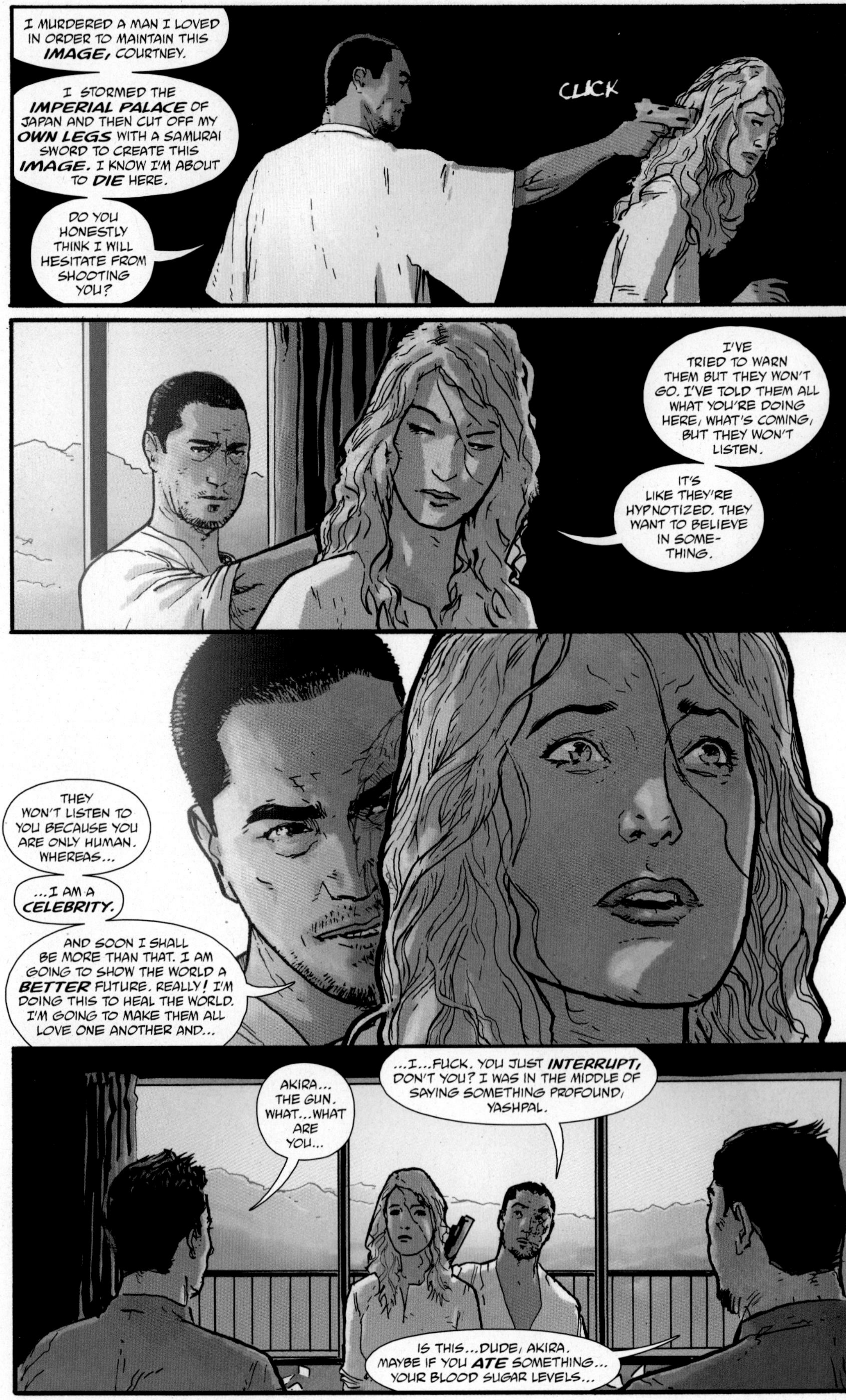
I MURDERED A MAN I LOVED IN ORDER TO MAINTAIN THIS IMAGE, COURTNEY.
I STORMED THE IMPERIAL PALACE OF JAPAN AND THEN CUT OFF MY OWN LEGS WITH A SAMURAI SWORD TO CREATE THIS IMAGE. I KNOW I'M ABOUT TO DIE HERE.
DO YOU HONESTLY THINK I WILL HESITATE FROM SHOOTING YOU?
CLICK
I'VE TRIED TO WARN THEM BUT THEY WON'T GO. I'VE TOLD THEM ALL WHAT YOU'RE DOING HERE, WHAT'S COMING, BUT THEY WON'T LISTEN.
IT'S LIKE THEY'RE HYPNOTIZED. THEY WANT TO BELIEVE IN SOME-THING.
THEY WON'T LISTEN TO YOU BECAUSE YOU ARE ONLY HUMAN. WHEREAS...
...I AM A CELEBRITY.
AND SOON I SHALL BE MORE THAN THAT. I AM GOING TO SHOW THE WORLD A BETTER FUTURE. REALLY! I'M DOING THIS TO HEAL THE WORLD. I'M GOING TO MAKE THEM ALL LOVE ONE ANOTHER AND...
AKIRA... THE GUN. WHAT...WHAT ARE YOU...
...I...FUCK. YOU JUST INTERRUPT, DON'T YOU? I WAS IN THE MIDDLE OF SAYING SOMETHING PROFOUND, YASHPAL.
IS THIS...DUDE, AKIRA. MAYBE IF YOU ATE SOMETHING... YOUR BLOOD SUGAR LEVELS...

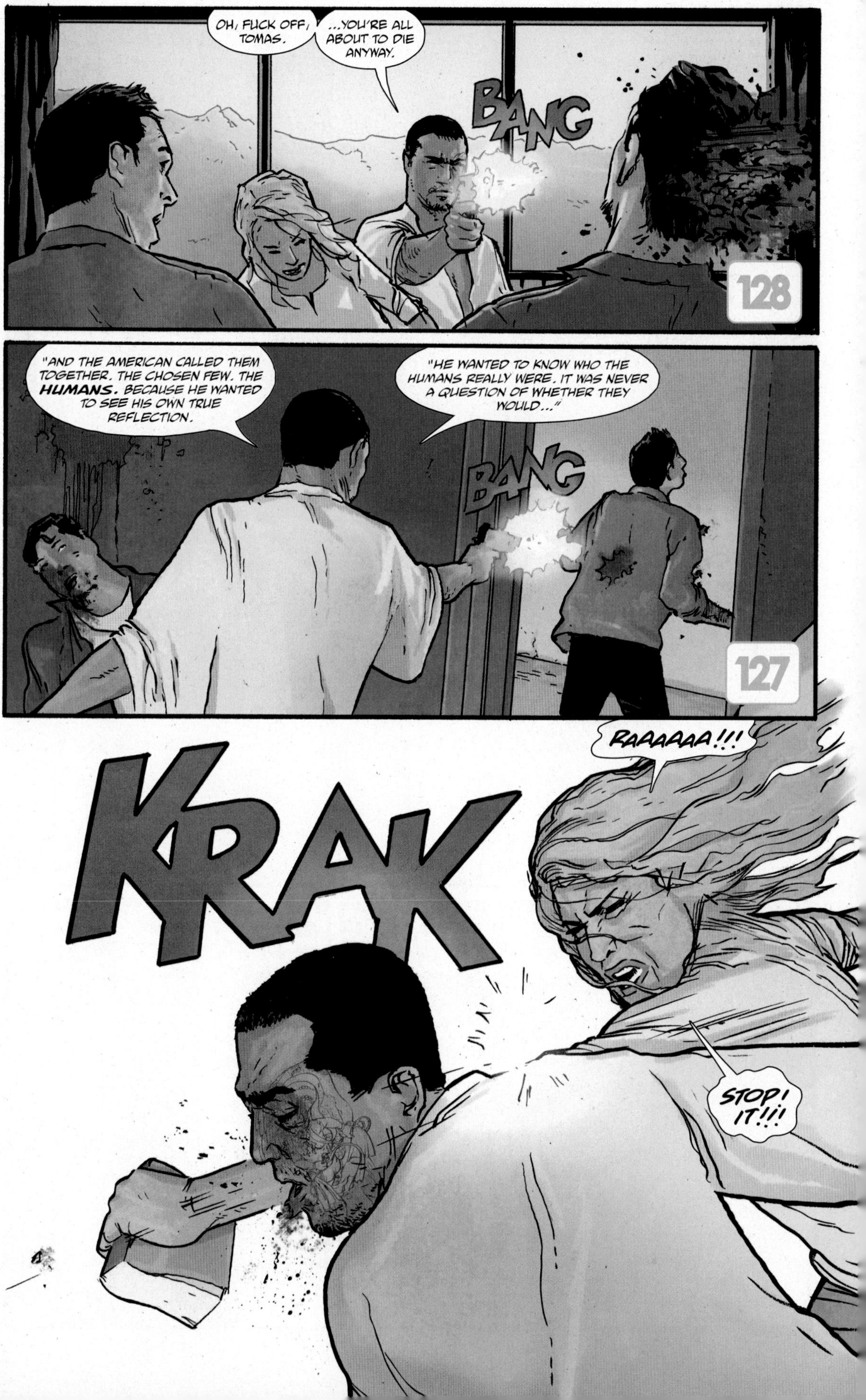
OH, FUCK OFF, TOMAS.
...YOU'RE ALL ABOUT TO DIE ANYWAY.
BANG
128
"AND THE AMERICAN CALLED THEM TOGETHER. THE CHOSEN FEW. THE **HUMANS**. BECAUSE HE WANTED TO SEE HIS OWN TRUE REFLECTION.
"HE WANTED TO KNOW WHO THE HUMANS REALLY WERE. IT WAS NEVER A QUESTION OF WHETHER THEY WOULD..."
BANG
127
RAAAAAA!!!
KRAK
STOP! IT!!!

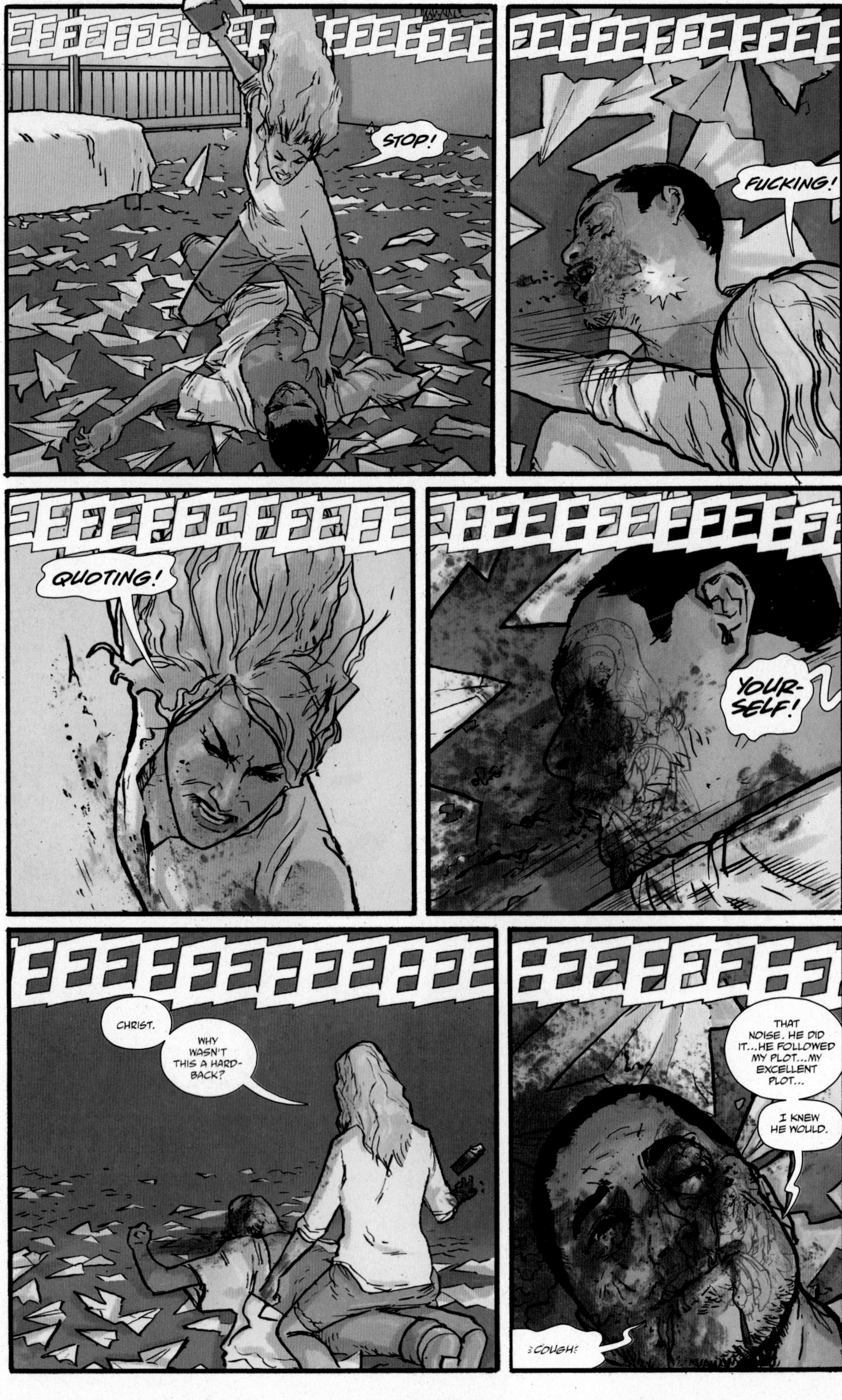
EEEEEEEEEEEEEEEE
STOP!
EEEEEEEEEEEE
FUCKING!
EEEEEEEEEEEE
QUOTING!
EEEEEEEEEEEEEE
YOUR-SELF!
EEEEEEEEEEEEE
CHRIST.
WHY WASN'T THIS A HARD-BACK?
EEEEEEEEE
THAT NOISE. HE DID IT...HE FOLLOWED MY PLOT...MY EXCELLENT PLOT...
I KNEW HE WOULD.
COUGH

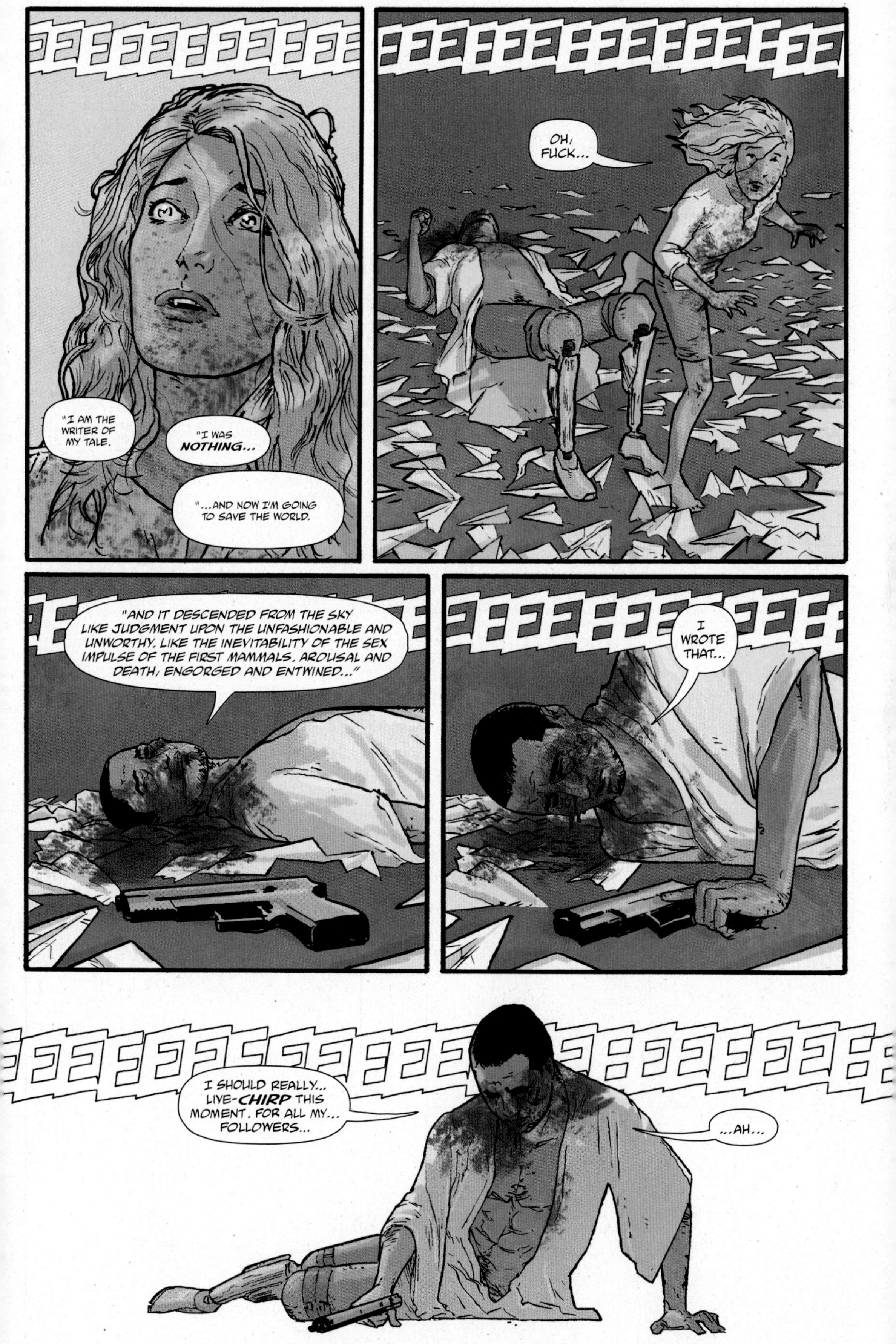
EEEEEEEEEEE
"I AM THE WRITER OF MY TALE.
"I WAS NOTHING...
"...AND NOW I'M GOING TO SAVE THE WORLD.
EEEEEEEEEEEEEE
OH, FUCK...
"AND IT DESCENDED FROM THE SKY LIKE JUDGMENT UPON THE UNFASHIONABLE AND UNWORTHY. LIKE THE INEVITABILITY OF THE SEX IMPULSE OF THE FIRST MAMMALS. AROUSAL AND DEATH, ENGORGED AND ENTWINED..."
I WROTE THAT...
I SHOULD REALLY... LIVE-CHIRP THIS MOMENT. FOR ALL MY... FOLLOWERS...
...AH...

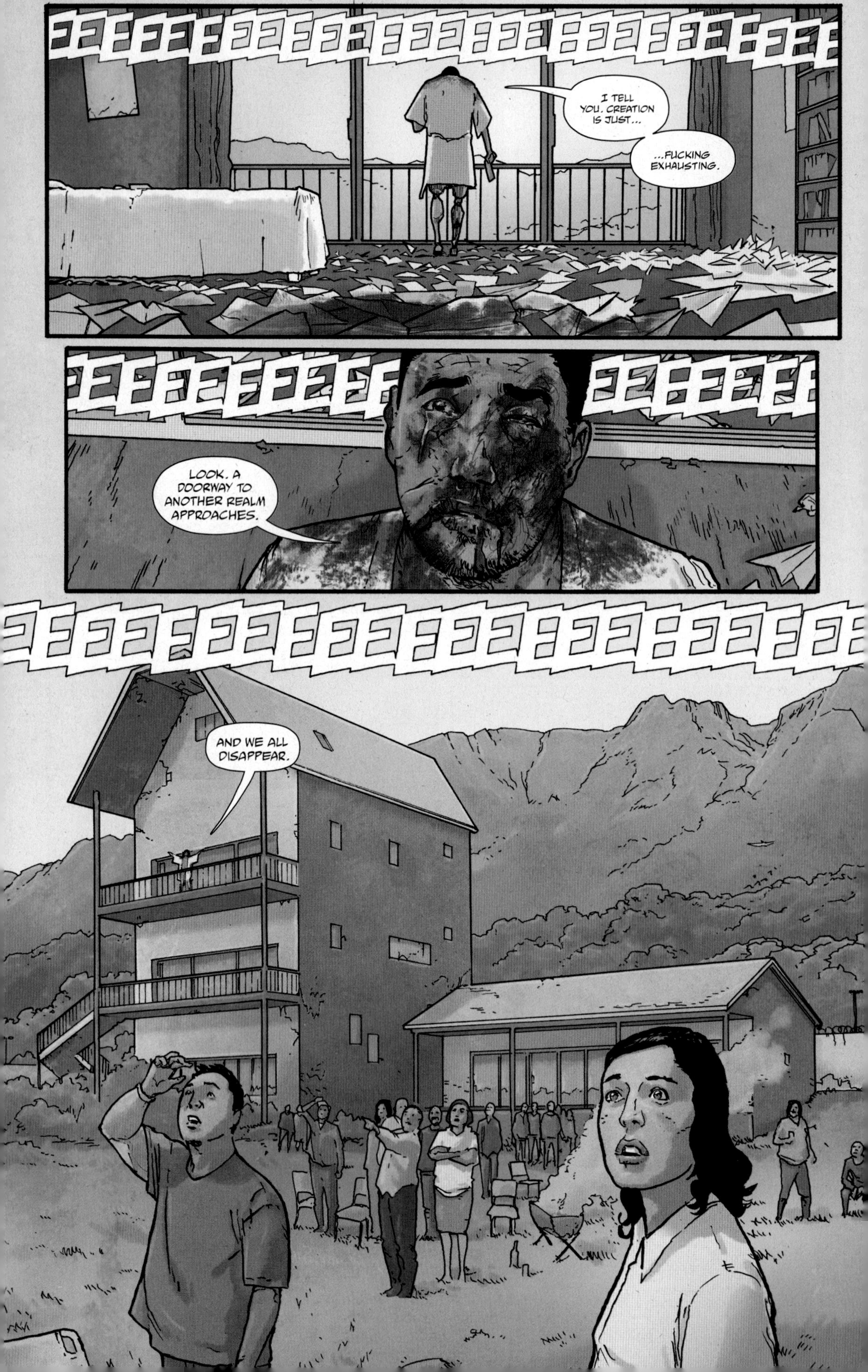
EEEEEEEEEEEEEEEEEEEE
I TELL YOU. CREATION IS JUST...
...FUCKING EXHAUSTING.
EEEEEEEEE EEEEEEE
LOOK. A DOORWAY TO ANOTHER REALM APPROACHES.
EEEEEEEEEEEEEEEEEEEEE
AND WE ALL DISAPPEAR.

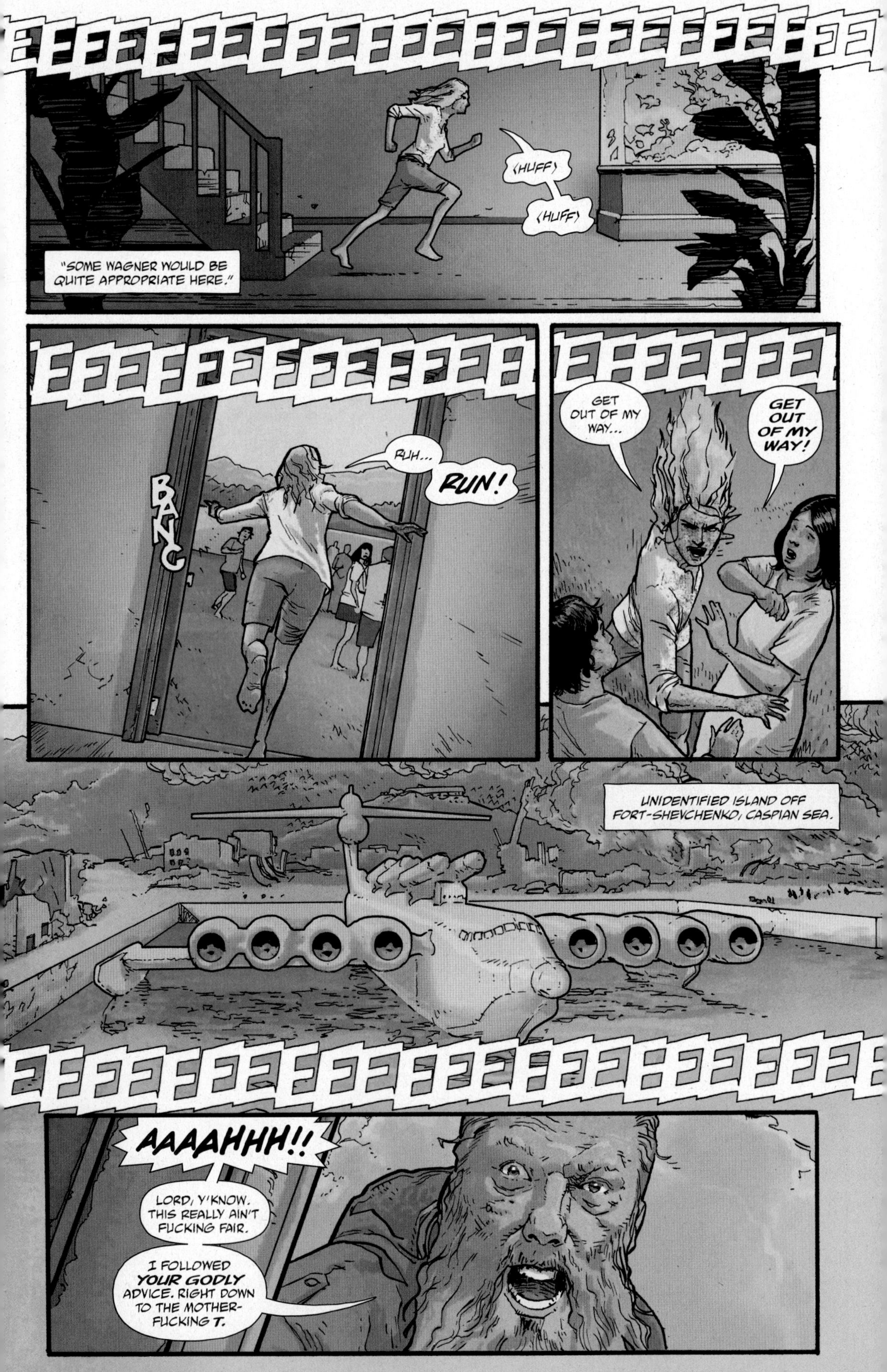
EEEEEEEEEEEEEEEEEEEEEEEEEEE
(HUFF)
(HUFF)
"SOME WAGNER WOULD BE QUITE APPROPRIATE HERE."
EEEEEEEEEEEEEEE
BANG
RUH...
RUN!
EEEEEEEEE
GET OUT OF MY WAY...
GET OUT OF MY WAY!
UNIDENTIFIED ISLAND OFF FORT-SHEVCHENKO, CASPIAN SEA.
EEEEEEEEEEEEEEEEEEEEEEEEEEE
AAAAHHH!!
LORD, Y'KNOW. THIS REALLY AIN'T FUCKING FAIR.
I FOLLOWED YOUR GODLY ADVICE. RIGHT DOWN TO THE MOTHER-FUCKING T.

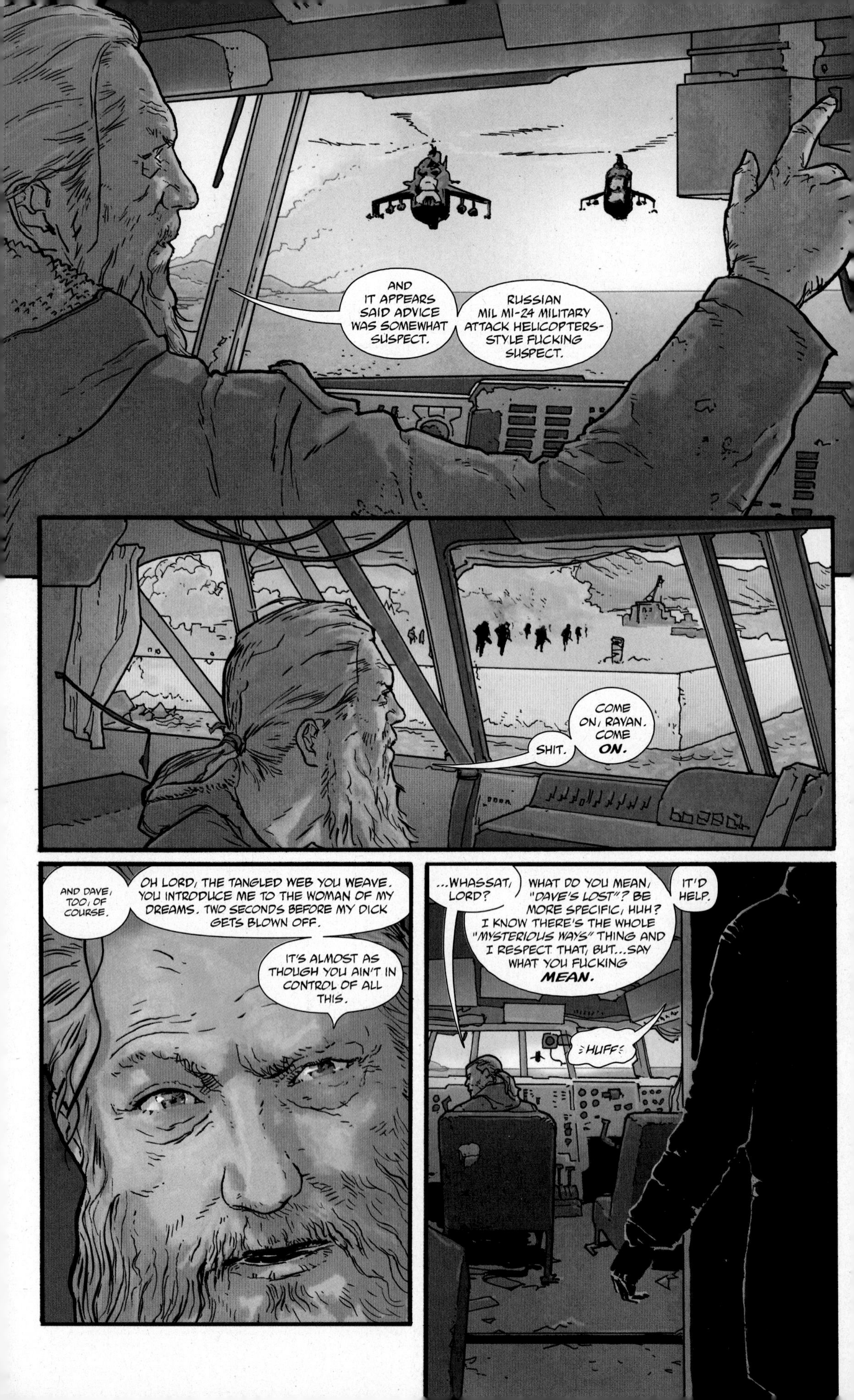
AND IT APPEARS SAID ADVICE WAS SOMEWHAT SUSPECT.
RUSSIAN MIL MI-24 MILITARY ATTACK HELICOPTERS-STYLE FUCKING SUSPECT.
SHIT.
COME ON, RAVAN. COME ON.
AND DAVE, TOO, OF COURSE.
OH LORD, THE TANGLED WEB YOU WEAVE. YOU INTRODUCE ME TO THE WOMAN OF MY DREAMS. TWO SECONDS BEFORE MY DICK GETS BLOWN OFF.
IT'S ALMOST AS THOUGH YOU AIN'T IN CONTROL OF ALL THIS.
...WHASSAT, LORD?
WHAT DO YOU MEAN, "DAVE'S LOST"? BE MORE SPECIFIC, HUH? I KNOW THERE'S THE WHOLE "MYSTERIOUS WAYS" THING AND I RESPECT THAT, BUT...SAY WHAT YOU FUCKING MEAN.
IT'D HELP.
HUFF

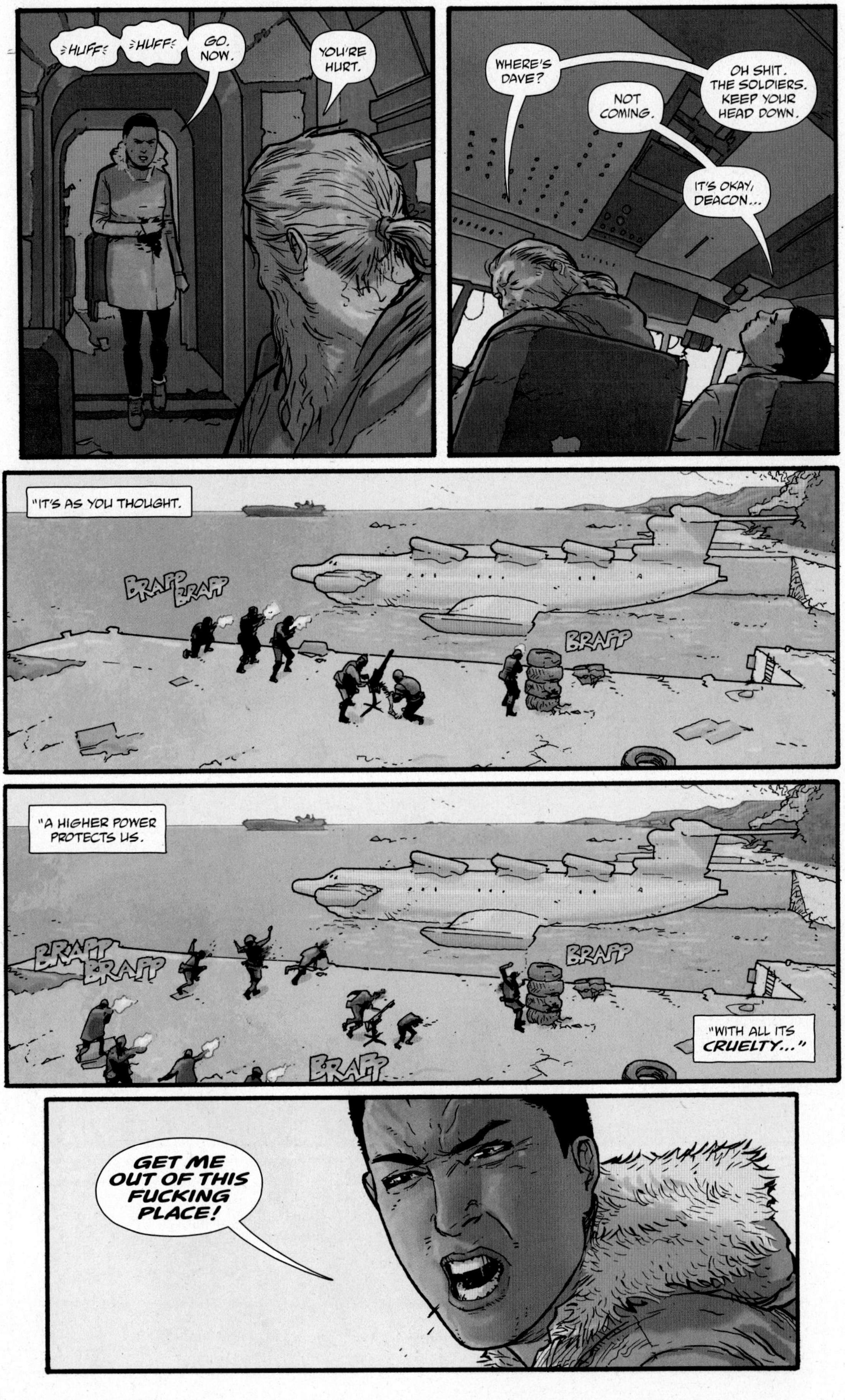
HUFF
HUFF
GO. NOW.
YOU'RE HURT.
WHERE'S DAVE?
NOT COMING.
IT'S OKAY, DEACON...
OH SHIT. THE SOLDIERS. KEEP YOUR HEAD DOWN.
"IT'S AS YOU THOUGHT.
BRAPP BRAPP
BRAPP
"A HIGHER POWER PROTECTS US.
BRAPP BRAPP
BRAPP
BRAPP
"WITH ALL ITS CRUELTY..."
GET ME OUT OF THIS FUCKING PLACE!

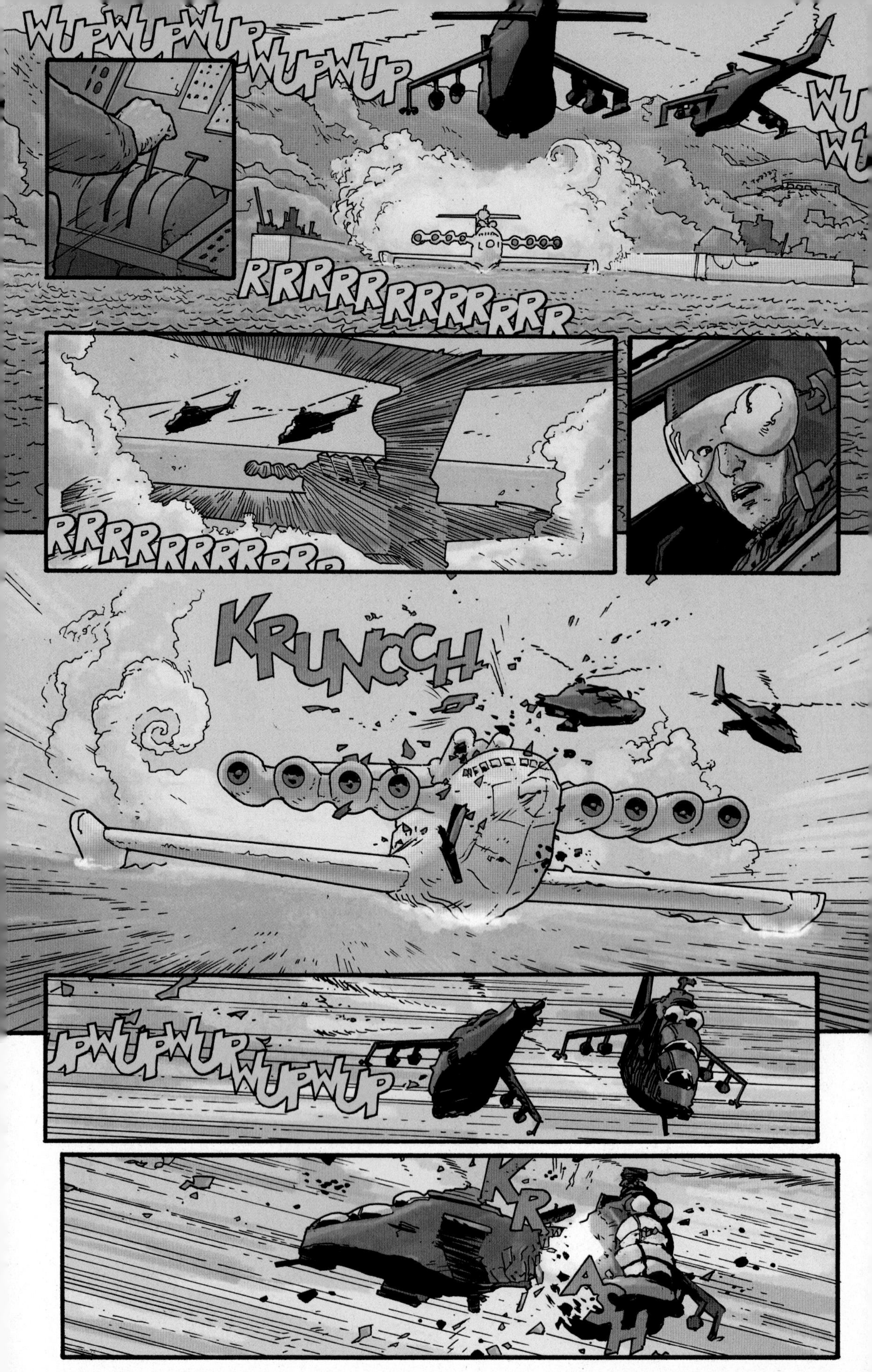
WUPWUPWUPWUPWUP
WU WU
RRRRRRRRRRRRR
RRRRRRRRRRRR
KRUNCCH
UPWUPWUPWUPWUP
KRAAH

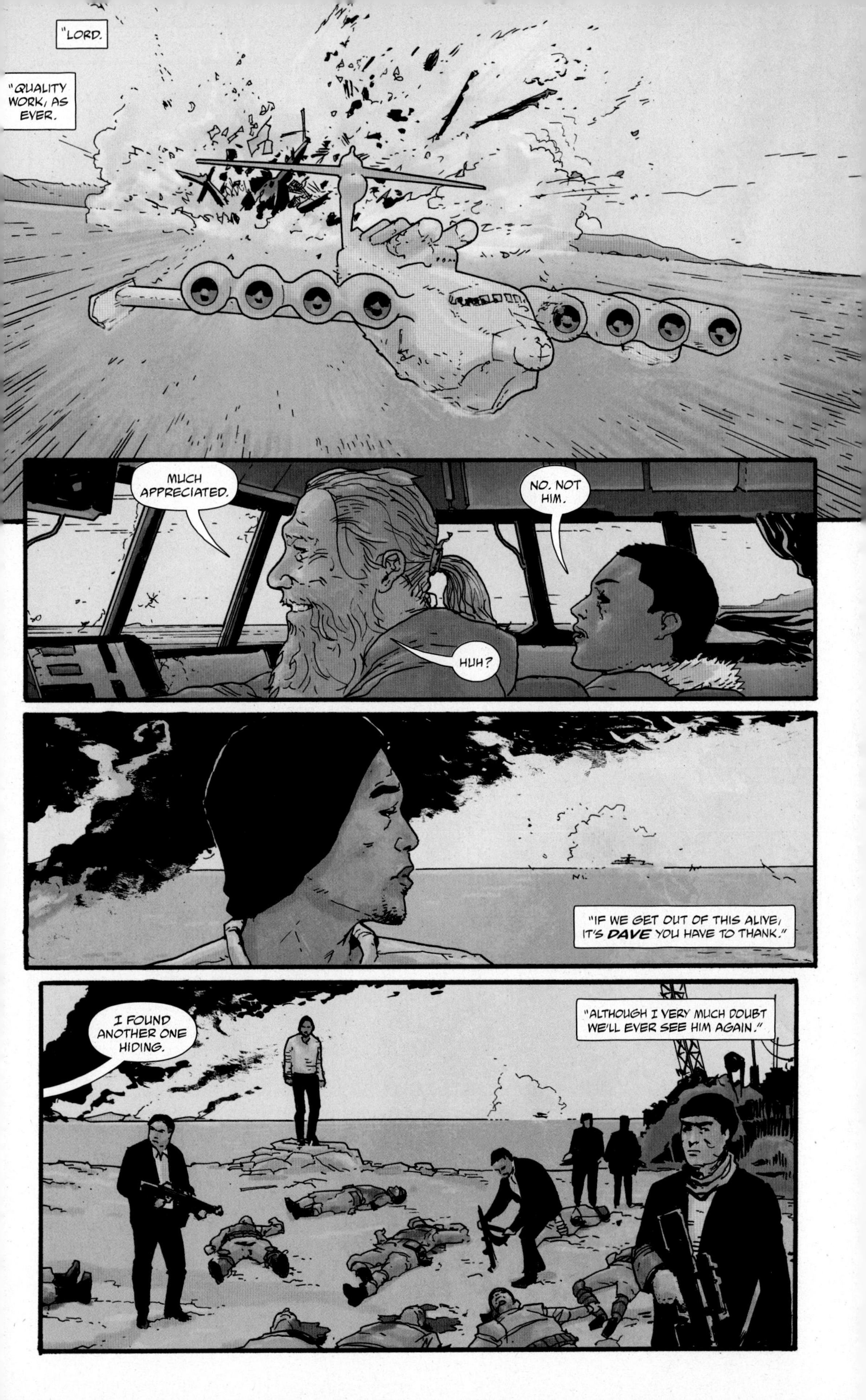
"LORD.
"QUALITY WORK, AS EVER.
MUCH APPRECIATED.
NO. NOT HIM.
HUH?
"IF WE GET OUT OF THIS ALIVE, IT'S DAVE YOU HAVE TO THANK."
I FOUND ANOTHER ONE HIDING.
"ALTHOUGH I VERY MUCH DOUBT WE'LL EVER SEE HIM AGAIN."

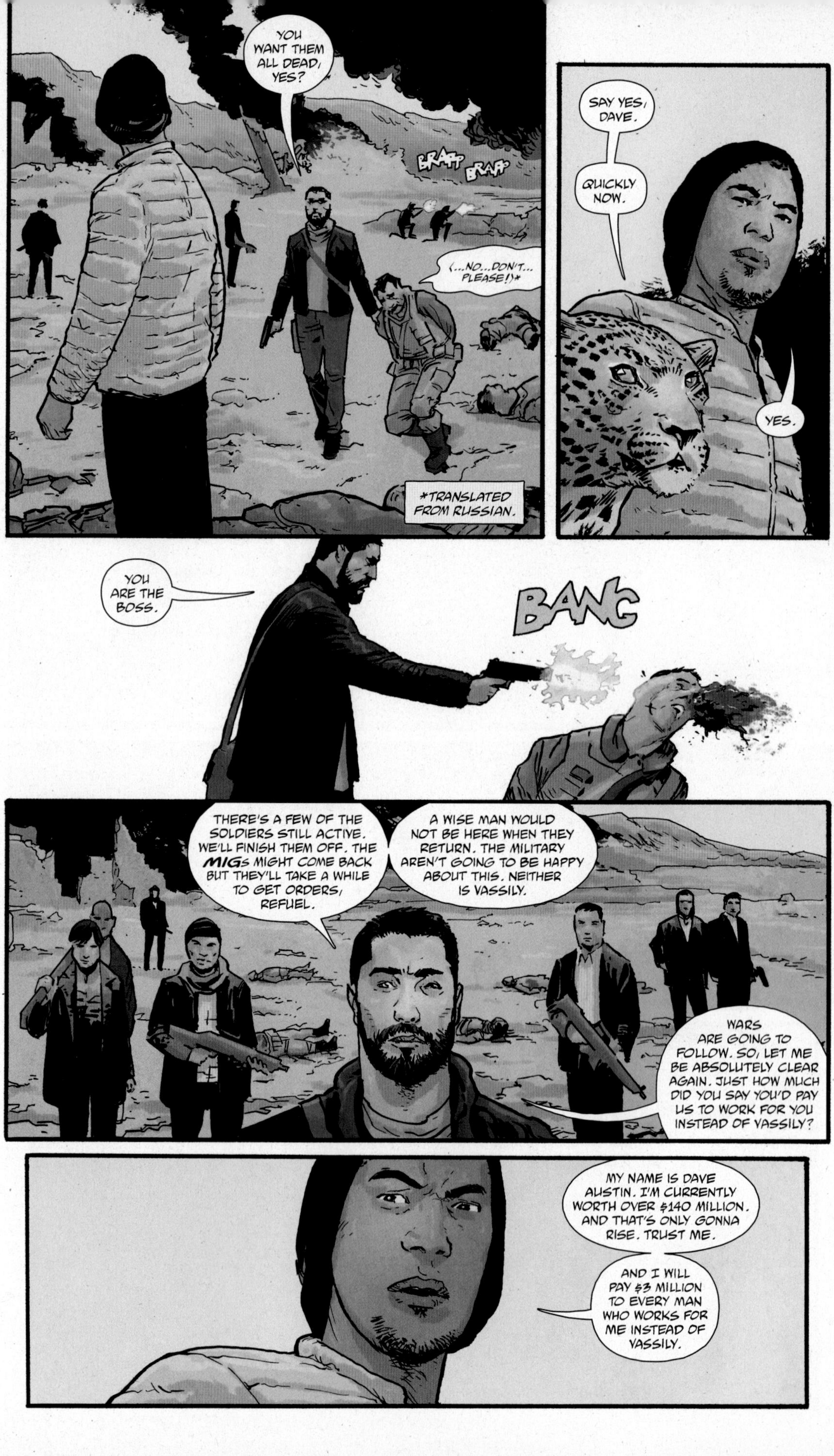

YOU WANT THEM ALL DEAD, YES?
BRAPP BRAPP
(...NO...DON'T... PLEASE!)*
*TRANSLATED FROM RUSSIAN.
SAY YES, DAVE.
QUICKLY NOW.
YES.
YOU ARE THE BOSS.
BANG
THERE'S A FEW OF THE SOLDIERS STILL ACTIVE. WE'LL FINISH THEM OFF. THE MIGs MIGHT COME BACK BUT THEY'LL TAKE A WHILE TO GET ORDERS, REFUEL.
A WISE MAN WOULD NOT BE HERE WHEN THEY RETURN. THE MILITARY AREN'T GOING TO BE HAPPY ABOUT THIS. NEITHER IS VASSILY.
WARS ARE GOING TO FOLLOW. SO, LET ME BE ABSOLUTLY CLEAR AGAIN. JUST HOW MUCH DID YOU SAY YOU'D PAY US TO WORK FOR YOU INSTEAD OF VASSILY?
MY NAME IS DAVE AUSTIN. I'M CURRENTLY WORTH OVER $140 MILLION. AND THAT'S ONLY GONNA RISE. TRUST ME.
AND I WILL PAY $3 MILLION TO EVERY MAN WHO WORKS FOR ME INSTEAD OF VASSILY.

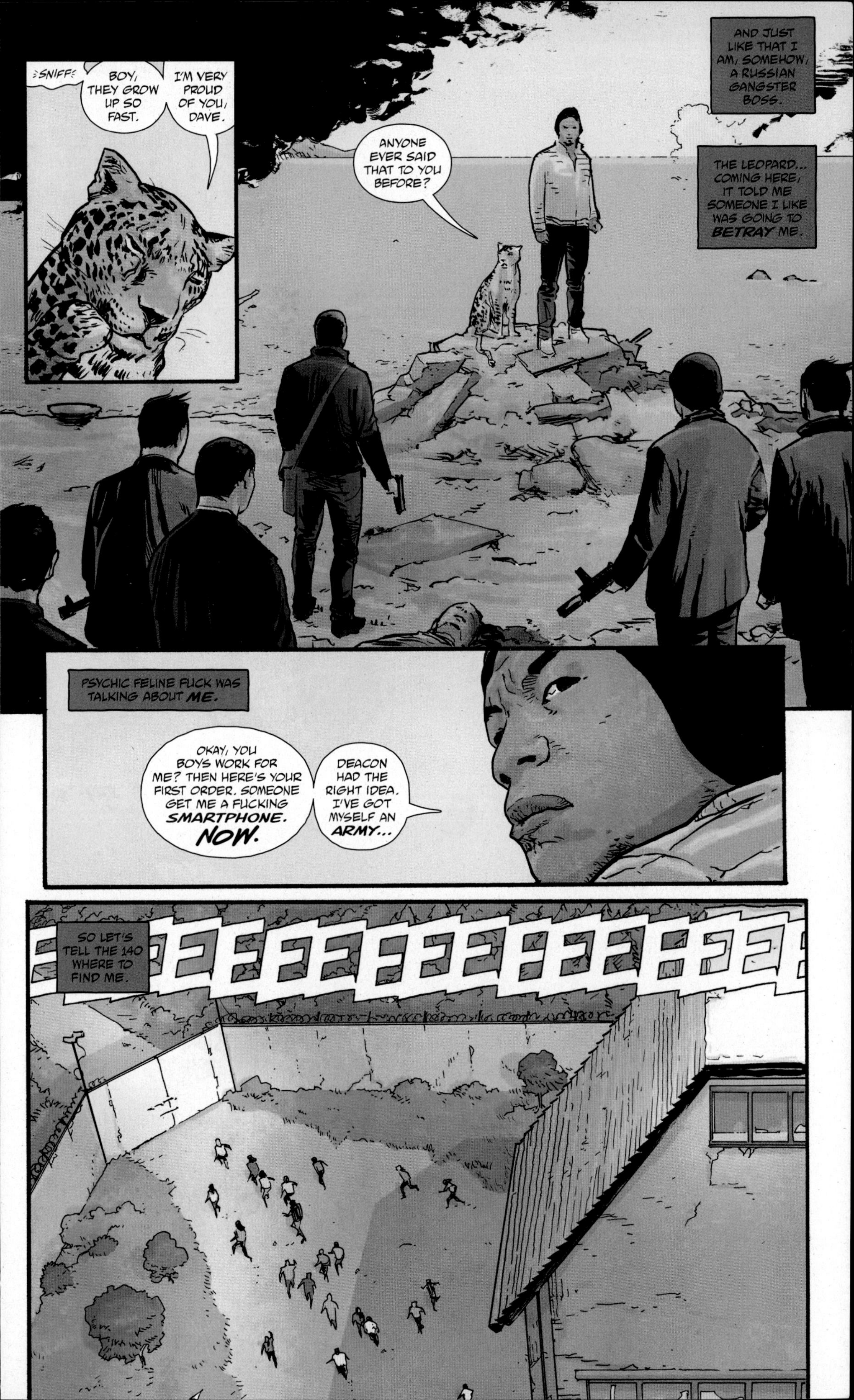
AND JUST LIKE THAT I AM, SOMEHOW, A RUSSIAN GANGSTER BOSS.
SNIFF
BOY, THEY GROW UP SO FAST.
I'M VERY PROUD OF YOU, DAVE.
ANYONE EVER SAID THAT TO YOU BEFORE?
THE LEOPARD... COMING HERE, IT TOLD ME SOMEONE I LIKE WAS GOING TO BETRAY ME.
PSYCHIC FELINE FUCK WAS TALKING ABOUT ME.
OKAY, YOU BOYS WORK FOR ME? THEN HERE'S YOUR FIRST ORDER. SOMEONE GET ME A FUCKING SMARTPHONE. NOW.
DEACON HAD THE RIGHT IDEA. I'VE GOT MYSELF AN ARMY...
SO LET'S TELL THE 140 WHERE TO FIND ME.
EEEEEEEEEEEEEEEEE

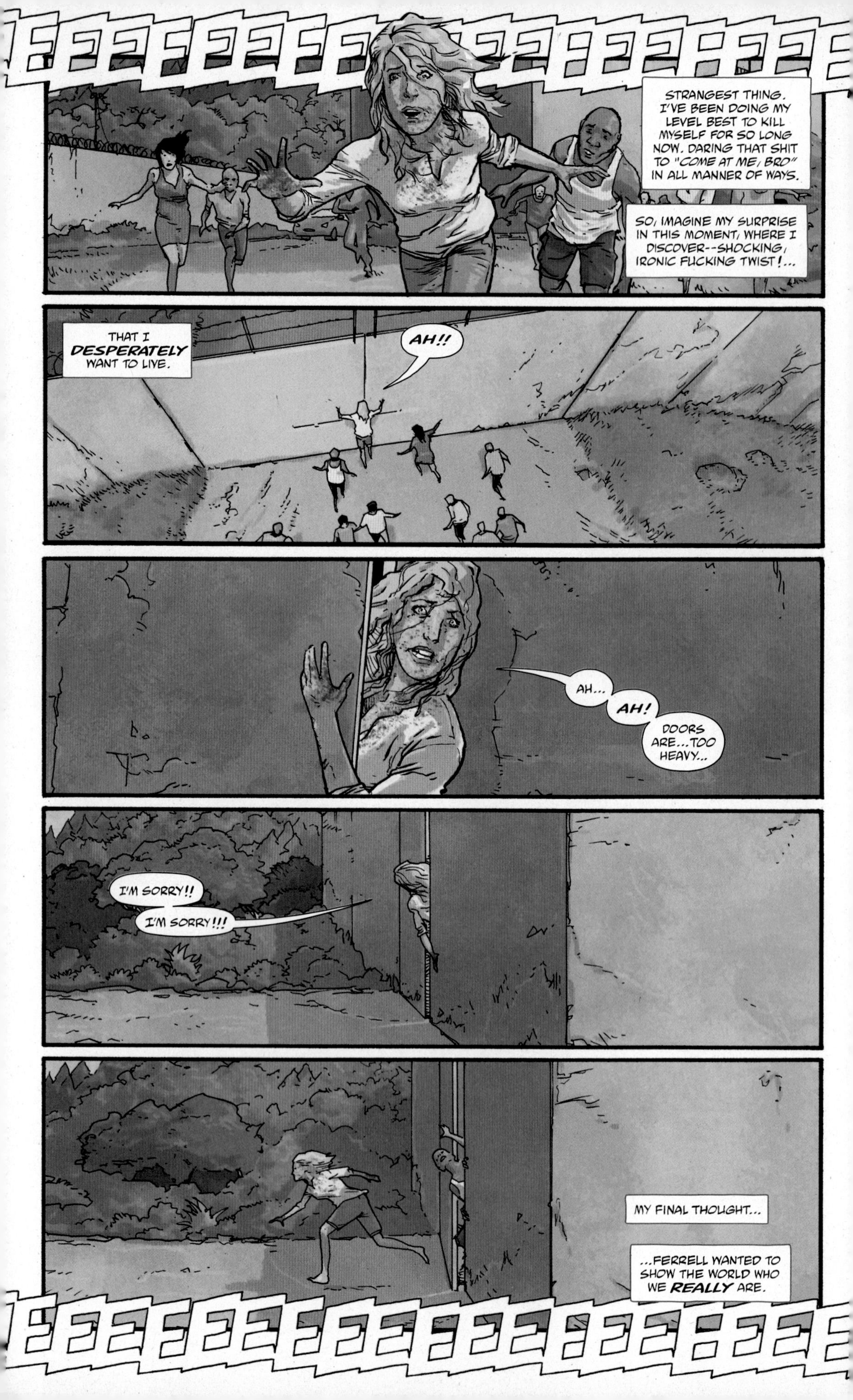
EEEEEEEEEEEEEEEEEE
STRANGEST THING. I'VE BEEN DOING MY LEVEL BEST TO KILL MYSELF FOR SO LONG NOW. DARING THAT SHIT TO "COME AT ME, BRO" IN ALL MANNER OF WAYS.
SO, IMAGINE MY SURPRISE IN THIS MOMENT, WHERE I DISCOVER--SHOCKING, IRONIC FUCKING TWIST!...
THAT I DESPERATELY WANT TO LIVE.
AH!!
AH... AH! DOORS ARE...TOO HEAVY...
I'M SORRY!!
I'M SORRY!!!
MY FINAL THOUGHT...
...FERRELL WANTED TO SHOW THE WORLD WHO WE REALLY ARE.
EEEEEEEEEEEEEEEEEE

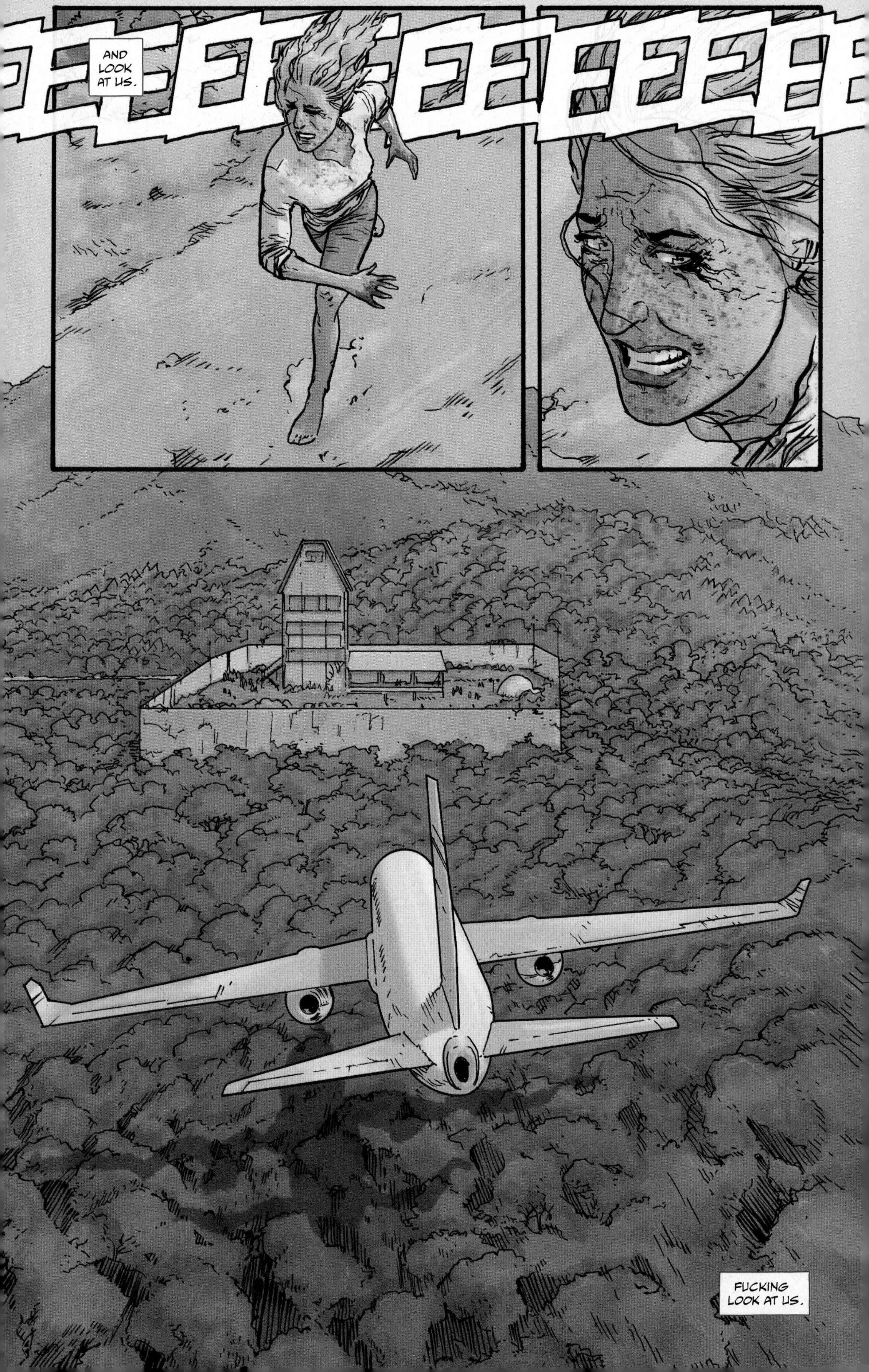
EEEEEEEEEEEEEEEEEE
AND LOOK AT US.
FUCKING LOOK AT US.

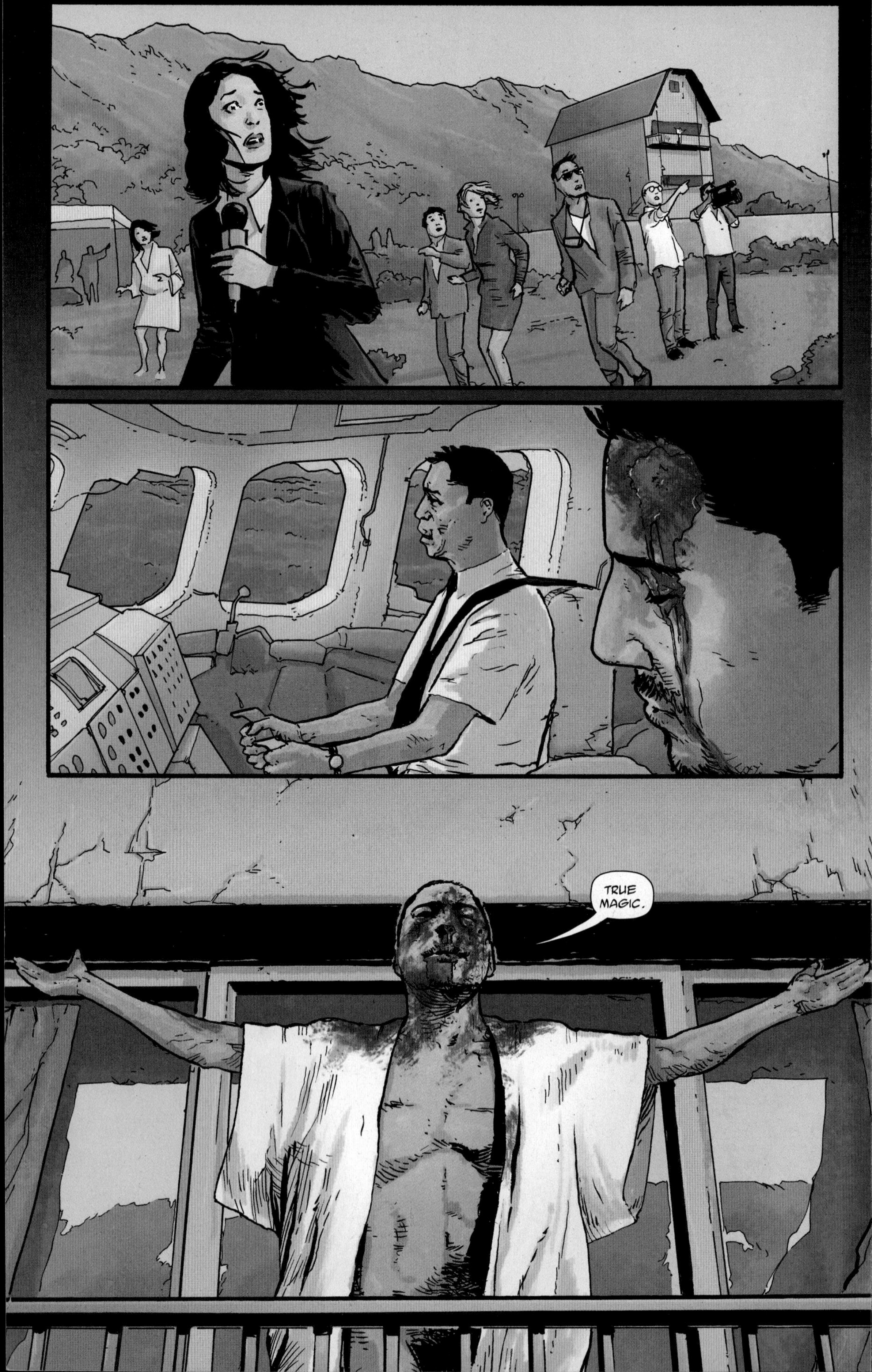
TRUE MAGIC.

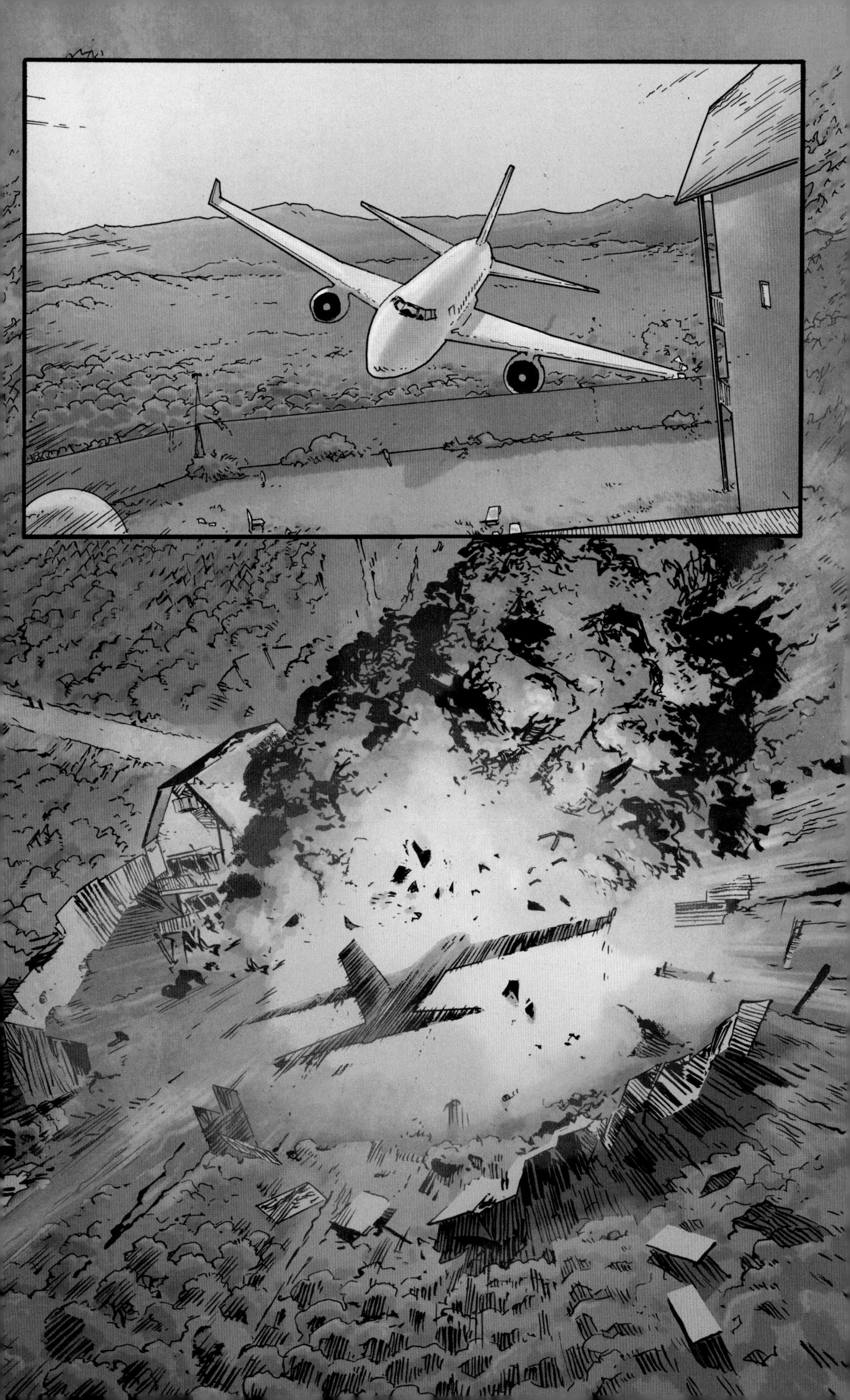

JESUS CHRIST!
IT JUST FUCKING MISSED US!
XF1
KEEP FILMING!
KEEP FILMING!

86

@CourtneyOMG 140 Verified

(Followers: 179,394 Following: 1)

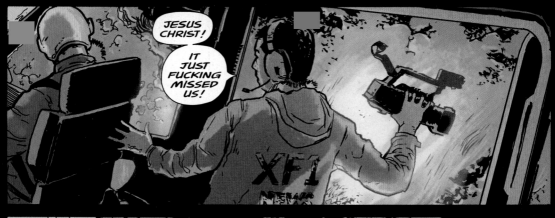

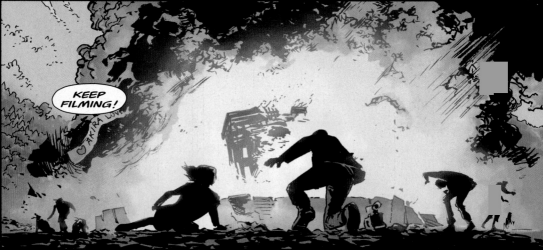

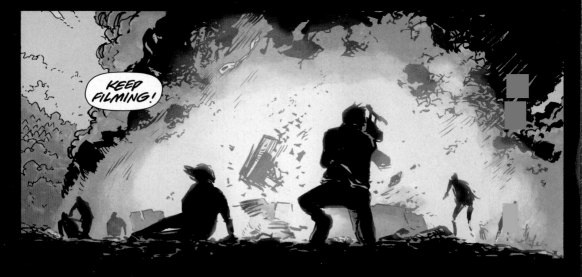

VERTIGO

"A seriously funny, nuanced fable. Grade A."
—ENTERTAINMENT WEEKLY

"Complete and utter comic gold."
—PUBLISHERS WEEKLY (STARRED REVIEW)

"Funny and scary. An utterly believable critique of society. A+."
—WASHINGTON POST

Y: THE LAST MAN VOL. 10: WHYS AND WHEREFORES

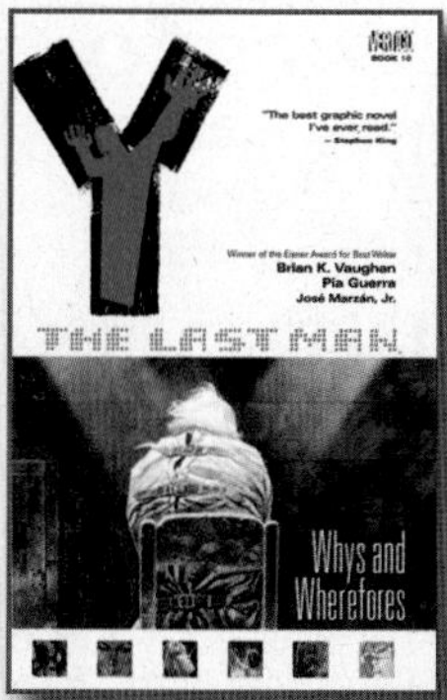
THE LAST MAN
Whys and Wherefores

FROM THE *NEW YORK TIMES* #1 BEST-SELLING AUTHOR

BRIAN K. VAUGHAN

with PIA GUERRA

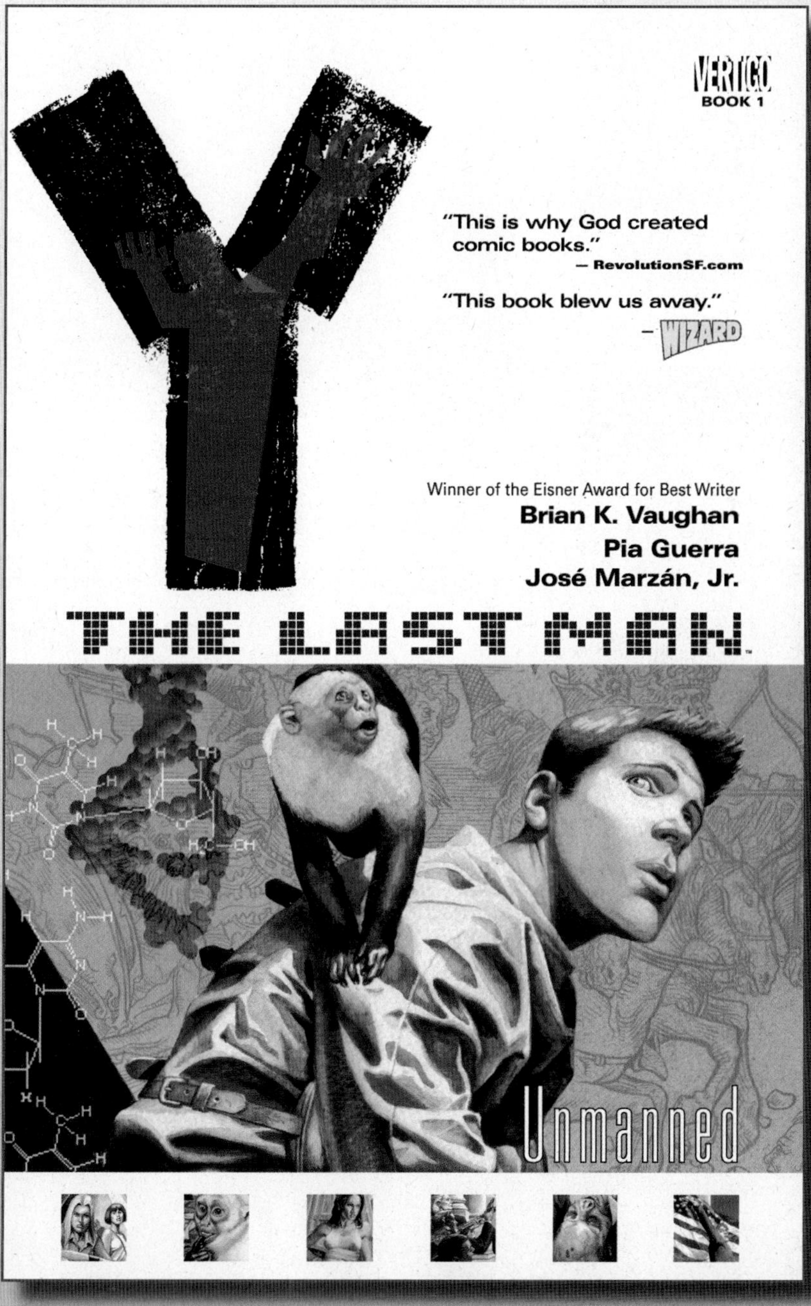
VERTIGO
BOOK 1
"This is why God created comic books."
– RevolutionSF.com
"This book blew us away."
– WIZARD
Winner of the Eisner Award for Best Writer
Brian K. Vaughan
Pia Guerra
José Marzán, Jr.
THE LAST MAN
Unmanned

READ THE COMPLETE SERIES!

Y: THE LAST MAN VOL. 1: UNMANNED

Y: THE LAST MAN VOL. 2: CYCLES

Y: THE LAST MAN VOL. 3: ONE SMALL STEP

Y: THE LAST MAN VOL. 4: SAFEWORD

Y: THE LAST MAN VOL. 5: RING OF TRUTH

Y: THE LAST MAN VOL. 6: GIRL ON GIRL

Y: THE LAST MAN VOL. 7: PAPER DOLLS

Y: THE LAST MAN VOL. 8: KIMONO DRAGONS

Y: THE LAST MAN VOL. 9: MOTHERLAND

Y: THE LAST MAN VOL. 10: WHYS AND WHEREFORES

Y: THE LAST MAN: THE DELUXE EDITION BOOK ONE

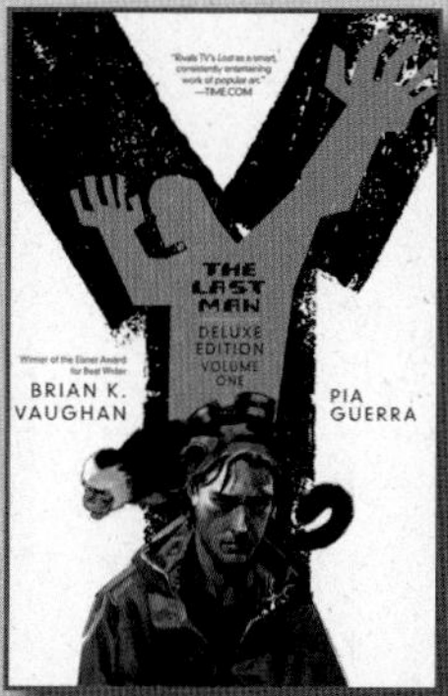
THE LAST MAN
DELUXE EDITION
VOLUME ONE
BRIAN K. VAUGHAN
PIA GUERRA

ALSO AVAILABLE AS DELUXE HARDCOVER IN A 5-VOLUME SERIES